James K. McGuire

IRISH STUDIES
James MacKillop, *Series Editor*

James K. McGuire campaign pin.

JAMES K. MCGUIRE

Boy Mayor and Irish Nationalist

Joseph E. Fahey

Syracuse University Press

For a listing of books published and distributed by Syracuse University Press, visit
our website at www.SyracuseUniversityPress.syr.edu.

ISBN: 978-0-8156-1032-8 (cloth)   978-0-8156-5277-9 (e-book)

Library of Congress Cataloging-in-Publication Data
Fahey, Joseph E.
    James K. McGuire : boy mayor and Irish nationalist / Joseph E. Fahey. —
First edition.
        pages cm. — (Irish studies)
    Includes bibliographical references and index.
    ISBN 978-0-8156-1032-8 (cloth : alk. paper) — ISBN 978-0-8156-5277-9
(ebook) 1. McGuire, James K., 1868–1923. 2. Mayors—New York (State)—
Syracuse—Biography. 3. Syracuse (N.Y.)—Biography. 4. Nationalism—Ireland—
History. 5. Irish Americans—New York (State)—Syracuse—Biography. I. Title.
    F129.S8F228 2014
    974.7'041092—dc 3
    [B]   2013049663

Manufactured in the United States of America

To my mother, Mary McGuire Fahey,
Who was his biggest fan

and

To my wife, Terri, and my daughters,
Meghan and Kate,
Who inspire me every day

and

To Claire, the next generation

Joseph E. Fahey is a judge in the New York State Unified Court System and an adjunct professor of law at Syracuse University College of Law. He is a member of the American Conference of Irish Studies, the American Irish Historical Society, and the Irish American Cultural Institute. He has published numerous articles dealing with legal and political subjects. He lives in Fabius, New York.

JMK

Contents

J M K

Illustrations

J M K

Acknowledgments

When I began to undertake the task of trying to recreate the life and times of my great-uncle, James K. McGuire, I was faced with several formidable problems. The first was that he had been dead for more than eight decades and, other than anecdotal glimpses that were part of family lore, no family members, friends, or contemporaries of his were alive and able to be interviewed. The second was that, unlike many prominent figures of his day, he left behind no papers, diaries, or correspondence as part of his legacy or if he did, they have long since perished. Therefore I was left to learn all that I could from the news accounts of his public life, correspondence from his three terms as mayor, and that which could be obtained from the archives of those who dealt with him.

I consider the news accounts of his life and those of his family members during his life in Syracuse to be a particularly valuable historical source since they are contemporaneous accounts of the events that occurred during those periods. I am deeply indebted to the staff of the Local History Section of the Onondaga County Public Library for their assistance in copying the hundreds of news accounts I obtained from their microfiche files. In particular I am grateful to Tom Howard, who copied and read each one for me and who was constantly on the lookout for any news items I might have overlooked.

I am indebted to Dennis Conners and the Onondaga Historical Association for the access they provided to their records. I owe a debt of gratitude to John Copanas, Syracuse city clerk, for the unfettered access he gave me to the City Hall Archives and the records and correspondence from the McGuire administration. I will always be grateful to Pat Mosely, assistant deputy commissioner of Corrections for Onondaga County, who combed the ancient records from the Onondaga County Penitentiary dealing with James McGuire's brief periods of incarceration there. I am appreciative of the efforts of my friend Bob Langan, retired from the New York State Unified Court System, who obtained a copy of the court file concerning James K. McGuire's indictment in New York County from Alan Murphy, the clerk of the New York State Supreme Court in Manhattan.

Outside of central New York, I was fortunate to have the help of the Irish American Historical Society, which provided me with access to the correspondence between McGuire and John Devoy and Daniel Cohalan. I am indebted to my friend Congressman James T. Walsh, whose staff provided me with the testimony from the House of Representatives committee inquiry into McGuire's World War I propaganda. I am also extremely grateful to Seamus Helferty, principal archivist at the University College Dublin's James Joyce Library, who culled the collections of Éamon de Valera and Harry Boland and provided me with the correspondence involving McGuire that came from the UCD-OFM Partnership.

I owe special thanks to Bill and Marge Hamler, who on two occasions retrieved my manuscript from some black hole in the Internet to which I had inadvertently sent it. I was also fortunate to have the advice and counsel of my friend Mike Grogan, an editor at the *Syracuse Post-Standard*, concerning the content of the biography. Finally, I'd like to thank Jim MacKillop, Irish Studies Series Editor for Syracuse University Press. His enthusiasm for the project and his patience and guidance helped me see it through to conclusion.

JMK

Introduction

The history of the Irish in America is replete with success stories, particularly in the political arena. In the decades following the Potato Famine between 1845 and 1855, when thousands of Irish immigrated to the United States, the Irish in the American major cities took control of government and erected political machines that ultimately culminated in the election of an Irish-Catholic president a century later. Legendary political bosses like James Michael Curley, John "Honey Fitz" Fitzgerald, and Patrick Kennedy ruled Boston. In New York, Richard Croker, "Honest John" Kelly, and later Edward Flynn wielded power with an iron fist. They rewarded friends and punished foes. Their successes paved the way for the next generation, perhaps best exemplified by Joseph P. Kennedy, to enter the Ivy League institutions and the business and banking worlds of America, so that their children could enjoy even greater success and one ultimately could be elected president of the United States.

During the last half of the nineteenth century and the first half of the twentieth, these politicians and machine bosses were aided by any number of Irish immigrants, who having arrived in America published newspapers catering to the needs of their fellow immigrants. Patrick Ford published the *Irish World*. John Devoy founded the *Gaelic American* in New York City and Joseph McGarrity established the *Irish Press* in Philadelphia, keeping the Irish abreast of the news and events in both America and Ireland. While the political bosses were careful to pay lip service to the cause of Irish independence and the publishers were vigilant about those who did, each of these groups, although influencing the other, largely kept to their respective field. The political bosses did not publish and the publishers did not run for public office. It was a rare individual who tried to navigate both seas.

One individual, who inhabited both worlds and exercised enormous influence in each, is largely unknown in the contributions he made to the successes of the Democratic Party and to the cause of Irish independence. Born in New York City, reared in upstate New York, and forced to leave school at an early age, he would become the youngest mayor of a major American city at the age of twenty-seven. He would pursue higher elective office, publish his own newspaper, establish his own news service, author two books, and write countless political and economic tracts that influenced the events of his day. Indicted twice and investigated by Congress once, both publicly and clandestinely, he would dedicate himself to the cause of Irish freedom, never shrinking from any opportunity, legal or illegal, to drive the British from Ireland. James K. McGuire's rise from poverty to power and his journey through life, both at home and abroad, is the quintessential odyssey that only life in America can provide.

James K. McGuire

1

July 12, 1868

July 12, 1868, dawned hot and humid, as most July days do in New York City. As the sun rose higher in the sky, the temperature rose with it and the humidity pressed oppressively down on the city and its people like a suffocating, wet, steamy blanket. It seemed like all of the country existed in a cauldron. Even the northernmost states, like Minnesota, were sweltering under the record heat this July.

It had been a little more than three years since the end of the "War of the Rebellion," the surrender at Appomattox Courthouse in Virginia, and the assassination of President Lincoln on April 14, 1865. His successor, Andrew Johnson, had been impeached and acquitted by the U.S. Senate only the past May.[1] The Republican Party had nominated the hero of the war, General Ulysses S. Grant, for president shortly thereafter. The Democrats had met in New York only the week before to nominate former New York governor Horatio Seymour on the twenty-second ballot to oppose him, and a delegation to ratify that selection had met in Philadelphia only the day before.

Locally, the results of a coroner's inquest into a murder in Brooklyn were made public in which it was reported that "The only serious incident that took place in the city on the Fourth of July, was the murder of Francis Kerrigan, an old man who kept a boarding house near the corner of Warren street and Underhill-avenue, who drank whiskey, beat, cut and bruised his drunken boarders, and was frequently engaged in quarrels such as are unusual in sober society."

The newspaper, apparently quoting Coroner Slattery, reported that it was the "result of Drinking Bad Whiskey." Pickpockets unsuccessfully accosted one Edward D. Cope of Philadelphia while he was riding in a stagecoach on Broadway and Bleecker Street, resulting in the arrest of all four members of the gang. Elsewhere in the city, Officers Moran and Moody arrested four men who robbed the stateroom of Henry Haywood of Gardner, Massachusetts, on the steamer *City of London* as it docked in New York.[2]

In lower Manhattan, Mary Jane Kennedy McGuire, twenty-three, was giving birth to her firstborn, a son. The young woman had been born in the upstate New York village of St. Johnsville, in Montgomery County, just west of Albany. Her father, John Kennedy, was a prominent farmer there. She was the youngest of six children. Like many families of that period, the Kennedys had been scarred by the war. Her two oldest brothers, Mathew and John, had been Union Army soldiers in Company B of the 34th New York Volunteer Infantry mustered at Little Falls, New York. Both had perished in the Battle of Bull Run. She had two older surviving sisters, Winifred and Margaret, and a brother, Michael.[3]

Mary Jane had met the tall, dark-haired, dark-eyed Irish shoemaker who became her husband five years before. They had been married in 1864 but, unlike most young Roman-Catholic couples of that era, had not been blessed with children immediately.

Her husband, James, had been born on March 3, 1843, in Enniskillen, Ulster, Ireland, two years before the great Potato Famine of 1845–47. The famine so devastated the Irish in Ireland that by one account, "In the west whole families walled themselves into their cabins and died."

Thousands more fled the island, emigrating to the United States, settling in the cities on the eastern seaboard, most notably Boston and New York. The sudden surge of Irish immigrants changed the makeup of the cities dramatically. In New York, "In 1850 26 percent of the population of New York City consisted of persons born in Ireland: some 133,000 out of 513,000."[4] This trend would continue, so that "by 1855 Irish immigrants made up 28 percent of the city's population, and five years later the New York Irish made up 13 percent of all of the Irish in the United States; making it the Hibernian center of the country."[5]

James McGuire was one of them.

The precise year in which James McGuire came to New York City is unknown. His obituary notes only that "he came to New York when a boy." Following his arrival in New York City, James McGuire entered the trades as a shoemaker. He was, by all accounts, "a remarkably skillful mechanic and considered a master-hand at the trade."[6] His skill in this field led him into employment with Burt & Co., a shoe manufacturer, located at 21 Warren Street in lower Manhattan, where he rose to the position of foreman at the age of twenty-three.

On July 12, 1868, Mary Jane and James decided to memorialize their union by naming their newborn son James Kennedy McGuire.

In 1869 James moved his family upstate, to Syracuse.[7] This move may have been precipitated by an offer of employment from Gray Brothers, a Syracuse shoe manufacturer, or by looming labor unrest at Burt & Co.,[8] or both. Whatever the reason, 1870 found the new family in a new city, with a new employer and a future with limitless potential.

2

Life in the Salt City

Optimists in 1870 believed that Syracuse might be destined to become "perhaps, the largest inland city in the state." It had grown swiftly and consistently throughout the previous fifteen years, from a population of 25,107 in 1855 to 28,119 in 1860, to 31,784 in 1865. Growth in the next three years had been even more dramatic. By 1868 the population had risen by 7,226 to 39,010. The following year, 2,440 came, including James McGuire with his wife and son, and the year after that saw 3,346 follow.

Recounting the history of Syracuse in 1870, the publishers of *Boyd's Syracuse City Directory*, noted,

> The city commenced its incipient growth in 1795, by the emigration from the State of Massachusetts of Mr. William Dean, who built a log house on the road leading to Salina, which was the continuation of Clinton Street, running on the low land part of the way on the west and for some distance on the east side of where Oswego Canal is now channeled. Mr. Dean located on this road near where the Van Buren Tannery is now situated, and this was the first house and the first settler of what is now the attractive and the extensive city of Syracuse.[1]

Development initially proceeded at a snail's pace. By 1811, there was a "single place of human habitation, Cossett's tavern," located in the area. Until 1825, when the Erie Canal was completed, the Village of Syracuse had a population of only 300.[2]

Upon arriving in Syracuse, the McGuires took up residence at 149 North Salina Street near Butternut Street on the city's near north

4

side.[3] They found a city teeming with life and ripe with opportunity. Bisected by the Erie Canal with various subsidiary canals running north and south of it, Syracuse boasted 5 hotels, 38 manufacturing concerns, 36 churches, 13 newspapers, 22 bakers, 10 flour dealers, 10 dry-goods dealers, 85 boot and shoe stores, 173 grocers, and a saloon or liquor dealer for every 190 people. It had a new limestone courthouse erected on West Genesee Street, facing the canal; St. Joseph's Hospital, run by the Sisters of St. Joseph on "Prospect Hill"; and St. Joseph's Asylum, an orphanage for boys, which included a boarding school run by the Christian Brothers, four miles west of the city. The city offered education in a school system that had a new high school built on the corner of West Genesee Street and Wallace Street on the eastern bank of Onondaga Creek, which ran north and south through the city, emptying into Onondaga Lake on the city's northern boundary. The system also included eighteen other neighborhood schools including two that served orphanages in the city. The school year was forty weeks, divided into three terms. There were 16,004 children between the ages of five and twenty-one living in the city that year. Approximately half, 8,001, were enrolled in the school system. Daily attendance was even lower, averaging only 5,180. The Board of Education employed 171 teachers with a teacher/student ratio of one teacher for 30.29 students attending per day. The average amount expended per student who attended daily was thirteen dollars and twenty-seven cents per year. Teachers were paid salaries ranging from as low as two hundred dollars per year to as much as two thousand dollars for a high school principal and teacher of languages and English literature.

In addition to the students in the city school system, another 1,639 were educated in private or parochial schools. That year, according to the 1870 *Boyd's City Directory*, an institution of even higher learning was contemplated:

The establishment is to be in the interest of the Methodist denomination, and will lend additional importance, as well as architectural attractions to the already imposing public buildings of the city. It will

be under the control of the Board of Trustees, composed of prominent men among the citizens of Syracuse, and others selected from
different parts of the State. The enterprise is in the incipient stages
but it has been fully inaugurated as to insure its permanency and success, and is a matter of the deepest interest to all concerned therein.

It was to be named Syracuse University.

Along with the Erie Canal and the surrounding canal systems,
Syracuse was also served by a variety of railways and other carriers.
There were four regional railroads: the New York Central and Hud-
son River Railroad, the Syracuse Binghamton & New York Railroad,
the Oswego and Syracuse Railroad, and the Syracuse Northern and
Chenango Valley Railroad. All of them had passenger depots located
in downtown Syracuse and made daily runs through the city. City
dwellers also had available five city railways that operated within the
city. The General City Railway, which commenced at South Salina
Street and terminated in the First Ward on the city's north side; the
Genesee Street and Fourth Ward Railroad Company, which commenced at the New York Central Railroad Depot on Franklin and E.
Washington Street and ran through downtown and northeast to the
James, Lodi, and Green Street neighborhood; the Syracuse and Geddes Railway, which ran from the corner of Salina and Fayette Streets
west to the town of Geddes; the Syracuse and Onondaga Railway,
which ran east from Washington Street to Oakwood Cemetery, then
in the town of Onondaga; and the Fifth Ward Railroad, which ran
southwest from Washington Street to South and Geddes Street.

Stage lines supplemented the railroads in transporting people into
and out of the city from all four directions. Eight stage lines brought
people from Brewerton, Cardiff, Euclid, Navarino, Central Square,
Collamer, Pompey Hill, and the Fayetteville-Manlius-Cazenovia
areas. The horse and buggy rides typically took three and one-half
hours each way.

Three freight companies carried cargo that wasn't human—American Merchants' Union Express Company, U.S. Express Company,
and City Baggage Expresses—all located in the commercial district

near the center of the city. Messages into and out of the city were carried over the wires of the Western Union Telegraph Company and the rival Atlantic and Pacific Telegraph Company, both located on South Salina Street. Culturally, the city took pride in a new Opera House located in the Barton Block on East Genesee Street. The sobriquet "Salt City" was embodied by the thirteen salt companies located in the city and more in the outlying towns. Geddes had seven, Liverpool two, and Salina two more.

John Greenway had erected a brewery, seven stories high, on West Water Street, which backed up to the Erie Canal. It had a daily output of two hundred barrels that were exported throughout the country, the western territories, and Canada.

Thirteen newspapers kept the citizenry abreast of developments in the city, at home, and abroad on a daily and weekly schedule. Among these were the *Syracuse Daily Journal, Syracuse Daily Standard, Syracuse Daily Courier, the Syracuse Union,* and *Syracuse Central Democrat,* the latter two of which were in the German language. Subscriptions were priced from two dollars to eight dollars per year.

The spiritual needs of the faithful were met by congregations of every creed. There were eight Methodist churches, in addition to five Lutheran, four Presbyterian, four Roman Catholic, three Episcopal, two Baptist, two Congregational, one Reformed, one Independent, one Unitarian, and one Universalist. There were also three Jewish congregations and, lest God not have received word of the Emancipation Proclamation seven years previously, the Zion Methodist Episcopal Church existed for the "Colored" population of the city.

Religious and charitable organizations of every purpose abounded. The Syracuse Home Association located at Townsend Street and Hawley Avenue offered refuge and was "open at all hours for the benefit of the virtuous but destitute friendless poor." A variety of Roman Catholic societies such as the St. Vincent de Paul Society, the St. Francis Society, the St. Joseph's Society, the St. Michael's Society, and the St. Stephen's Society offered similar aid to the needy. There was a Catholic Young Men's Association as well as a Ulysses S. Grant Lodge American Protestant Association.

The German community organized its own social network around the Social Turnevin located at 196 North Salina Street and the Schuetzen Verein (Sportsmen's Club).

Independent and secret organizations flourished. The Independent Order of Odd Fellows (IOOF) had six lodges. The Free Masons, not to be outdone, had ten.[4]

As the number of saloons multiplied, so the temperance organizations formed, and, if the churches were segregated by race, the temperance societies were segregated by religion. Temperance had always been a virtue encouraged by the Roman Catholic Church. In Ireland, however, a more stringent temperance movement had swept the country in the decade preceding the Potato Famine, led by a Capuchin friar, Father Theobald Mathew. Thus, while the Syracuse Temperance Union met at City Hall every Sunday afternoon, the Father Mathew Total Abstinence Society met on Sunday evenings at St. John's on Lock Street and on Thursday evenings at St. Mary's on Montgomery Street and Madison Street.[5] It was a city that offered something for everyone.

For the McGuires, the new decade in their new city started out much like the last decade in their old city, New York, had ended. The family had moved into 149 North Salina Street, the first block north of the Erie Canal, which ran east and west through the city. Each day James left his residence, crossed the canal on one of the many bridges, and made his way to Gray Brothers, located on the north side of West Washington Street near the Central Depot where the various railway lines that served the city had their offices.

On April 10, 1871, in a move reminiscent of his experience at the Burt Shoe Factory in New York City, the St. Crispin Society, which James had joined, struck Gray Brothers as well as Leonard, Vroman and Bowers, another shoemaker. In a letter published in the *Syracuse Daily Journal* of April 11, addressed to the Gray Brothers, the Strike Committee informed them as follows:

> Gentlemen:—It is alleged that your firm, or someone in your employ, has discharged some girls formerly in your employ, because said girls belonged to an order known as "The daughters of St. Crispin." If

this is so, you are hereby notified that the workmen employed by you, cannot do any more work for you, until such girls are reinstated, and fully restored to their former condition. This is not addressed to you as a threat, but as the result of a fair conviction on the part of the working classes, that they know their rights, and will maintain them at all hazards; and believing that, on more mature deliberation, you will not deny any person the right of self-protection.

The working classes of these United States may be made of clay but they are not made of mud; and a blind submission to the tyrannical dictates of a few cannot be tolerated.

Hoping that you examine this matter calmly on its own merits, and arrive at a conclusion honorable and satisfactory to both parties, we remain very respectfully your fellow citizens.

The letter was signed by John A. Burns, Samuel A. Hagerman, John Ferguson, Patrick McCarthy, and James McGuire as the "Committee." It was further "attested" by one James Brown, who was identified as the secretary of the Knights of St. Crispin.

That same day, the employers replied in a letter addressed to Brown:

Your communication received, and contents noted.

We discharged three girls this morning for reasons which we think were sufficient, and which any firm in our business would do, (as we think), if placed in a like situation.

We positively did not know of any organization of *Daughters of St. Crispin* (in Syracuse) until after they were discharged and then did not know it until you all left work, and we think, without cause or provocation.

But now as we know you have such an organization, and wish to make issue with us on this point, we will here say that we will not recognize or employ any person or persons belonging to such order of Daughter of St. Crispin.

And we cannot, under any circumstances, reinstate the persons discharged.[6]

The article went on to report that the workers removed their tools and struck Gray Brothers.

Unlike the *New York Times*, which covered developments during the strike against the Burt Shoe Factory as it unfolded, no additional news about the progress or the particulars of the strike against Gray Brothers was reported until eleven days later, on April 21, that the strike had ended with the rehiring of the women employees.[7]

With the strike resolved, life returned to normal in the McGuire household and James continued in his employment with Gray Brothers uneventfully throughout the remainder of the decade. News accounts from this period suggest that relations were uncomplicated between the employer and employees since all that made news were the various charity balls that the Gray Brothers employees sponsored for various causes that they deemed worthwhile.

As the decade unfolded, James and Mary Jane were blessed with four more sons. Charles Matthew, named for James's father and Mary Jane's brother killed at the battle of Bull Run, was born in 1871. John Francis, who would be called "Frankie," was born in 1873. George Henry Moore was born in 1877; and Edward Sarsfield was born in 1880.

In 1874, James moved his family into 69 Lock Street,[8] which would be their home for the next fifteen years. Lock Street, like North Salina Street, began at the northern edge of the Erie Canal and ran northeasterly to Lodi Street on the city's north side. The home was situated between the Church of Saint John the Evangelist, where the family would become parishioners, and across the street from a Lutheran congregation, the First Church of the Evangelical Association at 66 Lock Street.[9]

James K.'s earliest education was in a private school on the Simon Block of Lock Street in which the classes were taught in German.[10] He next attended another German school in the basement of a Lutheran Church located on Butternut Street.[11] In addition to becoming fluent in German, his experience at the hands of German teachers had a great influence on him, as he recounted later in life: "The writer attended two German schools in Syracuse when a boy and was trained to think in the German way. The writer will remember the first and last thought of the German professor was to teach the child his lesson thoroughly."[12]

Upon completing the early grades with the Lutherans, he was next enrolled in a school located at Saint John the Evangelist taught by the Christian Brothers.

The Christian Brothers, founded by St. John Baptist De LaSalle (1651–1719), first made their appearance in central New York during the late 1860s when they founded a school at the St. Joseph's Asylum and Orphanage located in the town of Geddes, on the western edge of Syracuse.[13] The school was "on the farm of the old City Poor House, about four-tenths of a mile south-west of the city on the Split Rock Road. A roomy school is attached for pupils whose parents are able to pay for tuition and receive all the benefits of a quiet, retired course of mental and moral training, removed from the noise and excitement of city life, and is destined to supply a need long felt in this connection."[14]

In 1870, the Rev. John Guerdet invited them to teach at St. John the Evangelist on Lock Street, where they organized the Boys Department of St. John the Evangelist School or "the Brothers School" as it was more generally known. They would teach all males there for the next two decades. It was here that James and Mary Jane sent their sons after they had completed their early education in the German schools on Butternut Street. Study was rigorous and discipline was swift and harsh.

On one occasion, Charles McGuire came to school with a wad of chewing tobacco in his mouth. Confronted by one of the Brothers, he was asked, "What do you have in your mouth, McGuire?" "Nothing, Brother," he responded. "Then swallow," he was told. Obediently, he swallowed the whole mouthful of tobacco, and shortly became deathly ill. He never chewed tobacco again.[15]

Life was pleasant and uneventful for the McGuires during the decade of the 1870s. James worked regularly at Gray Brothers and was "a man of striking presence" and "one of the best known men in the city." At his death he was described "as erect as a grenadier and admired by all for his many exceptional qualities of mind and heart."

Like many young men, he liked to get out of the house in the evening and seek the company of other men in the various pubs and taverns in the city, which were restricted to men only during that era. There, over drinks, they would argue politics and the issues of the day. Despite his lack of formal education, James McGuire was self-taught, well read, and considered a "brilliant conversationalist and quick at repartee." On one occasion, during the early part of the 1870s, he was in the Old Syracuse House

> engaged in an animated discussion with three friends whose pres-
> ence in those days would invariably attract a crowd of interested
> listeners. They were the late Patrick Corbett, James D. Garfield
> and James McGuire, the first two professional men and the latter
> a mechanic. In those days the two lawyers were of the Republican
> faith and Mr. McGuire, was a Democrat. His replies to the attacks
> of the great orators stamped him as a thinker, pleased his friendly
> opponents and surprised his auditors. He was happy a few years later
> when both Corbett and Garfield went over to the opposite party.[16]

Mary Jane was described "as an energetic woman and a remark-ably good mother."[17] She "devoted most of her time to looking after the welfare of her children, for whom she was ready to make any sac-rifice."[18] Unlike her self-taught husband, she was "well educated and early in the life of [James K.] taught him speeches and recitations by her side."[19]

When he wasn't learning the art of speaking from his mother, James K. became a leader and role model for his younger brothers. One of his first jobs was peddling papers to the many mansions that fronted James Street nearby. As he trudged up the hill lined with Dutch elms that formed a canopy over the street, his brothers fol-lowing along behind, he would regale them with his plans to become wealthy, successful, and an owner of a mansion of his own someday.[20]

Throughout the decade of the 1870s, the future looked bright and promising for James and Mary Jane, who had hopes and dreams for their children, and for the McGuire boys, who had hopes and dreams of their own.

3

The Early Years

Tragedy, Triumph, and the Rise to Power

Saturday, May 21, 1881, had been a wet and warm day. The temperature had risen into the low seventies and a rain shower had fallen earlier in the day. "Frankie" McGuire, age eight, was playing with Georgie Stanton and Johnnie Ryan, both age eight, on the banks of the Oswego Canal near the swing bridge of the Chenango Valley Railroad,[1] a few blocks northeast of the McGuire home at 60 Lock Street. A short time later, Charles McGuire, Frankie's older brother, encountered Johnnie Ryan coming toward him on Lock Street. He noticed he was carrying his younger brother's hat. "Your brother Frankie fell into the canal and went under," the youngster told him. The older brother turned and ran back to Lock Street where he got his father and returned to the scene at the canal. There was no sign of his brother.

James McGuire frantically summoned Mullin, the undertaker who serviced the Irish community. Together they searched both sides of the canal looking for the little boy. After a half an hour they found his body on the bottom of the canal on the opposite side. With tears streaming down his face, James McGuire carried his dead son home.

Due to the nature of the death, a coroner's inquest was required. The coroner, who was an elected official named Knapp, had to empanel a jury, present evidence of what occurred, and have the jury render a finding on the manner and cause of death. Despite this official-sounding process, the proceeding was quite summary in nature.

13

It was held that Saturday evening at the Mullin Funeral Parlor and a verdict reached at its conclusion. The only two witnesses to the occurrence at the canal were the two youngsters, Johnnie Ryan and Georgie Stanton.

According the account they provided, the three lads were playing on the bank of the canal near the swing bridge of the Chenango Valley Railroad, which crossed over the canal. The bridge was open, which meant that boats could pass through the canal. In this position, the boys were able to step down into the circular masonry into which the bridge swings when it closes.

At first, they amused themselves by dipping their hats into the canal water and watching the water pour through them.[2] After a short while, they began to see who could dip his head deepest into the water. During this contest, Frankie saw a bug skimming on the surface and reached out to grab it. Losing his balance, he fell into the water. Frightened, Georgie Stanton ran away, leaving Johnnie Ryan alone to fend with the situation. According to young Ryan, he picked up a stick as Frankie surfaced and held it out to him. The stick was too short, however, and Frankie was unable to grasp it. After looking at Ryan and saying "Oh," he sank back under the surface never to re-emerge.[3] After hearing this account, the coroner's jury rendered a verdict of "accidental drowning."[4]

There is probably no more painful, tragic, and grief-producing event in life than the death of a spouse or a child. The sudden, unexpected, accidental death of a young child produces profound grieving, often complicated by the different ways in which the surviving parents try to cope with it. The guilt felt by the parents over their inability to have prevented the child's death only deepens the sense of loss. This guilt can be compounded by the perception, real or imagined, that the other spouse and perhaps the surviving children blame one parent or the other for failing to keep the lost child safe. While the grief and guilt may be borne by both parents, it is often not shared between them. Thus, while one parent may be coping with the loss, the other may not be, and each may be oblivious to the pain of the other. Layered upon this pain, a certain paranoia may arise concerning the safety and well-being of the remaining children and an irrational fear that the parent cannot keep them safe from impending danger or death. In time, emotional walls may go up, a distance may grow, and the easy intimacy that the couple once enjoyed with each other and with the children can be lost forever.

The McGuire family was emotionally devastated by the sudden drowning of Frankie, but James was particularly destroyed by the death of his son. For while the coroner and his jury had received one account of the death of Frankie McGuire, James had heard another, and whether it was accurate or not, it served to only drive him deeper into the depths of his pain, loss, and guilt. The source of the account of the death of Frankie McGuire that plagued James McGuire for the rest of his life is unknown. Presumably it is an account provided by the boys who were playing with his son, and it differed greatly from the one presented to Coroner Knapp on the night of the little boy's death.

According to James McGuire, his son Frankie was indeed playing on the banks of the Oswego Canal with his playmates that May afternoon. But rather than accidentally falling into the canal, he was thrown in by a pack of bullies, who proceeded to step on his fingers, breaking them as he tried to crawl back up out of the water. Unable to climb out, and becoming exhausted, the little boy sank back under the water and drowned. Charles McGuire, the second oldest, vividly recalled his father carrying his lifeless brother into the home at Lock Street, crying and muttering, "Don't ever forget what they did to Frankie."[5] While the account appears implausible in light of the coroner's verdict, it might illuminate the reason behind the unexplained flight of the Stanton boy from the scene, and may have been withheld by both youths out of fear of retaliation. Ultimately, whether it was true or not, it had a profound effect on James McGuire, who would never be the same man again.

In the months and years that followed Frankie McGuire's death, his father would seek deeper and deeper into a stuporous depression, fueled by alcohol, which would cripple him for the rest of his life and alter the future of his older children irrevocably. In some ways, James McGuire had died along with his son.

Author William V. Shannon, in his classic work *The American Irish, A Political and Social Portrait*,[6] described the impact on the family of the loss of the father during these times, observing,

> The death of the father in his late thirties or early forties was common. These premature deaths of so many of the heads of families left their mark. The family held together; the youngest children were kept in school; the oldest helped all they could. After the first bitter impoverished years, the survivors resumed on the same economic level of pinched but not desperate existence as before. The calamity of the father's loss, however, had invisible psychological costs. It pulled the family inward. It curbed and frustrated individual ambitions to an extent that was abnormal in the larger American society which was increasingly committed to individualism, the emancipation of women, and the relaxation of parental control. It was a reversion in an urban setting to a family-centered life that most Americans migrating from farm to city were moving away from.
>
> The younger members of a family deprived of its chief male support began at the age of five or six to peddle papers, pick coke, run errands, and rummage through junkyards for useful and salable items. Upon the older children, just entering adolescence, were thrust the heavy burdens of maturity. At twelve or thirteen, boys took on full-time jobs wrestling freight or carrying a hod. From the oldest to the youngest, the members of the family were inculcated with the conviction that the family must maintain a united front if it were to survive. Sticking together was the only basis of hope for the future at all.[7]

While James McGuire was not physically dead, his paralyzing depression resulted in his oldest son and namesake's having to leave the Christian Brothers and enter the job market the following year, at the age of fourteen. His younger brother Charles would do the same at the age of fifteen.

James K. McGuire was luckier than most young men entering the job market for the first time. Unlike the youths described by Shannon in *The American Irish*, he did not have to wrestle freight, carry a hod, or engage in the backbreaking manual labor open to the Irish during this period. *Boyd's City Directory* for the year 1883 lists him as being employed in the capacity of a "clerk" at J. S. Atwell & Co., "Hosiery and Fancy Goods," 28 West Washington Street, which was a short walk from 60 Lock Street on the other side of the Erie Canal.

Various biographical profiles of him throughout his lifetime have him leaving school at the age of twelve and hawking newspapers on the trains belonging to the New York Central Railroad.[8] Indeed, some mythology grew up around this early employment, with one New York City newspaper at the height of his popularity going so far as to claim that he "was born in a downtown tenement. He sold papers in the daytime and picked up what schooling he could at night. An orphan, he lived in the Newsboys' Lodging House. As he grew bigger he went to Syracuse and there sold papers, continuing to attend night school."[9]

McGuire himself could sometimes burnish this legend, as noted in a 1947 news story almost a quarter-century after his death, in which it was reported, "After having many jobs—as many as 40, he claimed—he became a bookkeeper with a hardware concern in S. Clinton St., which within a few years was Kennedy, Spaulding & McGuire."[10]

Some of this legend was amplified in his profile in the *Dictionary of American Biography*,[11] which recounted that "he left school to earn his living before the age of twelve, worked as a newsboy on trains between Syracuse and New York, was employed in a candy factory, fed a printing press in a printing office, tried the baking trade, worked in a machine shop, was office boy in a law office, and at thirteen secured employment with Messrs. Kennedy, Spaulding & Co., wholesale hardware merchants in Clinton and West Washington Street."[12] Needless to say, this would have made for a very busy year. Since *Boyd's Directory* for the year 1882 does not list him as being in the labor market, as it does in each succeeding year after 1883,[13] it is safe to assume that he did not leave school until sometime in 1882, the year following his brother's drowning as his father's depression deepened. In the first public profile of him published in a Syracuse newspaper, in 1893,[14] two years before he sought public office, it was reported that he left school at the age of fourteen, corroborating the information in *Boyd's*.

Following his stint as a clerk at Atwell's, he obtained a position as a clerk with the firm of Bradford & Kennedy, which sold hardware, in 1884.[15] In 1885 he was promoted to the position of bookkeeper, and in 1887 he would become the cashier.[16] He would remain with Bradford & Kennedy, becoming a partner in 1893.[17]

In 1883 the last of his siblings was born, a sister, named Mary Elizabeth, on May 5.[18] She would be called Elizabeth.

The following year, 1884, he took a position as a clerk for Bradford & Kennedy, located at 32 South Clinton Street. During this period, he would begin to mature and evolve into the most gifted and compelling speaker that the area had ever heard.

The years between 1883 and 1885 were relatively uneventful, except for the developments in the McGuire household. The presence of his only infant daughter did not alleviate the depression that James McGuire had fallen into as a result of his third son's death. His addiction to alcohol increased and began to affect his work at Gray Brothers. He was not listed in the 1883 city directory and was omitted from the listing "Bootmakers" in the business section of the directory from 1884 on.[19]

In 1886, James K., at the age of eighteen, became the local correspondent for the *Irish World*.[20] The *Irish World* was founded by Patrick Ford, a native of Galway, in New York City in 1870.[21] This position would expose him to the struggles of the Irish in their native land, which would become one of the passions of his life. As he studied and mastered the issues surrounding the Fenian struggle for independence being waged in Ireland, he wrote articles about it, as well as penned letters to other newspapers on the subject. During that same year, he began to speak on labor issues to various labor organizations throughout the city.[22]

The following year, 1887, would prove to be eventful for both McGuire and his younger brother Charles. That year he drew notice for a speech to a labor convention at the old City Hall.[23] Later in the year he spoke to a group of farmers on the shore of Onondaga Lake.

This speech led to his election as the state secretary of the Farmers and Industrial Union, an organization he abandoned when it became involved in third-party politics.[24] That fall he made speeches before a number of ward committees of the Democratic Party.[25] That same year, Charles, sixteen, left school at the Christian Brothers and entered the labor market. His first job was as a clerk for G. N. Crouse & Co., a wholesale grocer, located at 32 West Water Street,[26] around the corner from Bradford & Kennedy where his older brother was employed.

The year 1887 would also begin James McGuire's steepest decline. In June the first of a succession of arrests occurred at the home located at 309 Green Street involving disturbances resulting from his drinking.[27]

Eighteen eighty-eight would prove to be a continuation of the previous year, as James K. McGuire became more active and involved in politics at all levels. On the local level, he became secretary of the Democratic Party.[28] He also became secretary of the Tariff Reform Club.[29] The issue of protective tariffs would be paramount in the 1888 presidential election, in which Grover Cleveland would stand for reelection.[30] McGuire wrote a number of pamphlets, including "Labor and Protection," supporting Cleveland's efforts to have the tariffs repealed. These became campaign documents in the western states.[31] The campaign was largely conducted by surrogates,[32] one of whom would be James K. McGuire. Stumping for Cleveland on November 3, 1888, he told the crowd,

The greatest political battle to be fought tomorrow is not merely a partisan political scramble for the spoils of office or the control of public patronage, but it is the fight of the common people against the ever increasing power of the protected vested interests of the nation. If ignorance, prejudice, and the influence of money should encompass the defeat of Grover Cleveland, as the red orbs of the sun pass silently beyond the clouds on the morrow, the man who would rather be right than be ruler of the land has fallen, and the cause of justice will receive a powerful blow and the commercial progress of our country checked and arrested. But it will be the Bull Run of the movement for tariff reform, not a Waterloo.

But we hope for victory and we will not anticipate defeat. And so supreme in our confidence and trust in the honor and intelligence of the American people that like Paul the Hermit in the first crusade of old, in the enthusiastic zeal that comes from a knowledge of right we could almost cry out, "God wills it!"[33]

Despite his best efforts, his candidate, Cleveland, went down to defeat on Election Day.

While 1888 was a year in which her oldest son's phenomenal accomplishments brought both pride and joy to Mary Jane McGuire, it was also a year that brought her great pain as a result of her husband's continuing mental state. The previous year he had been arrested for the first time, as a result of his drinking too much at the family home. While the Police Court justice, Thomas Mulholland, had been lenient and imposed only a five-dollar fine,[34] the family felt the situation at home had become too chaotic and had him involuntarily committed to the state asylum at Utica, New York, approximately forty miles east of Syracuse. Involuntarily committed to the Utica asylum, he was not amenable to staying. Twice he escaped,[35] and during one such occurrence, he walked the forty miles back to Syracuse, arriving at his home on Lock Street, instructing his family, "Don't ever send me there again!"[36] Each time, he was captured and returned. During the last week of March, he escaped again, making "a daring leap through a window." Again he was taken into custody, but after being held by the Syracuse police for a judicial examination, he was certified as sane and released.[37] Although legally sane, as events would prove, he was no better. Four months later, on August 20, 1888, he was arrested for breach of the peace at the family home on Green Street. This time, he was sentenced to ninety days' confinement at the Onondaga County Penitentiary but released on payment of a nominal fine.[38]

Throughout this period, the two eldest McGuire boys continued to support the household. James had been promoted to the position of cashier at Bradford & Kennedy, and Charles had moved to a clerk's position at C. E. Crouse & Co., another wholesale grocer, at 53 West Water Street, across the street from his former employer.[39]

The year 1889 would prove to be almost a mirror image of the previous year, except that the triumphs and tragedies in the McGuire family would be starker. For James K. and Charles McGuire, it would be another year of sustained accomplishment. At Bradford & Kennedy, now located at 210 South Clinton Street,[40] James, now twenty-one, continued to be a reliable and valuable cashier. His employers, perhaps recognizing his increasing prominence and enormous gifts, were generous in allowing him to pursue civic endeavors that must have impeded his employment responsibilities. He was sent to the Tariff Reform Convention in Indianapolis, Indiana, that year, and made a number of speeches on that issue in other states.[41] During all of his addresses, McGuire urged the renomination of Grover Cleveland by the Democrats at the next presidential election, three years off.[42] On September 17 of that year, in Buffalo, New York, where Cleveland had been both mayor and county sheriff prior to his ascension to governor,[43] McGuire told a crowd,

> Never was there so triumphant a defeat as that of Grover Cleveland and tariff reform in 1888. It was the Bull Run of the movement, not its Waterloo. The discussion aroused latent thought in the minds of professional men, doctors of divinity, college men and others of that class of our citizens who hitherto have been indisposed to advocate thoughts that savored of politics. These men will be of great assistance to us in the great political battle the lines of which are already forming. Revolutions never go backwards. The cause of tariff reform and her dauntless champion are bound to win in 92.
>
> It always appears to me that so long as only eighteen dollars and ten days ride on the water separates us from the "pauper" labor of Europe, from our own home labor, protection oppresses taxes, restricts, does everything but protect. This system enriches the few and enriches the many. It is not in accord with our Constitution. Our wise forefathers never intended that Congress should have the power to turn the protection of wealth from its natural channels, to tax the

many that the few may be benefitted, or that the American citizen should be deprived of the inalienable right to enhance the fruits of his labor where it will be most beneficial to himself and his family.[44]

He was also elected state secretary of the Farmers and Industrial Union, as well as the Tariff Reform League, but declined both offices due to the pressure of other activities. McGuire proved to be a prolific writer during this period, writing numerous articles on current events. One such article on tariff reform won first prize from the *Tax Reform Advocate*. Another subject that kept his pen active was the Irish Land League and the struggle being waged by the Fenian leader Charles Stuart Parnell. During fall 1889, he accepted the position of secretary of the Ballot Reform League and traveled to Albany to advocate for the adoption of the secret ballot. Among the converts to this issue he was able to make was the former president Grover Cleveland. He compiled a series of letters on various subjects relating to economics into a small book of fifteen chapters. This would prove to be the first of several books he would write over the course of his lifetime.

He also was active on issues of more local interest, giving a series of speeches in favor of municipal ownership of facilities to bring water from Skaneateles Lake to Syracuse. In a more partisan vein, he made several speeches on behalf of Mayor William B. Kirk, who was seeking reelection as mayor of Syracuse. He was nominated for the New York State Assembly in the First District but declined the nomination. During 1889 his younger brother Charles, eighteen, took a position as bookkeeper with A. D. Gregory Building Supply at 120 North Salina Street.[45]

As James K.'s fortunes continued to rise, the elder James's continued to decline. He was arrested and fined again on January 8, 1889, for breach of the peace and intoxication. On February 26, 1889, he hit bottom. He was arrested and charged with breach of the peace, public intoxication, and using insulting and abusive language in violation of Section 3 of Chapter 27 of the Ordinances of the City of Syracuse. Unlike the previous incidents, which occurred at home, this one took place at Lewis and Whelan's "Segars, Tobacco and Newsroom" located

1. James K. McGuire, ca. 1917, courtesy of the Fahey family.

at 7 and 8 Granger Block on Warren Street between East Washington Street and East Genesee Street It probably did not help that the owners, Edward Lewis and Michael Whelan, were police commissioner and city treasurer, respectively.[46] He was brought before the Hon. Thomas Mulholland, police justice for the City of Syracuse.[47] James, who had never denied being an alcoholic, again pled guilty. This time Judge Mulholland sentenced him to sixty days confinement in the penitentiary.

Penitentiary life in 1889 was not easy. Unlike the asylum, where patients had "dances, and theatricals and . . . kind treatment,"[48] the penitentiary operated under the "code of silence" in which inmates were forbidden to talk to each other.[49] Horizontal stripes were the uniform of the day,[50] and prisoners were assigned to work details such as clearing away earth and rocks. The work could be hard and back-breaking for a forty-four-year-old man who was not accustomed to it. Accidents, sometimes fatal, could occur.

Just nine years before, the Onondaga County Penitentiary had been rocked by a scandal when it was discovered that inmates, both male and female, had been "flogged, 'bucked,' suspended head downwards and otherwise subjected to cruel punishments."[51] It was not a place for someone as recalcitrant as James McGuire. It left young James no choice but to take legal action, which must have come with no small amount of public embarrassment and humiliation.

James K., only twenty years old, retained the services of Hopkins & Boudy, lawyers with offices also located in the Granger Block, to seek his father's release. On March 15, 1889, after James had been imprisoned for slightly more than two weeks, his son filed a petition for a Writ of Habeas Corpus in the Onondaga County Court, before the Honorable A. J. Northrup, contesting his father's imprisonment. While the legal grounds contesting the sentence appear somewhat dubious, in that the sentence was unauthorized, Judge Northrup, perhaps recalling James's history of asylum commitment, may have used the argument as a pretext to order James to be released that afternoon.[52] Notwithstanding his good fortune, the elder James would be involved in several more disturbances at home during the next year, but none of them would result in anything more serious than a fine's being imposed by Judge Mulholland.[53]

Despite the fact that life continued to be tragic and chaotic in the household, both James and Charles continued to achieve success outside the home during 1890. James authored a number of "tariff tracts for farmers of the west," and a paper was published from his pen that year entitled "The Democratic Party's Relation to Tariff Reform."

In the business world, James maintained his position as cashier with Bradford & Kennedy, while Charles took a position as a bookkeeper with Robert McCarthy & Son, a wholesale hardware and cutlery concern, located at 219 West Water Street.[54] Charles's life and career, however, were about to take a dramatic turn.

Eighteen ninety-one proved to be a watershed year for both young men. James's speeches on the Irish took him far and wide, from Chicago to New York City. On August 15 he addressed a crowd of more than ten thousand in Ogden Park in Chicago.[55] The *Chicago Sun-Times*, chronicling this appearance, recounted, "Mr. McGuire was introduced to the vast audience by M. J. McKean, and was greeted with tumultuous applause. His speech occupied 55 minutes in delivery, and held the audience almost spellbound until the close. His youthful appearance contrasted greatly with his polished oratory and depth of thought; which belong generally to those of more mature years. He pointed out that the Irish people were battling for the same principles [for] which the American colonists fought over a century ago."

A Syracuse paper was sufficiently impressed with McGuire's Chicago oratory that a profile of him accompanied the piece, which related,

James K. McGuire who was the main speaker at the great Irish gathering at Ogden's Grove, Chicago, yesterday, is cashier for Kennedy & Spaulding, wholesale hardware, of this city. He was born in New York City July 12, 1868, and has lived in Syracuse nearly twenty three years. His education was received in the Christian Brothers school, Lock street. After graduation he entered the employ of Kennedy & Spaulding. He has been a trusted and efficient employee and now occupies the position of cashier for that extensive establishment. Mr. McGuire is a thorough student and deep thinker who spends his leisure moments reading and writing. He is an orator of great promise who has spoken before multitudes of voters before he was able to exercise the franchise on account of his youth. He has made the tariff question a study and is a great admirer of Cleveland's tariff ideas. In 1888 he addressed a meeting on behalf of Cleveland. During 1888, 89, 90, he was the Secretary of the Ballot Reform Club.

During the agitation in favor of Skaneateles Lake as a water source, Mr. McGuire delivered a number of addresses in favor of the scheme.

He delivered a series of speeches throughout New York State and Ohio in September, 1889, on the tariff question under the auspices of the Tariff Reform Club.

He has contributed many valuable articles on the tariff and labor questions to the principal New York and Chicago papers during the past three years.

His ideas on the tariff issue and articles published have been commended by ex-President Cleveland, Roger Q. Mills and other Democratic leaders. He has taken a great interest in Irish affairs, and his writings on the Irish question have been read with interest by the leaders of the Irish movement in America. The subject of our sketch was nominated twice for member of the Assembly in the First Onondaga District by the Democrats, and has declined in each instance. He is Secretary of the Tariff reform and Ballot Reform clubs, and is Vice-President of Division No. 1, A.O.H.[56]

Reporting on the Ogden Park appearance in a later profile, the *Syracuse Sunday Herald* noted,

In the summer of 1891 he spoke at several fairs and on August 15th delivered two addresses, afternoon and evening, on "Irish Nationality" before 15,000 people at Chicago. These addresses aroused great enthusiasm and were highly commended by the Chicago newspapers. The *Chicago Interocean* said, "Mr. McGuire's eloquent appeal stirred the audience to the greatest pitch of excitement it had yet reached." The Chicago demonstration gave him a wide reputation and he is constantly in demand by Irish societies. He has spoken in many cities, including New York where his addresses were delivered in Parepa hall and in Germania hall.

Later that year, on November 27, 1891, in New York City, he again held forth on the Irish cause, telling his audience,

"The truest test of civilizations," says Emerson, "is not the census or the size of the cities, nor the crops, no, but the kind of men that the country turns out." And from the humble cabins on the sides of the hillsides of Ireland have emanated men who, although handicapped by poverty and ignorance, have broken their fetters and shackles and attained the highest position of eminence, trust and responsibility. The oppressor gravely informs a wondering world that coercion laws are absolutely necessary to govern the Irish people, who are unable to govern themselves. That dungeons, prisons and scaffolds are needed to curb the rebellious spirit of the wild and imaginative Celt.

Where would English literature rank in art without Irish imagination. They forget Swift, Mangan, Berkely, Griffin, Goldsmith, Burke, Steele, Sheridan, Stern, and Maria Edgeworth and the hundreds of illustrious Irishmen and women who adorn the pages of English literature. Have these people committed a crime because, in spite of persecution and oppression, they have outstripped the more phlegmatic English?

The policy of England destroyed Irish literature and the Irish language. Their cruel tyrannical laws, by keeping the people in ignorance and superstition, aimed to sap the mental development of the race. But genius reached the surface under any and all conditions. They tell us the Gael is impracticable and not blessed with a scientific mind. But let us see. Abernethey, the first surgeon of England, was an Irishman. I recall to mind, Ball, the naturalist, Barry, the artist, Dr. Joseph Black, the distinguished chemist, Robert Boyle, the philosopher, Cairnes, the economist, Crozier, the explorer, Doctor Flood, the anatomist, Hamilton, the mathematician, Harvey, the botanist, Hogan, the sculptor, Parsons, the astronomer, and Wilde, the great oculist. Each and every one of these illustrious men ranked first in their various pursuits, and they were all Irishmen.

And surely in our own beloved America the Irish people have demonstrated their fitness for government. Last year the Mayors of forty out of eighty cities were men of Irish blood. We point with pardonable pride to the long and honored roll of illustrious Irishmen in America who have achieved distinction in every branch of art, science, invention, manufactures and commerce.[57]

Unlike other prominent political personalities and officials of his era, McGuire's oratorical skills came naturally to him. Jack Bellamy in his biography of Boston mayor James Michael Curley recounts the training and lessons Curley received in elocution and oratory during his lifetime.[58] There is no account of McGuire's receiving any type of similar coaching. While he was capable of utilizing colorful metaphors and biblical analogies, for the most part he addressed his audiences in simple, basic, understandable language that more than adequately conveyed his message. His electoral successes were conclusive testament to those gifts.

That same year, 1891, Charles McGuire, twenty, bought an insurance agency. The McGuire Insurance Agency, in which he held the title of president, would become an important part of the McGuire family and would be intertwined in the highs and lows of James's career for the remainder of his life.

Eighteen ninety-two would mark the beginning and the end of two important chapters in James K. McGuire's life: his entry into the publishing business and the death of his father, James, at age forty-nine.

On June 24, 1892, the *Catholic Sun*, Syracuse's first Catholic newspaper, made its debut. James K. McGuire was listed on the Board of Directors and as secretary-treasurer of the Syracuse Catholic Publishing Company. The two new owners of McGuire Insurance, Charles M. and John McGuire, who was not a relative, were on the "grand list of gentlemen" listed as stockholders in a "company capitalized at $20,000."[59] In a front page story titled "How We Start," the paper told of its inception, relating, "Four months ago a few enterprising Catholic gentlemen assembled together to consider the question of establishing and publishing a thoroughly Catholic newspaper worthy of this city and the Syracuse diocese."[60]

The *Catholic Sun*, in addition to providing James K. a position of some prominence and respectability, would also be another medium through which his future exploits and accomplishments would be reported. While the weekly newspaper was designed to be primarily a news organ of the Catholic community, it occasionally strayed into national politics. Less than a month after its maiden edition, it came to the defense of McGuire's hero Grover Cleveland in an unsigned editorial that read suspiciously like a McGuire piece.

On October 21 that year, James McGuire died at the family home at 309 Green Street. Despite his tragic and somewhat public descent into mental illness, fueled by alcohol, the Syracuse newspapers were surprisingly kind to him. The *Syracuse Daily Journal* in describing him wrote, "At one time he possessed considerable property and was regarded as a man of keen intellect."[61]

An obituary in the *Catholic Sun* described him in a similar complimentary fashion. This article is noteworthy in several other disclosures. It contains the first mention of the James K. McGuire Democratic Association.[62] The James K. McGuire Democratic Association was a "marching club of large membership" of which "he was the youngest member."[63] It also reported that James had ceased his employment with Gray Brothers in 1890, two years before his death. In addition to floral tributes from the mayor, W. B. Kirk; the Democratic County Association; and the Tariff Reform Club, there was one from Jennie Dolphin, a young lady who would eventually marry Charles and become James's sister-in-law.[64]

Despite these two monumental events in James's life, 1892 was just as hectic politically for him, if not more so. His primary mission that year was the renomination of Grover Cleveland as the Democratic Party candidate for president of the United States. This undertaking was complicated by the fact that Cleveland remained unpopular with the powerful Tammany Hall organization and its candidate, U.S. Senator David Hill, also of New York.[65]

The former president was, to say the least, a reluctant candidate. One of his biographers, H. Paul Jeffers, recounted that "when some went so far as to express their hope that he might run for president, he attempted to dissuade them by predicting that the outcome would be another party defeat."[66]

Cleveland's reluctance in no way tempered McGuire's zeal in this endeavor. As the *Syracuse Sunday Herald* noted, "From almost the hour of his defeat in 1888 he had been urging him as the logical candidate of the party for 1892."[67]

Indeed, his efforts to obtain Cleveland's renomination were a constant refrain in the speeches he gave on tariff reform during those years and resulted in his bucking the Democratic Party elders and establishment at both the New York State and National Democratic Convention in Chicago as 1892 unfolded. The leaders of the New York State Democratic Party attempted to convene a "snap" convention in Albany, one held on short notice, during the month of February when that city and much of the state were covered with snow, making travel difficult if not impossible. The strategy was to ensure that the delegates chosen for the party's national convention would be bound to the nomination of party boss and senior New York State senator David Hill, who would be a candidate for president.[68] Locally, former mayor and party boss William B. Kirk tried to secure delegates pledged to Hill.[69]

Despite his best efforts to deliver a slate of delegates totally committed to Hill, Kirk's worst fear materialized. An anti-Hill/pro-Cleveland delegate was chosen as an alternate from the Twenty-fifth Congressional District: James K. McGuire.[70]

How James came to be chosen as a delegate at this convention remained something of a mystery. Nevertheless, out of all of this controversy and confusion, he emerged as a force. As the *Syracuse Sunday Herald* reported, "In February 1892, Mr. McGuire refused to abide by the decision of the Democratic State convention, claiming that it had been called too early and that its result was unsatisfactory to the rank and file of the party, who he claimed, wanted Cleveland. For some reason he was made an alternate on the Hill delegation to Chicago, although his position was thoroughly understood at Albany. He refused to abide by his instructions, saying that he had not asked for the honor and could not be held responsible."[71]

Although the State Democratic Party had chosen delegates pledged to Senator Hill, James persisted in his quest to sway the party nomination to Cleveland. Upon his return to Syracuse, he organized a committee on Cleveland's behalf. As the *Syracuse Sunday Herald* described it,

> When the committee of fifteen was organized here, William Beach was made chairman and McGuire secretary. Together they started out to organize the county for Cleveland and the May Convention. Mr. Beach took care of the towns and Mr. McGuire perfected an organization in every ward in the city.
>
> The caucuses were largely attended and the enrollment in the county reached 7,000. Mr. McGuire also delivered addresses on other points urging Cleveland's nomination.[72]

This was, apparently, McGuire's initial break with William B. Kirk. Kirk was mayor of Syracuse from 1888 to 1889 and the Democratic Party political boss of Onondaga County. Kirk was born in Syracuse on June 6, 1850. He was both wealthy and privileged from birth.[73]

At this point in their respective careers, McGuire and Kirk were allies. Kirk, during his administration as mayor, sought to bring drinking water to Syracuse from Skaneateles Lake.[74] McGuire made speeches in support of the project on his behalf. When Kirk sought reelection in 1889, McGuire, twenty-one, made speeches in support of his candidacy.[75] The break between McGuire and Kirk during the Cleveland-Hill contest would not be the last time the two men clashed.

In addition to Kirk, McGuire made other powerful enemies during this contest. Hill, the favorite son, former governor, and current U.S. senator, was supported by other political bosses in the state. The *New York Times* reported that the Hill candidacy was supported by "Messrs. Murphy, Croker, McLaughlin and Sheehan, the new bosses of the party."[76]

Born in 1843, the same year as McGuire's father, in County Cork, Ireland, Richard Croker was brought to the United States in 1846 by his father, Eyre Coote Croker. Although he was descended from the English and Protestant by birth, he was commonly mistaken to be Irish, perhaps because the family settled in the Irish shantytown that is now the site of Central Park in New York City. His political trajectory was somewhat similar to that of William Magear Tweed, in that both men emerged as the leader of the Tammany political club at the same age, forty-six. In 1886 Croker became the leader of the powerful Tammany organization,[77] and as the *New York Times* reported, helped secure the New York State delegation for Senator David Hill. McGuire's bucking of the party leadership, and his support of Grover Cleveland, would have dire political effects on his future political fortunes.

In addition to the enmity of the party bosses, McGuire came to the attention of the newspapers that supported Hill's candidacy and that poured out their wrath and invective about him to their readers. The widely read *New York Sun* inveighed against him, as a "sample of Cleveland treachery." Although chosen as an alternate delegate at the February state convention, McGuire worked tirelessly organizing a second convention to be held in Syracuse that May and attacked the Tammany Hall bosses.

McGuire went on to the Democratic National Convention in Chicago that June, where he, although being the youngest delegate to the convention,[78] continued to make a lasting impression on friend and foe alike. If McGuire had gained an ally in the former mayor of New York City, at the same time he made an enemy in Lieutenant Governor William F. Sheehan, also a delegate from New York.[79] Their chance encounter before the Washington delegation led to an acrimonious exchange between the state's second highest elected official and the convention's youngest delegate.

Upon returning to Syracuse from the convention, James threw himself wholeheartedly into the presidential campaign. The local papers and his own *Catholic Sun* reported on his speeches for Cleveland. On Election night in 1892, Cleveland "won the presidency in a landslide the like of which had not been seen since Lincoln was reelected in 1864. The Democrats found themselves blinking in amazement at carrying New York, New Jersey, Connecticut, and Indiana, and almost winning all the electors in Republican bastions of Ohio and Michigan."[80] James K. McGuire's political star power was rising and burning brighter than ever.

The election of Grover Cleveland to a second presidency fueled public speculation about McGuire's future, whether he would take a post in the administration and share in the spoils of victory. On February 11, 1893, several weeks prior to Cleveland's inauguration, the *Syracuse Evening Herald* openly raised the question before its readers, reporting that McGuire had played such an instrumental role in Cleveland's victory that the president-elect was considering him for a position in his administration or a foreign posting, possibly in Guatemala. When confronted by a reporter, McGuire was concerned that such a position would "interfere with his business relations."[81]

In addition to his "business relations," there were other factors that might have militated against his accepting a consular position or other office in the Cleveland administration. At the top of the list is the fact that his father had been dead for only four months and there was the matter of his mother and younger siblings to support. Social Security and other "safety net" programs were almost fifty years in the future, and as author William Shannon pointed out, the responsibility for the support of the household usually fell to the eldest child. Although James had been listed as an employee of Gray Brothers in his obituary, it had been years since he had been genuinely productive, and both James K. and Charles had shouldered the burden of supporting the household for some time. While Charles was in the process of building a successful insurance agency, it is doubtful that he could have taken on this financial responsibility alone, with James living and working elsewhere. It is also possible that James harbored his own political ambitions. He had been nominated for public office twice,[82] and had declined both times. Whether his earlier decision not to seek the assembly seat had been motivated by his concern about his father's increasing notoriety resulting from his frequent arrests is open to conjecture. In this day and age, when every aspect of a candidate's upbringing is under a microscope, such a reason would be readily understandable; however, at no point in James K.'s career did his father ever become an issue. Indeed, James's father's life and death were treated both charitably and positively by the newspaper that ran his obituary.[83] Whatever the reason was, McGuire chose to remain in

Syracuse with Bradford Kennedy Sons & McGuire, and went about making his presence even larger in the community.

As 1892 turned into 1893, McGuire's life became even more active and successful. In spite of the widespread speculation that he might take a consular position in Guatemala in the Cleveland administration, he decided to stay in Syracuse and his employer, Bradford Kennedy and Sons, brought him into the business as a partner.[84] It is hard to say how much of this decision was driven by the need to help his mother provide for his younger siblings, now that her husband was dead, or whether it was motivated by a desire to pursue an active political career.

Although the 1895 mayoral campaign would not officially kick off until October, there was plenty of drama and activity in the months preceding it, particularly in the Democratic Party. Former mayor William B. Kirk, who controlled it or by some was considered the "Boss,"[85] sought to dictate the nomination. McGuire, however, had done a thorough canvass of all of the city ward committees and was convinced he had a sufficient number of votes to secure the nomination at the party convention.[86] The *Syracuse Standard*, which was house organ of the Republican Party, did a credible job of reporting on the contest, even if it could not resist characterizing the former mayor as "Boss" Kirk. In describing the contest, it reported that McGuire had thirty-six delegates of the forty-eight delegates required to win the mayoral nomination and that party elders were trying to dissuade him from running. In this regard it also reported that McGuire was reassessing his candidacy.[87] The article further reported that former mayor Thomas Ryan was prepared to become the Democratic candidate in McGuire's stead.

To paraphrase Mark Twain, reports of McGuire's political demise were greatly exaggerated. While the Kirk forces contended that their opposition to McGuire was based upon his youth and inexperience, it became increasingly evident that the dispute was about power, control, and ultimately future patronage. The fault lines in the party continued to deepen as the *Standard* reported that McGuire had the support of sixty-five of the ninety-five delegates elected at the caucuses earlier in the year but that the party bosses were confident that they could persuade many of them to support another candidate.[88]

McGuire's apparent indecision about seeing his candidacy through to conclusion may have been a feint to throw off his opposition about his real intentions and actual strength. Indeed, at a party meeting on September 30 to decide when and where the party convention should be held, he apparently failed in his preference to have the convention held in the evening rather than during the daytime working hours.[89] Emboldened by this victory, the Kirk forces sought to pass a resolution releasing the Ninth Ward delegates from their pledge to vote for McGuire and allowing them to vote for former mayor Ryan. This resolution, which failed, provoked a strong response from at least one of the Ninth Ward delegates, who was heard to remark, "Any duffer what makes a res'lution for to trow down Jim 'Guire will get a poke in the jaw from me. D'ye see?"[90] The tension surrounding this ward meeting escalated to a point at which the windows in the firehouse where it was being held were stoned, and the police were called out to keep order because of the size of the gathering crowd that could not gain entry.

As the date of the Democratic convention neared, Kirk advanced one candidate after another as an alternative to McGuire. In addition to former mayor Thomas Ryan, Henry Lyon, William Niver, and Duncan Peck were floated as candidates.[91] At a preconvention meeting, Kirk proposed that McGuire, Ryan, and Lyons serve as a committee to select a chairman for the convention. Kirk and McGuire held a number of meetings during which Kirk tried, without success, to get McGuire to withdraw as a candidate in favor of Niver. Realizing that McGuire was in the race to stay, Kirk went after as many of McGuire's delegates as possible, attempting to cajole or intimidate them into changing their vote. As one delegate characterized it, McGuire was leading the younger men who had been carrying the workload in the party activities against the Kirk machine. A member of the Kirk machine took a different view of McGuire's chances, contending that the organization was too strong for the young men of the party to wrest the nomination away from the leaders.[92]

On October 8, a test of strength of the two factions occurred on two procedural votes. McGuire's forces won, 53 to 41; Kirk threw in the towel and moved to nominate McGuire by acclamation.[93]

The following day the *New York Times* captured the action, the scene, and the mood, reporting that McGuire had prevailed over the party's power structure. It portrayed the result as a victory of one generation over a preceding generation. It described McGuire as a "magnetic speaker" who would go into the campaign as a "champion of municipal reform."[94]

If the Democratic Party appeared split at the time it went to choose its candidate, the fissures that continued to exist in the Republican Party between the Belden and Hendricks wings remained unbridgeable. The first inkling that trouble might be afoot appeared in the *Standard* on October 2, when it reported that the ex-congressman would be arriving in the United States from Europe and would be met by a delegation of local politicians on the dock in New York City.[95] At the same time, the incumbent mayor, Jacob Amos, was still undecided about whether to seek a third term, and those in the leadership of the Hendricks wing of the party were not tipping their hand about his candidacy. In some quarters this issue would be decided by whether McGuire became the Democratic nominee. The *Herald* reported that if McGuire were nominated the Party would choose Amos again; however, if another more senior Democrat were nominated, a different Republican candidate would be chosen.[96]

Despite McGuire's upset victory over the Kirk forces on October 9, Mayor Amos decided not to seek a third term and a new name was added to those of Lyman C. Smith and Hendrick S. Holden: Charles F. Saul, a school commissioner.[97] On the morning after the McGuire nomination, the leadership of the Hendricks wing met and decided that Saul would be the nominee.[98]

On October 10, the Republicans met at City Hall and made it official by nominating businessman Charles F. Saul.[99]

The election of 1895, like many of that era, was largely conducted through the newspapers of the day. The candidates themselves generally refrained from personal attacks on one another, leaving that

2. Francis Hendricks, Onondaga County Republican boss, New York State senator, and New York State insurance commissioner, courtesy of the Onondaga Historical Association.

task to surrogates and the publishers supporting them. Syracuse had six newspapers in existence, the *Syracuse Standard*, the *Syracuse Courier*, the *Syracuse Post*, the *Syracuse Herald*, the *Syracuse Journal*, and the *Syracuse Evening News*. Each of them supported a candidate in the race for mayor, and the distinction between editorial support and news coverage of the campaign was often blurred.

The *Courier* supported McGuire. It greeted his nomination with a generous editorial, describing McGuire as having a "personal and political record without stain." It lauded his "extended business career which has given him judgement and experience." It concluded that

3. James J. Belden, courtesy of the Onondaga Historical Association.

"it cannot be truthfully said that he is handicapped in any way."[100] Commenting on the Republican candidate the following day, it all but accused him of being a tool of Francis Hendricks.[101]

The *Standard*, which supported the Hendricks organization and its control of the Republican Party, promptly endorsed the candidacy of Charles Saul.[102]

The *Post*, which was a Belden enterprise, editorialized about both selections in a piece entitled "Time for the People to Act, in which it encouraged an independent candidacy. It characterized Saul's nomination as a "machine made" one, and while complimentary of

McGuire's abilities, charged he would have "obligations" to the Democratic organization.

The *Syracuse Journal* also supported Saul for mayor, and although it would produce some of the most heated controversies of the campaign as reported by the other four newspapers, its articles are not available for firsthand examination.[103]

The *Standard* struck back at the *Post*'s call for another candidacy in an editorial titled "The *Post*'s Pretense," in which it charged that the *Post* would not have supported any Republican candidate for mayor other than Belden.[104] In an editorial less pointed, the *Courier* too criticized the prospect of an independent candidacy, declaring that McGuire possessed all of the characteristics the *Post* wanted in an independent candidate.[105]

Democrats, Republicans, and reform-minded citizens of the Belden stripe were not the only ones interested in the mayoralty that year. Thirty-two Prohibition Party members met and decided to field a full slate of candidates. One of its leaders, the Rev. Amos Naylor, voiced some support for McGuire's ideas concerning the franchises. McGuire may have had even greater appeal to the Prohibitionists since he neither smoked nor drank, this latter character trait undoubtedly the result of his father's decline. There was, however, no indication that McGuire would advance it as his own policy as an elected official, and the party decided to stick to its principles and nominated its own candidates.[106]

The following day, a committee of nineteen representatives from each of the city wards met and selected Charles Baldwin, forty-nine years old, a lawyer and a Civil War veteran, as the candidate for mayor on the "Citizens Municipal Reform Party" ticket.[107] With less than three weeks remaining until the election, the field of candidates was complete.

The *Standard*, commenting on the Baldwin candidacy, ridiculed the choice of a lawyer rather than a businessman.[108] As expected, both the *Post* and the *Herald* immediately endorsed Baldwin's candidacy in their October 17 editions.

Unexpectedly, that same day McGuire received an endorsement from a segment of the community that typically voted Republican because it was the party of Lincoln. The *Colored-American*, an African American publication, endorsed him for mayor. In urging its readers to back McGuire, the newspaper recounted the treatment African Americans had received at the hands of the Republican Party leaders.[109]

Since the African American community of Syracuse from 1890 to 1900 never exceeded more than 1 percent of the population,[110] McGuire's courting this particular constituency clearly had little to do with seeking political advantage and more likely was motivated by what he believed was right.

The McGuire campaign trained its fire on the increase in the city budget, trumpeting the fact that spending now exceeded a million dollars.[111]

McGuire's handlers, apparently concerned about some of the comments he had made about "franchise grabbers," which could be construed as a veiled reference to former mayor Kirk, prevailed on him to change his approach to public speaking, giving shorter speeches of no more than ten minutes in length.[112]

On October 20, the *Standard* reported on a lengthy speech by McGuire at a Democratic meeting in which the candidate addressed a number of issues and told the audience that Saul was the candidate of Francis Hendricks, whom he called the "silent man" who nominates mayors, judges, and assemblymen without consulting anyone. He pledged a strong public school system, an end to "race feeling," and a promise that the city engineer and city contracts would be awarded without political favoritism.[113]

At this juncture in the campaign, Carroll E. Smith, the editor of the *Syracuse Journal*, managed to touch the third rail in politics, namely religion, by accusing the bishop of Syracuse, Patrick Ludden, of supporting McGuire because he was a Roman Catholic.[114]

Bishop Ludden responded to the *Journal* the following day in an extraordinary letter to the *Post* in which he denied endorsing McGuire and accused the *Journal* of covering up wrongdoing by the Republican machine.[115] Accompanying the bishop's letter was an editorial in which the *Post* took the *Journal* to task for implying that the bishop supported McGuire because both were Roman Catholics. It went on to observe that "Bishop Ludden's letter should be read by every voter in Syracuse. It is a dignified, able reply to the unwarranted and bitter attack from a paper that prefers epithets to arguments and abuse to reason."[116]

The other three principal newspapers remained silent on this controversy, the *Standard* perhaps sensing that it could only do its candidate further harm, the *Courier* sensing that it may have done McGuire some good, and the *Herald* recognizing that the *Post* had done all it could for Baldwin by featuring the controversy. It would not, however, be the last time that the editor of the *Journal* would make a foray into the quicksand of religion and politics.

The editor of the *Journal*, Carroll E. Smith, not content at having stepped on the political third rail once, stepped on it again when he charged that McGuire was anti-Semitic.[117] Smith had the dubious distinction of being the "first presidential postmaster in New York State to be removed by President Cleveland for 'offensive partisanship' on May 23, 1893 while editor of the *Journal*."[118] Responding to the accusation, McGuire was quoted as saying,

> You may say, that I am authorized to state that my friends will give a purse of $1,000 to the Hebrew Orphan asylum if a single statement in The Journal last night and to this effect is true: That I have opposed the Hebrews or have written a line against them, or against Mr. Rosendale, who was the Democratic candidate for Attorney-General two years ago, or that the Catholic Sun, of which I am the principal stockholder but not the editor, has ever printed a line derogatory to a Hebrew or the Hebrew people. The files of the Catholic Sun are open to all citizens at any and all times for inspection.[119]

One might expect that as the principal stockholder of the weekly Catholic newspaper in Syracuse, McGuire would have exploited that opportunity to use that weekly to further his own candidacy. The newspaper, after all, was a major source of news—religious, social, and to some degree political—for the Catholic citizens of Syracuse. An example of this is the more expansive obituary of McGuire's father and namesake, which appeared in the *Catholic Sun*, than that which appeared in the white Anglo-Saxon-Protestant–controlled dailies. Surprisingly, very little news of the mayoral race appeared in the *Catholic Sun*, and when McGuire did author an opinion, it was not about the race and bore his signature.

As November 5 fast approached, the various newspapers supporting each of the candidates continued to report that their candidate held a wide lead, and the papers supporting Saul and Baldwin continued to accuse each other of being the spoiler in the race. The *Herald* went so far as to accuse the Hendricks camp of hatching a nefarious plot in which the machine would plant lead pencils in the voting booths that would turn blue on paper, invalidating the ballots of others.[120]

No political campaign would be complete without some wagering on the outcome, and the *Courier* carried the news of the various bets that were being placed on the outcome. After reporting on certain individual wagerers and how much they were prepared to risk, it noted that betting between McGuire and Saul was about even, with Baldwin finishing third.[121]

On the eve of the election, the *Courier* took a very hard swipe at the opposition, accusing the editor of the *Syracuse Journal* of "unvarnished lying." It cited Smith's claims, among others, that McGuire was "a jew baiter" and a "socialist and anarchist," and that he owed his nomination to "Hibernian societies." It called Smith the "only jew-baiter in Syracuse."[122]

All three candidates expressed confidence that they would be elected the following day. McGuire observed, "You may say simply this: The indications are most encouraging. I have every reason to feel confident of my election. My strength has increased daily since my nomination." Saul was more expansive in his prediction that he would be elected with a 2,500-vote plurality. Baldwin too predicted victory.[123] After McGuire had made fifty-two speeches[124] and spent $2,443,[125] the campaign was over.

Election Day dawned, and the *Herald* reported perfect weather and a heavy vote.[126] When the polls closed and the votes were counted, it appeared that Saul's predication of a 2,500-vote plurality was almost correct. The only flaw in his calculation was that McGuire was the victor, with 9,123 votes; Baldwin had 7,930 to come in second, and Saul was last with 6,084.[127] The *Courier* described the election-night scene in which a crowd of three thousand waited outside the Vanderbilt House for the election results. As McGuire's margins piled up, the crowd became louder and more enthusiastic in their cheers. The victorious candidate had to shake two thousand hands in the corridors of the hotel. He received "Old Democrats with tears of joy running down their faces." As he emerged on a balcony of the hotel, the crowd cheered for fully fifteen minutes.[128] Informed that her son had been elected mayor, Mary Jane McGuire declared it to be "the proudest day in her life."[129]

McGuire's election provoked a number of different reactions among the newspapers in the city. The *Courier* was both muted and cautionary in its observations, celebrating the outcome and reminding the victors of the responsibility they had to remedy the wrongs of the past administrations.[130] The *Evening Herald* offered McGuire congratulations and held forth in a manner similar to that of the *Courier*, noting that the election of McGuire was a rebuke to both party machines, but to the Republican one in particular.[131] The *Post* struck a tone somewhere between the *Courier* and the *Evening Herald*, first congratulating the new mayor-elect on his triumph and then cautioning him that the victories of a Democratic executive and council should not be taken as an invitation to establish a Democratic machine.[132]

The *Standard* had nothing laudatory to say about the mayor-elect and lamented everything about the outcome of the election. It attributed McGuire's victory to a backlash against the anti-Catholic forces that were arrayed against him. In a convoluted fashion it suggested that his victory was because of forces that were un-American.[133] The editorial went on to suggest that the Baldwin ticket had been constituted to conform to the dictates of the American Protestant Association,[134] and that the "citizens reform" campaign had been designed to appeal to a bigotry that had backfired, resulting in the election of McGuire for no greater reason than that he was Catholic.

What is interesting about the *Standard*'s opinion is that it appears to be the first time, including throughout the entire campaign, that it ever accused the Baldwin campaign of bigotry or suggested that McGuire was a victim of it. Moreover, it seems that, at best, it had a myopic view of its journalistic partner's, Dr. Carroll E. Smith's, opinions of McGuire and his relentless religious baiting. It returned to this theme the following day, when it took to task those Republicans who supported Baldwin, whom it apparently viewed as spoilers despite their having finished ahead of their candidate, Saul.

Just as interesting to note about the *Standard*'s revisionist view of the election is how little it dwelt on the issue it had heretofore advanced: that there was a conspiracy between the McGuire and the Baldwin forces to defeat the Hendricks machine. It had hammered this theme on an almost daily basis throughout the campaign. What is even more astonishing is that it overlooked and never reported the one fact that might have converted even the most skeptical reader to its somewhat paranoid view. McGuire and Baldwin lived next door to each other, in a duplex at 201–203 Green Street, on the city's near north side.[135]

Once the newspapers had voiced their opinions about the outcome of the election, their attention was turned to the issue of patronage under the new administration, as well as to McGuire's future. After a brief meeting with his business partner, Bradford Kennedy, the mayor-elect left town to get a respite from the fatigue of the campaign and the demands of potential office-seekers.[136] While the *Herald* reported that McGuire was to visit New York City for several days, in reality he was much closer to home. The mayor-elect was being heralded as a political crusader and a rising star by newspapers across the state, such as the *Buffalo Examiner* and the *Auburn Bulletin*.[137] The *Rochester Herald*, the *Utica Herald*, and the *Buffalo Express* all promoted him as a candidate for lieutenant governor.

McGuire's respite from the campaign and the onslaught of potential office-seekers did not take him far nor last very long. Two days after departing, he gave an interview to the *Utica Press* in which he held forth on a number of topics, including patronage. Responding to the suggestion that Irish Catholics would make up a disproportionate share of his administration, he pointed out that he had defeated

4. James K. McGuire, official mayoral photograph, ca. 1896, courtesy of Fahey Family Collection.

Charles Saul in the German neighborhoods despite Saul's being German.[138]

One of the men who may have been swept into office because of McGuire was Alderman Frank Matty.[139] Despite the fact that Matty likely owed his reelection to McGuire's showing and the lip service he had paid to McGuire's campaign, close observers of both men reportedly had misgivings about the future. Matty had already begun to position himself as the future leader of the Common Council.

The mayor-elect had much more on his mind than appointments or Matty. At twenty-seven, he was single, a successful businessman, and the mayor-elect of a large city in America, and was being touted for statewide office. By all accounts he should have been the city's most eligible bachelor. In reality, he was spoken for. His secret started to leak out after his sojourn to Utica and the "North Woods."[140] Upon returning to Syracuse, he gave an interview to the *Herald* in which he discussed a wide range of topics but ducked the question about his rumored engagement.[141]

Notwithstanding his reluctance to confirm or deny the rumor, the story would not die. Less than a week later the *Herald* reported that he would be married to Frances McGuire of Forestport, New York.[142]

Exactly who Frances McGuire was, and how they met or became engaged, was a mystery. It was certainly the best-kept secret of the campaign, and one that would have never survived in today's political crucible. She was the second youngest of seven children born to Phillip McGuire and Mary Coughlin. Her father was born in Ireland in 1837 and emigrated to the United States at age twenty, settling in Oneida County. Her mother was born in Forestport, the daughter of John and Catherine (McGuire) Coughlin. Her parents were married in 1864.[143]

Despite the pressures to organize a new administration replete with patronage demands, McGuire found time to devote some attention to the cause near and dear to his heart, Irish independence. On November 24, he appeared on the speaker's platform in the Grand Opera House in New York City at an event sponsored by the Irish National Alliance. He was heralded as the "youngest mayor of a large city in the world." Owing to the lateness of the hour, he declined to deliver a speech on the Irish question but briefly extolled the beauty and qualities of Syracuse, which he encouraged the audience to visit. He shared his experiences on this trip with the readers of his news weekly, describing a dinner at which he was feted by the "young men of the Democratic Club of New York . . . at Marine's French restaurant . . . where I was unable to decipher the bill of fare, but found the food tasted good in spite of the terrible titles given each dish."[144]

The teenager who had been forced to drop out of school to support his family, who had never completed his formal education, who had educated himself on the Irish question and the tariff issue, and who had written pamphlets and made speeches on the great issues of the day, as well as for presidents, had adorned his study with "a hand-written motto, large and of ancient pattern," that said "'Knowledge Is Power.'"[145] Such was the makeup of the next mayor of Syracuse.

4

The Mayoral Years

Boy Mayor

McGuire's first message to the Common Council took the form of a fourteen-page letter that the new mayor read to the council at a much-attended public meeting. The letter touched on a wide range of topics. He advocated ending the practice of awarding franchises to the various transportation and utility companies without negotiating a fair return for the city coffers. He advocated the public ownership of these franchises. He proposed that the city negotiate a three-cent streetcar fare for working people during the hours that they travel to and from work. He called for the establishment of a "subway commission."[1] He proposed municipal ownership of the water and lighting companies, and the construction of a "free public bath system." He championed the construction of a new high school. He advocated abandoning the practice of designating an official newspaper, and proposed reducing the salary of the commissioner of public works by a thousand dollars.[2] Unfortunately for the new mayor, his proposals were addressed to a council that was now headed by President Frank Matty. McGuire's involvement in the leadership struggle in the council would plague him for the foreseeable future.[3]

The mayor's proposal that the city do away with "official" newspapers died in the council; however, he at least had the satisfaction of having the *Courier*, which supported him, designated as one of them.[4]

Ultimately the mayor was able to engineer the appointment of Melvin Z. Haven as city clerk by garnering the support of five Republican

members of the council. The selection of Haven, under these circumstances, opened up a subplot concerning the appointment of a deputy
city clerk.[5]

In the meantime, the mayor proposed the creation of a Public
Bath Commission,[6] and became embroiled in a controversy in which
he was asked to renege on a promise to help a constituent obtain a
saloon license over the objections of his neighbors. To resolve the
controversy, the mayor offered to personally compensate the would-
be saloon owner for his loss, declaring, "Personally I am a temperance
man. No man in this room is more rigid in his temperance than I
am. If I had my own way about it, I would not have a drop of liquor
drunk in any way. I stand ready to give $50 or even $100 to do away
with Schoen's place. My opinion is that in consequence of my experience with the Schoen matter you need not be troubled with fear in
the future."[7]

Among the places that the mayor traveled during this period was
New York City, where he visited the offices of the *Irish World* and
its publisher Patrick Ford, for whom he had previously worked. He
reported that "Mr. Ford is quite an old man, white hair and bent
form, with a worn literary countenance. Yet he enjoys rugged health
and labors in his little sanctum many hours each day. He is ranked as
one of the first editorial writers in the country and his journal is the
best as well as the largest circulated of its class in the country."[8]

A dispute with the Democratic members of the council arose when
McGuire refused to dismiss the superintendent of parks, Thomas
Bishop, because he was a Republican. Bishop, who was the only person
to have ever held the office, had been appointed by William B. Kirk, a
Democrat.[9] Explaining his reason for refusing to bow to the aldermen's
demand, McGuire justified his position based upon Bishop's satisfactory performance over the years and the fact that he had received more
than two thousand Republican votes, which required some bipartisan-
ship. It was not language that was likely to bind up the wounds that
had opened between him and some members of the council.[10]

Despite the ongoing battle between the mayor, President Matty,
and the council over patronage and issues of integrity, some positive

achievements managed to be accomplished. In May, after extensive public hearings and a threatened veto by the mayor, the mayor and the council managed to come to terms on the awarding of the suburban franchise, which involved linking the eastern towns and villages to the city by railway.[11] Matty, who had voted for the franchise, nevertheless found himself having to defend the integrity of his vote against an attack by the *Syracuse Standard*. On the morning after the vote, he denied that campaign contributions from John Gaynor, who controlled the franchise, had influenced his vote.[12]

On the heels of the suburban franchise's passage, the mayor decided to replace the Board of Police Commissioners.[13] This board was responsible for selecting the chief of police, setting the compensation of the members of the department, and overseeing its affairs. While the mayor could remove and appoint a new board under the existing law at that time, any replacement he nominated had to be from the same political party as the board member he replaced.[14] McGuire believed that the election results had been a repudiation of the previous administration and that a new board was in order. Among the men whom he would name was his opponent, Charles Baldwin. Some of the existing board were not inclined to go quietly and indicated that they might make the mayor remove them for cause.[15]

Notwithstanding these difficulties, McGuire was also able to come to terms with the council on the Lakeside Railway franchise that had been the subject of his bribery accusations.[16] The bribery allegations had now ripened into a grand jury investigation, with the mayor, City Clerk Haven, and various aldermen and company directors making appearances before the grand jury.[17]

If McGuire's political existence seemed bleak, his personal life was about to turn for the better. On June 24, he married Frances McGuire in the living room of her home in Forestport. The wedding was private, attended only by the bride's mother and sisters and John J. Cummins, the mayor's best man. The *Herald* reported the various gifts the couple received along with their plans to honeymoon in New York City and Europe. McGuire was expected to speak in Dublin before returning home. It also reported that Matty would assume the duties of mayor in McGuire's absence.[18] At the end of the day, Syracuse had a new First Lady. She was one month past her nineteenth birthday.

Unfortunately the mayor's European honeymoon was not to occur. Conflicting reasons were attributed to the mayor's inability to leave for an extended period, but it appears that the most likely reason he and his bride remained in the United States was the prospect of Matty's acting as mayor. To the world outside of the city, the need to sell bonds in New York City was the ostensible reason given.[19] The *Herald*, however, reported that the blame was being placed on Francis Hendricks, who rebuffed McGuire's request that legislation be enacted allowing another official to exercise mayoral authority in his absence.[20]

Upon returning from his abbreviated honeymoon, McGuire spent much of the summer addressing issues involving the various franchises being sought. He proved to be a hard bargainer when it came to the consolidation of two city railway companies, demanding that all back taxes be paid before the city's consent to the consolidation was given.[21]

That August the Democratic Party nominated William Jennings Bryan for president and politics became a preoccupation of the mayor. Once again he was in demand as a stump speaker for a presidential candidate, although he was not inclined to make too many speeches.[22] He likewise toyed with the prospect of running for Congress and took an active interest in the delegate selections in the various assembly districts in central New York. His activity had a dual purpose. First, the delegates would play a role in the selection of a congressional candidate. Second, he wanted state legislators who would be sympathetic to the city's needs.[23] McGuire's championing of Bryan and his endorsement of the "Free Silver" platform of the Democratic Party was not without cost to the city. The city was unable to sell $220,000 in bonds in New York City because of McGuire's endorsement. One of the New York City bankers, in a letter to one of his local counterparts, said that McGuire's endorsement of Bryan and the party platform would harm the city's ability to obtain credit.[24]

McGuire ultimately decided against running for Congress, but it appears that his decision was made largely on the basis that there would be a split in the Democratic Party between "Free Silver" Democrats, of which he was one, and those wedded to the gold standard.[25]

Despite her youth, Frances did not seem at all daunted by her newfound role as First Lady of Syracuse. On August 20, she led a contingent of two dozen prominent women from Syracuse on a two-day excursion to the Thousand Islands by railway.[26]

McGuire was one of the local delegates to the State Democratic Convention in Buffalo that September. This convention was particularly interesting from a local standpoint, since the mayor ended up seconding the unsuccessful nomination of William Sulzer for governor, but only after W. B. Kirk and former mayor Thomas Ryan disavowed any interest in the nomination.[27] Sulzer was not the candidate favored by Tammany Hall, and McGuire's speech on his behalf once again antagonized them.[28]

Shortly after his return from the convention, the mayor vetoed the Common Council's proposed budget. In a series of messages to the council, the mayor vetoed appropriations for three new firehouses and a bridge.[29] In his messages, he justified the vetoes for the firehouses on the basis that fires in the localities were infrequent and that all of the expenditures could not be justified due to the jobless rate in the city and the pain a tax increase would cause.[30] As predicted, the vetoes were overridden.

Another franchise veto, of the Hughes Company for electric light, telephone, and subway connections, was proving to be very popular with the general public. Even the Chamber of Commerce, led by Donald Dey, urged that the veto be sustained.[31] More than seven hundred people attended the council meeting at which the veto would be considered. When McGuire's veto message was read, the crowd cheered, and when Matty spoke in favor of an override, he was hissed. The meeting became so heated that the vetoes were tabled, and the aldermen who were inclined to change their votes refrained from doing so because of the insults heaped on them at the meeting.[32]

That November, William McKinley carried Onondaga County over William Jennings Bryan by a 12,000-vote margin. James J. Belden was swept into another term in Congress in the wake of the landslide.[33]

5. Donald Dey, courtesy of the Onondaga Historical Association.

It had been a mixed year for McGuire. It had held some joy. He had, after all, married the woman he loved. Politically, however, it was a disappointment. What had started with such promise, the announcement of his goals and dreams for the city he had been elected to lead, had become bogged down in bitter personal wrangling. What was worse, the obstruction of his program was being undertaken by members of his own party. The coming year appeared to promise more of the same.

The second year of McGuire's term, 1897, again began with the prospect of Matty's being elected president of the council. Although

Matty, again, protested that he would willingly pass up the honor, McGuire wisely refrained from trying to forestall the inevitable.[34]

While the aldermen denied that they would hold up the mayor's appointments to the Board of Health in order to exact patronage, it became clear that swift action on the appointments would not be taken and that they might either be rejected outright or allowed to languish into the summer. McGuire was probably not helping his situation by, at the same time, announcing that he would reappoint Thomas Bishop as the superintendent of parks.

Although the election was almost eleven months away, Frank Matty surprised the political world by announcing that he would challenge McGuire for mayor.[35] Before the month was out, the council went back to its practice of systematically overriding the mayor's vetoes, no matter what reason was provided for them.[36] McGuire tried to make light of the situation, remarking, "No vetoes this week," as he signed legislation after one of the council's meetings.[37]

McGuire offered an interesting observation concerning a feature of a bill that Senator Horace White was sponsoring in the state legislature that would increase the length of the mayor's term to either three or four years. McGuire observed, "Two years are too short a term for the mayor to secure good results, especially with the tremendous responsibility which the bill would place on him." McGuire need not have cared. The bill was unlikely to pass.

As McGuire began to contemplate reelection later that year, he also began to point out the forces that were arrayed against him on all fronts. He publicly complained about the aldermen who overrode each veto, contending that they were trying to create a fiscal crisis that would drive up the tax rate. He added to the list of aldermen two unnamed assembymen.[38]

Another issue that reared its head was the pollution of Onondaga Lake by Solvay Process. The Process, also known as "Solvay Works," was a chemical company that manufactured soda ash from salt brine and limestone in the area. A large employer for the area, it was founded in 1880 on the shore of Onondaga Lake, and was dumping its residue and waste into the lake. Corporation Counsel James

Newell sought the assistance of Attorney General Theodore Hancock, also a Syracusan, but the latter referred it to the State Board of Health for its consideration, and the dumping of ash into the lake continued without abatement.[39]

With an eye toward the coming election, a committee was formed to explore the prospect of an independent reform candidate for mayor. It was headed by Syracuse University Chancellor James Day; George Driscoll, a Democrat and attorney; and Gates Thalheimer, a Republican and police commissioner during the Amos administration.[40]

That May the city received a check for $5,000 from the Syracuse & Suburban Railway Company. It was the first money ever received from one of its franchise holders.[41]

In a surprise move, one of the Democratic aldermen admitted that the mayor's claim that the council was passing construction measures in order to drive up the tax rate to hamper McGuire's reelection was true.[42] With an eye on the coming election, both sides appeared to settle into an uneasy cease-fire.

As the summer months unfolded, McGuire saw an opportunity to both improve the city parks and make a dent in the city's unemployment. Commenting on a $20,000 appropriation for work in the parks, he noted that he was bombarded with requests for employment in the parks both at his office in City Hall and at home.

If there was any question that McGuire intended to seek reelection, he put an end to it with a speech he gave in early June defending his administration and attacking the Hendricks Republican machine. On the subject of the city's finances, he called attention to the city's low tax rate, top credit rating, and lack of any corruption or scandal.[43]

In the wake of the first organizational efforts to form a municipal reform ticket, Francis Hendricks had his loyalists infiltrate the reform movement, in the hope of presenting a unified ticket against McGuire.[44] While W. B. Kirk remained silent on the renomination of McGuire, his willingness to relinquish the chair of the city Democratic Committee indicated that the mayor was likely to be renominated without a fight.[45] The McGuire forces began to confront the municipal reformers and their alliance with Hendricks more directly.

M. Z. Haven intimated that one of its leaders, Col. Austin Chase, was a hypocrite for holding himself out as a reformer while serving as a director of the Rapid Transit Railway Company, which was seeking a franchise from the city without paying it any percentage of its revenues.[46] At the same time, one political observer was quoted as saying, "It looks to me as if one of two things will happen to the municipal reform movement—it will die or it will become a tender to the Hendricks machine."[47]

Among the measures that were subject to the mayor's veto was a $25 tax on bootblacks. In his veto message he declared, "This tax appears to be an unjust hardship on ten men who make a living in the summer months only. If enforced, it will practically drive these men out of the occupation. I am informed that the people who patronize these chairs are not the same class who have their shoes shined in barber shops."[48] Like every other veto that year, it was overridden, this time by a margin of 16 to 0.

The courtship of the municipal reform movement by the Hendricks machine appeared to be a bumpy one. Hendricks appeared to favor former mayor Amos as the candidate but he could not be cast as a reformer.[49]

The strong language contained in the mayor's veto appeared to have some effect. At its next meeting the aldermen only had thirteen votes to override and the Rapid Transit Railway Company franchise was tabled.[50]

The dance between the municipal reformers and the Hendricks machine continued. Perhaps stung by the criticism that it was a tool of Hendricks, the group declared its intention to announce its candidate before either of the political parties. Close observers of the scene, however, understood that no matter who the candidate was, he would also be acceptable to the Republican Party and its nominee too.[51]

In August McGuire got the kind of publicity that a politician seeking reelection dreads. Deciding to inspect a paving job on James Street, the mayor directed his brother George to obtain a horse from the police stables and transport him in a wagon to the job. George had been employed in two different positions during two different time periods since the beginning of his older brother's administration. Both times he had quit after being criticized by McGuire's opponents.

En route to the job site, the horse was frightened by a freight train and the mayor told his brother to hitch it to a fence until it calmed down. Before it did, another train came by; the horse broke its strap, dragged the wagon into a canal, and drowned. George was able to jump free before the horse and wagon went into the water. When McGuire realized what had occurred, he chastised his younger brother, telling him, "You are the most unlucky boy I ever saw. You will be the death of me." George, in reply, said, "Yes, I have lost two jobs on account of the newspapers, and I guess to-morrow morning they will drive me out of town." McGuire took a streetcar back to town and offered to pay the city for the loss of the horse. He later observed that he was lucky not to be "sticking feet upward in the mud of the steamboat basin" and that George was a "hoodoo," a person cursed with bad luck.[52] McGuire had no idea how unlucky George would prove to be in the years to come.

Before taking a three-week recess, the council approved a garbage disposal contract let by the Board of Health for John Dunfee.[53] This approval provoked one of the most scathing veto messages yet.[54]

Despite the forcefulness of his language in the veto message of the garbage contract, the Common Council overrode it by a vote of 15 to 1.[55]

On August 27, McGuire and his wife celebrated the arrival of their first child, a girl, named Frances Gertrude after her mother but would be called Gertrude. Discussing the event with a reporter,[56] McGuire said, "The title 'Boy Mayor' vanishes today." Turning to the effect that being a father might have on his priorities, the mayor observed, "I shall now take a larger interest in the school children's picnic—more of a personal interest." The new father waxed eloquent on having a daughter, saying, "Yes, we both wanted a girl. Why? Well, because it is easier to bring up a girl. There isn't so much anxiety, so much worry over opportunities for going wrong. Women, as a rule, are better than men. Yes, I know a bad woman is probably worse than a bad man, but I repeat that the women, as a class, are better than the men."

McGuire humorously compared the task of raising a daughter in comparison to his younger brothers, noting, "With a girl I won't have to hustle to get her a place as I do for George and Sarsfield.[57] She won't put any of the police patrol horses in the lake, and she won't do a lot of other things that boys will do in spite of all protest." McGuire concluded the interview by noting that it was his wife's twentieth birthday.

On September 3, the municipal reformers, going by the name Citizens Union, nominated Donald Dey for mayor. The two Republican factions led by Francis Hendricks and Congressman James J. Belden quickly fell in line behind the nomination.[58] McGuire was now faced with a single opponent who had the backing of the reformers and a united Republican Party.

As the campaign unfolded, McGuire was relentless in his criticism of the aldermen and the Hendricks ring, often tying them together in the same speech. In a speech at a Democratic rally on October 8, he told the audience that if his vetoes had been sustained, the city would have received "many hundreds of thousands of dollars."[59]

At times he was required to respond to criticism from some of his own appointees. Despite having been appointed police commissioner by McGuire, Charles Baldwin remained loyal to the Citizens Union and stumped for Donald Dey. McGuire found himself answering a critical speech made by Baldwin, telling his audience that Baldwin had overspent his department's budget by 10 percent.[60]

While McGuire hammered relentlessly at the Hendricks machine and questioned the commitment of the reformers aligned with it, Donald Dey ran a campaign reminiscent of the timidity that had plagued Charles Saul two years previously. Like Saul he relied on surrogates and the *Syracuse Standard* to carry out attacks on McGuire. When he was called upon to speak, like Saul, he resorted to platitudes about party unity.[61]

That Dey had not mentioned McGuire by name until there was less than two weeks to go did not bode well for the Republican Party no matter how united it was, with or without the reformers.

McGuire by contrast continued to hammer hard at Dey and his backers. At one rally he cried,

Behind Mr. Dey stands the "paving ring," a combination of a half a dozen greedy politicians who want to get back into the City Hall so that they can control fat paving jobs.

They bought the *Standard* and are losing thousands of dollars in that moribund newspaper. Great as their losses are, in that enterprise, the amount is a mere bagatelle as compared with the fortune they will make out of this city if you allow them to get into the saddle again.[62]

He went on to charge that the Citizens Union was "a mask for paving jobbers" and that the committee of nineteen that made up the Union was made up of contractors and "franchise grabbers." He labeled Syracuse University Chancellor James Day as only a "figurehead." He refused to endorse any of the incumbent aldermen who had opposed him, even if they were Democrats.

One of the surrogates who felt the sting of McGuire's lash was Chancellor Day, in a speech McGuire made at the Wigwam in the Fourteenth Ward, which he characterized as the "enemy camp." It was a rare man indeed who could alienate both McGuire and Matty. After castigating Donald Dey and the "franchise grabbers" backing him, he returned to the subject of the chancellor, remarking, "At no time in the history of the city has there been so much done for this section of the city as during my administration. Chancellor Day has come to me time and time again and asked for favors which I have granted."[63]

McGuire not only pushed himself hard, he was also not shy about reminding others about what they had gained and stood to lose if he was turned out of office. In an unpublished letter to Alderman Jeremiah Carey dated October 23, 1897, from his Green Street residence, he wrote,

Dear Jerry, Take off your coat and get to work. Two years ago I was elected mayor and the fight for Mayor pulled the whole ticket through including the Board of Aldermen.

Indirectly the fight I made for Mayor carried three doubtful wards. As a result the Common Council was Democratic and you got a position which has netted you nearly $2,000. In addition to that I prevented the appointment of Malone by refusing to sanction the combination of 2 Democrats and 2 Republicans who wanted to make him the Sealer of Weights and Measures. And if the Common Council is to be Democratic again it is I who must pull these Aldermen through. Besides it is in your business interests to work for me. Meagher says that he will take care of your brother in due time. But your family through your self has been pretty well recognized and I want you to get to work and hustle for the whole ticket. Mayor[64]

Sharing in the fruits of the "spoils system" was not limited solely to loyal supporters; his brother George was employed as an "Inspector" with the city government and his brother Edward also held the position of "Map Clerk."[65]

Despite the flaying that he and his supporters were getting each night from McGuire, Donald Dey just couldn't seem to give it back. At a rally near the end of October, the best Dey could manage was a pledge to work for the people of Syracuse. McGuire continued to distance himself from the aldermen, including those in his own party, although he walked a fine line between condemning them and urging their defeat.[66]

With only twenty-four hours left in the campaign, the reports of wagering, unlike two years previously, were sparse. What bets were to be had seemed to favor the challenger, Dey.[67] On the final day of the campaign, McGuire spoke at thirteen rallies.[68]

When the votes were counted on election night, McGuire soundly defeated Donald Dey. Indeed, against a united Republican Party augmented by the Citizens Union reform movement, he increased his majority in every election district over his plurality two years ago. He had polled 11,791 votes to Dey's 10,583 for a margin of 1,208.[69] McGuire told the crowd celebrating his victory on election night, "For Donald Dey, I have the most respectful and kindliest feeling. He was a brave soldier who fell fighting valiantly in a cause he was led to believe was right, but which was only the mask that hid the same element who were repudiated two years ago, and who wanted to crawl back into power masquerading as bogus reformers. They have been found out and the people are with us."[70]

A further vindication of sorts occurred in the Common Council elections. While Matty was reelected in his rematch with Richard Martin by a wider margin than in the election two years previously,[71] Aldermen John Troendle and James Maher, both Democrats and Matty supporters, were defeated.[72] The Republicans now held control of the council and presumably the presidency. The Matty revolt for all intents and purposes was over.

The mayor and Frances left for a ten-day trip to New York City, but not before McGuire gave a postmortem of the election results, observing, "The chancellor does not have much influence among his neighbors . . . The *Herald* was the only opposition paper which published my addresses, although in the last week of the campaign I addressed 12,000 voters not the remotest reference was made to these important gatherings by one of the opposition papers . . . The Common Council will be politically hostile for two years, but if the Aldermen read the handwriting on the wall rightly they will support me."[73]

In the afterglow of his victory, McGuire decided to withdraw from Democratic Party affairs and concentrate upon his duties as mayor. At the same time his supporters were floating a trial balloon for governor.[74]

As the year came to a close, Republicans began to organize to elect a president of the council, with an eye toward replacing some of the Democratic appointees with members of their own party.[75] The aldermen, frustrated by their inability to get any action by state agencies to stop Solvay Process from dumping into the lake, sought legislation to make it illegal.[76] The Common Council, fearing that they would lose the opportunity to appoint fellow Democrats to the Board of Health, confirmed the mayor's appointees Dolan and Mulherin, finally giving McGuire control of the board and its patronage.[77]

If McGuire thought that his relationship with his first Common Council was contentious, the relationship he was about to have with the incoming council would appear, at the outset, to be downright dysfunctional. Since the Republicans now had a 12 to 7 majority, observers expected that Alderman E. J. Mack, the senior Republican, would be the new council president. Even more astute observers, however, would not rule out a bid by Alderman Matty for reelection, "viewed as the slickest man in the Council to accomplish whatever he seriously undertakes."[78]

The observation about Matty would be borne out when the council met to elect a president at its first meeting of 1898. It did not select a president until 3:18 AM after seventy-seven ballots. On the last ballot, Matty was the victor by a vote of 10 to 9. The seventy-six previous ballots were occasioned by the fact that 21 votes were regularly being cast on each ballot. Someone was stuffing the hat with two extra ballots.[79] The following day, when heads had cleared, the Republican majority called a special meeting for that night to repair their situation. A notice was sent to all of the aldermen, with all but Democratic Alderman George Freeman attending. What followed was pure farce. M. Z. Haven, the council's clerk, declared that the meeting was invalid because the notice was not filed with his office until 6:02 PM, two minutes after the time for which the meeting was scheduled. Neither Haven nor Matty would recognize the legality of the meeting, so the Republican members proceeded to elect their own temporary chair and then elected Alderman Mack the council president.[80] The council now had two presidents, each recognized by their own party members only.

The Republicans, however, were not content to let matters lie there. Word leaked out the following day that eight Democratic members of the council and Clerk Haven had been indicted for conspiracy. While no official action had been reported, New York State Supreme Court justice Peter McLennan was required to reinstruct the grand jurors concerning their oath of secrecy and order an investigation into the leak.[81] At the same time, Alexander Cowie, an attorney and son of a former mayor, traveled to Albany to obtain permission from the attorney general to bring an action to nullify the election of Matty. A subsequent proposal by Matty that he and Mack both resign and a new election be held was rejected by the Republicans.[82]

Because the council's initial meeting ran so long, McGuire did not get the chance to read his annual message to the aldermen. Instead, he filed it with the clerk at 2:00 AM and left, telling Haven that if the aldermen ran out of paper, they could use it for ballot paper.[83] Unlike his inaugural message of 1896, it contained no broad outlines of goals and plans for the city. Instead it was cautionary in tone, telling them,

It is farthest from my thoughts thus ever to scold or admonish the new Council, but the lessons of the municipal election returns gives us sufficient cause to urge your honorable body to study the desires of the people manifested in the ballots of November 2, 1887.

It is now more than two years since my first annual message was sent to the Common Council. In that communication I reiterated the oft expressed opinion of the citizens that the streets of the city were the common property of all of the people. Municipal owner-ship and control of public privileges was urged and the Common Council was requested not to pass unpopular legislation over the executive veto.

From the first the advice of the Mayor was disregarded and two-thirds of his sixty vetoes were ruthlessly and heedlessly overridden, notwithstanding the fact that the Aldermen and the Mayor were elected on the same platform of municipal reforms. Although the majority of the Common Council were supposed to be of the same political faith as the Mayor, only two Democratic Aldermen stood by the executive. It is interesting to know these Aldermen were re-elected by a largely increased vote, while most of the Aldermen who fought the Mayor were overwhelmingly defeated. He who runs, may read. Of the fourteen Aldermen who most appeared to enjoy voting against my vetoes, three only have been returned to the Common Council.

I speak of these results with no idea of personal glorification, but rather to impress upon your minds the lessons of those elec-tion returns and to regard the political fate of a majority of those Aldermen who refused to heed the instructions of the voters of their

respective wards. We shall have no misgivings for the next two years
if the legislative and executive branches work together in harmony
and execute a broad policy of municipal economy and endeavor to
solve the pressing municipal problems of the hour.[84]

To McGuire's increasing frustration, the council continued to meet
and hold separate meetings simultaneously in the council chambers.
The machinery of the city government was slowly grinding to a halt.[85]
If the mayor could accomplish next to nothing with the council at a
stalemate, he turned his attention to trying to attract manufacturing
to the city.[86]

At the end of January, District Attorney Jay Kline announced that
the Democratic aldermen and Clerk Haven had been indicted for conspiring to effect the election of Matty as council president.[87] Reaction
to the news from the press was scathing. The *Herald* commented,
"An indictment is a serious affair but at times it is less serious than
at other times, and in the present instance it is somewhat difficult for
anybody with a sense of the ridiculous to maintain composure and
countenance, no matter how profound one's regard for the dignity of
the grand jury system."[88]

The politicization of the indictment was furthered when it was
discovered that the commissioner of jurors, Salem Hyde, had culled
the list of men eligible for grand jury service and denoted their political affiliation by placing a *D* for Democrat, *H* for Hendricks, and *B* for
Belden after their name. Hyde claimed he did so in order to ensure a
representative grand jury.[89]

During this period, the mayor continued, unsuccessfully, to
persuade at least four of the Republican aldermen to meet with the
Democrats so that some city business could be transacted.[90] African
American citizens lobbied for one of their own to be appointed to
the Police Department,[91] and legislation was introduced in the state
legislature to amend the city charter to create the elected positions of
comptroller, city treasurer, and president of the Common Council.[92]

The first thaw in the relations between the Republican and
Democratic aldermen occurred in late February when the Democrats

decided not to contest the appointments the Republicans were entitled to make because of their numerical superiority.[93] At the same
time, Hendricks proposed that the state senate form a committee to
investigate the city's finances and overdrafts. McGuire, in response
to the report, declared that the investigators would be welcome as
long as they included the overdrafts from the Amos administration.
Republicans in the senate further proposed that overdrafts in the
city's accounts would have to be made up in the existing budget, in
the hope that it would drive up the tax rate and damage McGuire's
popularity.[94]

During this period, the mayor experienced some personal financial strife that he disclosed in the *Catholic Sun*.[95]

Notwithstanding his personal difficulties, McGuire's gubernatorial ambitions began to bear fruit when observers began to speculate
that the Onondaga delegation to the Democratic State Convention,
to be held later that year, would be pledged to the mayor. At the same
time it was understood that the mayor would not accept any lesser
position on the state ticket that would result in a loss of city patronage
if he were elected.[96]

At the end of March, jury selection in the lawsuit brought by
Alderman Mack to annul the election of Matty as council president
was under way. The jury was composed of nine Republicans, one
Democrat, and "two who straddle the fence."[97] Testimony in the
trial included the surprising revelation that Mack had been one of the
aldermen who stuffed extra ballots into the hat. Mack contended that
he did so in order to "deceive" Matty that his plan was going awry.[98]
After two days of deliberations, the jury reported it was unable to
agree upon a verdict. In a vote that mirrored its party makeup, three
sided with Matty and nine for annulling the election.[99]

As McGuire's campaign for governor continued to take shape, an
ominous sign appeared on the horizon. Richard Croker, the "Boss" of
Tammany Hall, declared he was enthusiastic for McGuire for lieutenant governor but had others in mind for governor.[100]

McGuire must have had a sense of satisfaction when the *Syracuse Journal* was sold for $8,000 at a public auction. The sale of the

newspaper meant the retirement of one of his chief antagonists, Dr. Carroll E. Smith, its editor. Two weeks after the *Journal* went on the auction block, the *Courier* was up for sale, and prominent members of the Democratic Party made plans to purchase it. Local politicians saw it as an asset to McGuire's pursuit of the nomination for governor, with one remarking, "We couldn't very well demand the Governorship for Onondaga County if we couldn't afford a paper to help along with the state campaign."[101]

In addition to acquiring a newspaper, the McGuire campaign sent W. B. Kirk on a tour to all the major cities throughout the state to boost the mayor's candidacy. Kirk, by virtue of his service as mayor and later state committeeman, had numerous contacts throughout the state, and McGuire sought to exploit them.[102] McGuire was careful, however, to insist that the only place on the state ticket he would accept that fall was at the top.[103]

McGuire walked a fine line when it came to interacting with the clergy and guarding the public morals. His unwillingness to ban the playing of baseball in the parks on Sunday enraged the Ministerial Association and led to their threat to try and have him removed through the courts.[104]

His support for Sunday baseball notwithstanding, McGuire did have a bit of the puritan in him as evidenced by his demand that the council rescind the concert hall license of Austin's Electrical Garden. Writing to the council, he poured out his wrath:

> During the past two weeks my attention has been called to the orgies at Austin's Concert Hall in North Salina street. This concert hall has been turned into a dive of the worst sort where the lowest characters in the city visit. Of late, about midnight a woman described as "Little Egypt" nearly, if not entirely, naked appears in a disgusting dance, in imitation of the Seeley dinner scene. The place is frequented by street strollers and boys and the dance is performed for the gratification of the young bloods of the town.
>
> I complained of this exhibition to the Police Board and the Chief of Police, who inform me that the resort is regularly licensed.

I sent a man there recently to attend the performance and report the doings which are said to take place after midnight. He informed me that the dance is a vile exhibition and believes that the dive should be closed without delay. He offers that the minds of hundreds of young men are being poisoned through the lewd jokes and songs and the disgusting exhibition.

The license is granted by the Mayor and the Common Council and we possess the authority to revoke and rescind any license for cause. Austin's performance cannot possibly be classed under the head of "Concerts."

I would respectfully recommend the adoption of a resolution revoking Austin's concert license, No. 153.

A resolution revoking the license was not only passed unanimously, but the mayor warned that other halls offering similar fare would meet the same fate.[105]

As the summer months came and the fall campaign got closer, McGuire began to make his own forays throughout the state to raise his gubernatorial profile. On July 4 he traveled to New York City to participate in the Independence Day celebration of Tammany Hall.[106] Although he made a favorable impression on the club, he did not obtain any commitment furthering his gubernatorial campaign.[107] The mayor had a rock-solid commitment from the various central New York delegations, but his success was pinned on a split between two of his old nemeses, former senator David Hill and Tammany Hall boss Richard Croker.[108] McGuire had jousted with both men in brutal political combat as far back as Grover Cleveland's campaign and as recently as the previous State Democratic Convention in Buffalo. One of McGuire's campaign managers optimistically summed up the situation, declaring that McGuire would pull one-third of the Tammany Hall vote on the first ballot and would be the party's eventual nominee for governor.[109]

One of the additional complications the McGuire candidacy faced was the activity of the "Free-Silver" Democrats. McGuire had been an avid supporter of William Jennings Bryan in the last presidential

6. James K. McGuire, ca. 1898, courtesy of Onondaga
Historical Association.

campaign and a strong supporter of his "Free Silver" platform. He
had successfully avoided having this issue injected into the mayoral
election of the previous year and had fended off criticism that his support for the issue had impaired the city's creditworthiness with the
banking industry. Now the Free Silver proponents in the Democratic
Party were back demanding allegiance to this principle and castigating anyone who would not support it. Two of their most prominent
targets were former senator David Hill and Richard Croker, whom
McGuire was trying to win over. On August 10, they held a meeting in

Rochester at which they floated the candidacy of Robert Titus, a judge from Buffalo, New York, and scored both Hill and Croker. The representative of the Onondaga County Democratic Party refrained from joining the attacks on Hill and Croker. The gathering did support an early Democratic State Convention, which most observers believed would aid McGuire's candidacy before the Hill and Croker elements could coalesce around a single candidate.[110] Shortly after the gathering, Syracuse was selected as the site of the state convention to be held on September 28. Opinion was split on the question of whether this location would help or hurt McGuire. One camp believed it would be the only concession to his candidacy, while the other considered it as evidence that his stock was rising.[111]

In the midst of all of the turmoil in the Democratic Party, the Republicans had some surprises of their own. Despite the fact that the current governor, Frank Black, was a Republican who could run for reelection, another candidacy was blossoming. Colonel Theodore Roosevelt, fresh from his heroic charge up San Juan Hill, was emerging as a potential candidate. Black had weathered a minor scandal involving patronage and the Canal Commission and was considered by the rank-and-file Republicans to have been a good governor. Roosevelt, however, was viewed as having the star power to run the strongest campaign.[112]

As all of the various candidates in both parties continued to jockey for position, McGuire found himself having a backup plan to campaign for another candidate with the same name, James G. Maguire, who was running for governor of California. The two men had become friends after McGuire met the California congressman in New York City. They made a pact that if one lost his party's nomination and the other won, the losing candidate would visit the other's state and campaign for him.[113]

Theodore Roosevelt's candidacy for governor on the Republican ticket was virtually assured when he won the backing of Senator Thomas Platt, who controlled the Republican State Committee. Knowledgeable observers confirmed that the current governor could not overcome Roosevelt's popularity and Platt's backing.[114]

In the midst of all of this frenetic political jousting, Frances McGuire gave birth to their second child, a daughter, whom they named Mary Frances.[115]

One week before the convention, the cream of the Onondaga County Democratic Party went to New York City to persuade Richard Croker that the mayor would be the party's strongest candidate. The delegation included M. Z. Haven, Charles Hughes, Duncan Peck, William T. Gaynor, Daniel O'Brien, John Dunfee, Alderman George Freeman, and W. B. Kirk.

As the convention neared, speculation arose that the Tammany candidate would be Robert Van Wyck, the mayor of New York. Sentiment for McGuire as a candidate for lieutenant governor increased everywhere but in Onondaga County.[116] Van Wyck, a member of the Tammany club, was a highly regarded mayor of New York City. His candidacy, however, was viewed with greater trepidation by Tammany leaders than was McGuire's by Onondaga leaders. While the Onondaga party members were willing to chance that McGuire could be successful as a candidate for governor and bring them greater spoils, the Tammany leaders were not willing to take the chance that Van Wyck might be elected as governor, depriving them of the New York City patronage and requiring them to field another candidate for mayor of New York the following year.[117]

That same week in Saratoga Springs, the Republicans turned aside the incumbent governor, who had spent hours greeting his fellow Republicans, and nominated Theodore Roosevelt for governor. Another casualty of that convention was Francis Hendricks, who was the early front-runner to be Roosevelt's running mate. The Republicans instead stuck with the current lieutenant governor, Timothy Woodruff.[118] Hendricks's misfortune must have given McGuire some joy during a frantic period.

The first dramatic event of the Democratic Convention was the bolting of the "Free Silver" contingent, which decided to field their own slate of candidates for statewide office.[119] This development may have hurt McGuire's prospects since he was viewed as a candidate who could represent both factions of the party. As the delegates waited to see who would prevail as the candidate for governor, factions began to form. Hugh McLaughlin, the leader of the Kings County delegation from Brooklyn, aligned himself with former Senator Hill in opposition to Mayor Van Wyck, dooming that candidacy.[120] Croker then joined McGuire for a lengthy carriage ride around the city, a development that must have elated the mayor's supporters. While Croker rode with McGuire, Hill won several battles before the Credentials Committee concerning delegates from western New York, giving him control of the State Committee. A late-night meeting was held with Hill, Croker, McLaughlin, and Senator Edward Murphy in attendance. At the conclusion of the meeting, a Van Wyck was the nominee for governor but it was not Mayor Van Wyck. Instead, Croker and McLaughlin had agreed upon the mayor's brother, Augustus Van Wyck, a New York State Supreme Court justice, as the nominee for governor and Hill's candidate, Elliot Danforth, as the candidate for lieutenant governor. It was claimed that McGuire was opposed by Senator Murphy, who feared that an Irish candidate for governor might doom his chances for reelection.[121]

In retrospect, it is hard to see how McGuire could have emerged as the nominee for governor in a convention dominated by Hill and Croker. He had been an early and constant antagonist of Senator Hill during the Cleveland campaign, and no attempt to reconcile with Hill was ever reported. During the same period he had supported Cleveland and his ally Mayor Grace, both of whom were anathema to Tammany Hall. Two years previously his speech at the state convention in support of William Sulzer for governor had been characterized by Croker as an "insult." The idea that either man would have placed McGuire at the head of the state government and its patronage seems a bit far-fetched.

One person who did come out of the convention with his profile raised was M. Z. Haven. The *New York World* praised and published in red ink a portion of his nominating speech for the mayor in which he excoriated Roosevelt for becoming the candidate of Platt and other Republican Party bosses.[122]

In the aftermath of the convention, there was plenty of political activity on the local front. Congressman James J. Belden initially announced that he would not be a candidate for reelection, which prompted Republican attorney Michael Driscoll to seek the nomination. Then Belden, after the McKinley League endorsed him, reversed himself and accepted the Democratic Party nomination while still pursuing the Republican one.[123] Ultimately he reversed himself again and declined all nominations, creating further disarray among the Democrats.[124] McGuire, who had been away on vacation during this period, approved of the attempt at fusion politics and lamented the loss of Belden as the Democratic Party nominee.[125]

Despite his defeat at the state convention, McGuire was a loyal and gracious campaigner for Augustus Van Wyck. When Van Wyck arrived in Syracuse by train in late October, McGuire was the first man to meet and shake hands with him. Van Wyck was at best a very wooden campaigner. He declined to speak to the press or others about the campaign unless he was on a platform.[126] Once he was on a platform, he read his speeches gripped in both hands and "delivered it as he . . . might have delivered a carefully prepared charge for a jury."[127] Roosevelt, by contrast, arrived the following day and filled both City Hall and the Alhambra.[128]

On the eve of the election, McGuire dutifully traveled to New York City, where he spoke at an overflow rally of 16,000 at Tammany Hall. At this event he became embroiled in a controversy that would ultimately cost Van Wyck the election.

That fall, Richard Croker refused to nominate New York Supreme Court justice Joseph Daly for another term on the bench. Croker was angry with the justice because he refused to appoint a Croker loyalist to the position of chief clerk of the Court of Common Pleas. The legal community was outraged, and Roosevelt seized upon the issue as one of "judicial independence," excoriating Croker as corrupt in his speeches across the state. As the campaign came to a close at Tammany Hall, McGuire "compared Croker favorably to Republican Boss Thomas C. Platt, who, he claimed, named the judges and clerks in 50 New York counties."[129]

Upon his return to Syracuse, impressed by the size of the turnout at the rally and apparently blind to the potency of the controversy,

McGuire told the press that all signs portended a Van Wyck victory.[130] Whether he was posturing or genuinely believed such a prediction was known only to him.

On Election Day, Roosevelt was the victor by 20,000 votes. In the greater New York City area, Van Wyck defeated Roosevelt by 85,000 votes. North of the city and throughout upstate, however, Roosevelt had a plurality of 105,000. The Democrats had gained between 190,000 to 195,000 votes from its showing against Governor Black in 1896. Justice Daly was defeated by the Tammany-backed judicial candidates.[131] Croker would eventually admit that the Democrats made the wrong choice in nominating Van Wyck and that had they chosen McGuire the outcome of the election would have been different.[132]

One week after the election, McGuire, citing business pressures, told a reporter that he would not be a candidate for mayor in the next election.[133] Reaction to McGuire's announcement that he would not run again was swift. Democratic Party activists began calling on the mayor to reconsider, arguing that they had no other candidate that could win. At the same time, speculation began to mount about whether M. Z. Haven would secure another term as city clerk when his term expired the following February.[134]

As the year began to come to a close, McGuire gave a very revealing interview concerning his views about the treatment of inmates in the county penitentiary. The interview was occasioned by the county's anticipated construction of a new penitentiary in Jamesville to replace the one on the city's north side. McGuire had no interest in discussing the construction issues involving the new structure, but had many thoughts about what programs should occupy the inmates. As the interview continued, it became clear that his views concerning the worth and dignity of the inmates had their seeds in his father's experiences as he observed them growing up:

> The penal machinery of New York is in a very bad way when the only
> occupation suggested in the proposed Penitentiary is the breaking of
> stone by prisoners . . . Let us imagine, if we can, several of the gro-
> tesque features of this ridiculous and ill-fitting proposition. Nearly

one-fourth of the prisoners are known as short-term "drunks," confirmed inebriates, shaken and broken from the effects of liquor. What sense is there in putting a 6-pound hammer in the hands of these trembling drunkards and sitting them on top of a pile of stone? They are scarcely sober before they are discharged. . . . I have before me the Penitentiary report of last year. Among the prisoners were broken-down actors, artists, cooks, domestics, agents, type-writers, more than 400 mechanics, including 20 blacksmiths, 14 boilermakers, 12 bakers, 13 bricklayers, 12 butchers, 32 carpenters, 21 cigarmakers, 7 clerks, 8 bookkeepers, 7 engineers, 18 firemen, 11 iron workers, 34 machinists, 35 molders, 53 painters, 23 printers, 18 polishers, and 23 shoemakers.

Those with sparrow brains and wooden hearts will say that these mechanics ought to be breaking stone. But I want to say to you that the loss of employment in many cases, the failure to get an honest month's work, drove these men to drink or made them vagrants, and if they could have found work at their trade in the first instance, they would not be in the Penitentiary.[135]

He went on to make an additional observation whose poignancy could only have come from one who witnessed and experienced it firsthand: "I presume the report will show nearly 2,000 prisoners in the Penitentiary during the year 1898. This is not the end of the suffering. There are the mothers, sisters, wives or families of these unfortunates, the disgrace and sorrow affecting from 10,000 to 15,000 people outside the jail."

McGuire's empathy for the plight of the unemployed, as articulated in the penitentiary interview, was demonstrated at City Hall before the year concluded. Confronted by fifty men chanting, "We demand work or bread," the mayor admitted them to his office, sent out for twenty-five dollars in half-dollars, and gave each man one for food. He invited them back the following day with the promise that he would try to find work for them. At the close of the scene, McGuire told a reporter that he would investigate the feasibility of establishing a soup kitchen.[136]

McGuire ended the year by proposing the abolition of the mort-gage tax, which he felt "falls heaviest on widows and minor children."[137]

Eighteen ninety-nine opened on a tragic note for McGuire. On January 19, his mother, Mary Jane, died from pulmonary tuberculo-sis at the age of fifty-four. The mayor told the *Post-Standard* that his "proudest boast is that all he is, is due to the good advice and care of his mother."[138]

Unlike the turmoil of the previous year, the council selected Alder-man Mack as the president of the council without any controversy.[139] Despite the fact that the Democratic aldermen were not going to put up any opposition to the Republicans' naming a replacement for M. Z. Haven as city clerk, no candidate could be agreed upon. Although the year was barely a week old, speculation was under way about who would be the Republican candidate for mayor that year. Attention was being particularly paid to this election because a new city charter would take effect the following year, giving the mayor much more power. Political observers pronounced former mayor Jacob Amos the front-runner for the nomination.[140]

It was not until early February that McGuire delivered his annual message to the council. He started with a valedictory tone, announc-ing that he expected it to be his last one. He discussed the changes that would come with a "strong mayor" form of government under the new city charter that would take effect. Under the new char-ter, known as the "White Charter" after its legislative sponsor, Sena-tor Horace White of Syracuse, the mayor would have the power to appoint department heads; establish a Board of Estimate that the mayor would control to award contracts; and establish the elective offices of controller, treasurer, commissioners of education, and ases-sors.[141] He went on to address the "overdrafts" in the city funds, noting that out of thirty different funds only two were overdrawn. McGuire continued to demonstrate his empathy for the homeless in his advocacy for establishing a "Municipal Lodging House" to pro-vide shelter for the "tramps" that frequented the city. Rather than jailing them, he specifically proposed converting the "old Irving school" for such a purpose.

After reviewing all of the successful programs and achievements of his administration, he extolled the bright future he foresaw for the United States in the next century.[142]

Speculation about who might succeed McGuire as mayor continued to mount in the wake of his announcement that he would not run again. The prevailing wisdom was that McGuire was the only Democrat that could be elected mayor, although some said that Water Commissioner Daniel Ackerman might be McGuire's choice to succeed him.[143]

Meanwhile, the city's deficit continued to grow. Alderman Hill, the mayor's chief critic on this subject, reported that it had grown from $170,000 to $180,000 as a result of certain bills having been withheld from the overseer of the poor for a year and a half.[144] Within a day, it would grow by another $20,000 as more unpaid bills were uncovered.[145] In a speech on "Municipal Ownership," the mayor told his audience that one of the evils of granting public franchises to private companies was that the owners, in turn, paid the campaign expenses of the officials whose favor they were seeking.[146]

In late April, members of the North Side Citizens Association, tired of poor service and cavalier treatment at the hands of the Rapid Transit Company, tore up several sections of track on Butternut Street and damaged some of the trolley cars. McGuire, who had been locked in a bitter disagreement with the company over a variety of issues concerning service and the payment of taxes and fees, took the side of the north-side residents.[147] The company immediately declared that the city was liable for the damage owing to its failure to provide police protection.[148] Republicans, seeing an opportunity to be rid of the mayor once and for all, dispatched Francis Hendricks to Albany to see about having McGuire removed from office. McGuire not only dismissed the company's claim for damages as greatly exaggerated, but put his imprimatur on the tearing-up of the tracks, declaring that the citizens were within their rights to remove the tracks.[149]

Hendricks denied that the purpose of his trip was to seek the mayor's impeachment, observing that there was no provision in the city charter or the general law that would allow for such a step. Governor

Roosevelt, on the other hand, voiced his belief that he could remove the mayor of any city for sufficient cause regardless of the absence of a charter provision.[150] In the meantime, the Rapid Transit Company obtained an injunction preventing anyone, including the mayor, from interfering with its service on Butternut Street, despite the mayor's declaration that the "franchise was dead."[151]

As if this fight was not enough, McGuire signed and returned a deficiency bill to Albany, but not before issuing a statement in which he declared that the deficits were the result of spending incurred by prior city administrations.[152]

As the election drew closer, Francis Hendricks and James J. Belden met to see if they could agree upon a mutual candidate to do battle with McGuire. Hendricks favored former mayor Jacob Amos and Belden favored John H. Moffitt, the former general manager of the Rapid Transit Railway Company. This latter choice must have left McGuire salivating at the prospect of such a contest. Moffitt, however, was unlikely to get the support of Hendricks, and additional spec-ulation settled upon District Attorney Jay Kline, formerly a Belden candidate for mayor, and upon former New York State attorney gen-eral Theodore E. Hancock, who was not inclined to run.[153] Repub-licans were particularly concerned about McGuire's popularity in the large German community on the city's north side. Fluent in German, McGuire often campaigned in their native tongue. This proved to be an added plus for the Amos boom, and two other members of that community, Nicholas Peters and Charles Listman, were touted.[154]

Despite his expressed unwillingness to seek the mayoral nomina-tion, Theodore Hancock began to emerge as the consensus candidate of the Republican Party. A leader of the Belden wing of the party pre-dicted that Hancock would "bury" McGuire by two thousand votes. It was also thought that if the nomination were tendered, Hancock would accept since the office of mayor could be a stepping stone to a high judicial office.[155] Hancock, however, continued to disavow any interest in the nomination.[156]

In July, McGuire embarked upon a multicity tour that included Detroit, Pittsburgh, Allegheny City, and Chicago with Alderman Mack

7. Theodore Hancock, courtesy of Onondaga Historical Association.

and others to study the ownership of municipal lighting. Like all other types of franchises, McGuire became convinced that municipal ownership was preferable to awarding franchises to private companies.[157]

While the Republicans waited for their eventual nominee, McGuire, on the eve of the city Democratic convention, announced his own candidacy for reelection. Repudiating his declaration of the previous year that he would not be a candidate, he declared himself to be the best qualified person to wield the enhanced mayoral powers under the new charter.[158]

McGuire opened his campaign by seeming to offer an olive branch to Hancock, but on closer examination it was more of a fig leaf, which barely concealed the criticism that was about to come as he paid tribute to Hancock's career while branding him a tool of Hiscock and Hendricks. McGuire, with the help of a slide projector, went on to review the accomplishments of his administration in what the newspapers would call his "stereopticon" campaign.[159] McGuire would stick with this theme for a while, adding a charge that the *Post-Standard* was controlled by "the millionaire bosses trust" and that it was falsely charging that there were no overdrafts before 1895. He expanded his slide show to include slides on this subject as he lectured his audiences on the true history of the city's finances.[160]

In contrast to the overflow crowds that McGuire was drawing wherever he spoke, the Hancock campaign was disappointed at the meager crowd he drew for his maiden campaign speech. Hancock poked fun at McGuire's campaign, calling the slide projectors "a vaudeville show" and predicting a landslide victory for himself. Like Dey and Saul before him, Hancock left the attacks on the mayor to others and laid out his general themes of good government and no deficits if he were elected. He appeared to play into the criticism that McGuire seemed to imply about electing a lawyer as mayor, telling the crowd that they would be his "clients."[161] He would then proceed to criticize in lawyerlike fashion that the McGuire administration was lacking and that he could deliver more efficient government.

McGuire, on the other hand, warmed to the challenge of running not just against the attorney general, but rather a whole army of lawyers, characterizing one of Hancock's rallies as a "slimy and bloodless affair."[162]

On October 17, McGuire's political alter ego, M. Z. Haven, took the campaign into a new domain, pure class warfare, in a speech he delivered in the city's Fifteenth Ward, where he told the crowd,

> Did you gentlemen ever stop to think what a very peculiar thing it is that every time the Hendricks-Hancock political organization starts out after a candidate for Mayor of this city they always go

hunting up James street, Genesee street or West Onondaga street? You know that four years ago they went up James street and nominated a decent fellow for Mayor, Mr. Saul. You all know what happened to Saul. Then two years ago they went up James street again and nominated a decent fellow, a nice and a bright fellow, a man who was the head of a large business house. You all know what happened to Donald Dey.

Now, this year they have gone into the fashionable precinct of Genesee street and selected as a candidate Mr. Hancock and I think you people know what is going to happen to Hancock. . . .

Now, I have no prejudice, fellow citizens, against the residents of these streets. They are good, respectable people, but, somehow or other, the people of this municipality have conceived the idea—and I believe they are right—that the people of those streets are not sufficiently in touch with the plain, common people of the city to be familiar with their likes and dislikes or their necessities.[163]

In the remaining days of the campaign it was only going to get worse. McGuire himself took up the class warfare in a speech before a German audience, telling them, "If this corporation lawyer who claims to be the special champion of the workingmen in this campaign ever manifested any special interest in your behalf, I cannot recall it."[164]

Hancock continued to hammer at his belief that McGuire had mismanaged the city's financial affairs, charging that under the mayor, the cost of governing had risen by $1,100 per day.[165] He likewise continued his criticism of the overdrafts.[166] The mayor responded by pointing out that there was a 30 percent increase in the cost of operating the city between the years 1891 and 1896.[167] He went on to point out that the expenses of the attorney general's office doubled during Hancock's tenure.[168]

Hancock vigorously defended his record as attorney general, reminding his audiences that he was reelected in 1895 by more than 100,000 votes and a huge majority in both the city of Syracuse and Onondaga County. He did, however, seem to play right into McGuire's class-warfare strategy in addressing the municipal lodging issue, criticizing the amount of money expended to feed its occupants, declaring that "tramps are a county charge" and that the lodging house was a "very expensive experiment."[169]

Apparently oblivious to the class warfare McGuire was waging in the campaign, Hancock continued to stoke the image that he was a wealthy lawyer, out of touch with the needs of the unfortunate, as he continued to denigrate the mayor's municipal lodging house. His criticism became even more strident than before as he told a crowd that McGuire was turning Syracuse into a "Mecca for tramps."[170] Meanwhile McGuire continued to hammer at the "millionaires machine."[171]

McGuire kept up a relentless schedule of appearances as the campaign came down to the wire. He took no segment of the electorate for granted, appearing at a meeting of African American voters in the Fifteenth Ward, where he claimed to be the first mayor to recognize that they were entitled to share in patronage too.[172] As the campaign came to a close, those who wagered on the outcome had the race about even.[173]

The issue of "illegal registrations" for voting became front and center at the close of the campaign. District Attorney Jay Kline claimed that there might be as many as five hundred men illegally registered and vowed to prosecute and punish those who did so.[174] McGuire responded to this claim by telling his audience that he would deputize his campaign workers as "special policemen" to ensure every voter's right to exercise his franchise.[175]

After a day of very heavy voting,[176] McGuire had 12,470 votes to Hancock's 10,349. Approximately 3,000 Republicans had crossed over to vote for the mayor, despite the fact that the Republican Party had a registration edge of 2,000.[177] Unlike the two previous elections, McGuire had no kind words for his defeated opponent nor did Hancock have any for him.

McGuire's victory over Hancock was stunning by any standard. The thought was almost unthinkable that this young son of an Irish immigrant, who was forced to leave school in his teen years, could upset a blue-blooded Columbia University Law School graduate who had been elected twice to the position of the state's chief legal officer

8. Jay B. Kline, courtesy of the City of Syracuse.

and who had carried the city with a plurality almost twice as great as any other candidate on the ballot just four years before.[178]

As the year drew to a close, Francis Hendricks was faced with the realization that three times he had tried to defeat McGuire and had failed. Now he would have to find another way to rid himself of his nemesis.

The new administration, entering the new century and operating under a new city charter, was getting off to a slow start. The mayor, after being besieged by more than a thousand office-seekers, announced his appointments in the newspaper. The only real suspense surrounded the appointment of the corporation counsel, a position that went to M. Z. Haven.[179] Some suspense surrounded the naming of a new city clerk, but McGuire decided to play no role in that decision, since the appointment belonged strictly to the council under the new charter.[180] McGuire had become ill during his postelection trip to Old Point, Virginia, and was still plagued with the effects of his illness. He was finding it hard to accomplish all the work required to operate under the new charter. The year was only three weeks old, and he was contemplating a March trip to California to rest and recuperate.[181] Frances McGuire not only had to cope with the lingering effects of her husband's illness both at Old Point and upon returning to Syracuse, but had to do so in the last trimester of her third pregnancy. On January 10, 1900, she gave birth to their third child and only son, whom they named James Phillip.[182]

In the meantime, the mayor concentrated on the size of the overdrafts in the city accounts, which he estimated might reach $350,000.[183]

Early in the year, a group of prominent central New York Democrats held a secret meeting to promote McGuire's most ambitious political undertaking yet: his nomination for vice president of the United States as William Jennings Bryan's running mate. The meeting was inspired by talk that Theodore Roosevelt would be President McKinley's running mate, and the plan was to have McGuire confine his campaigning to central and western New York to hold down the Republican majority and carry the state for Bryan. The leaders attending the meeting claimed that Bryan was receptive to the idea and that Tammany Hall would support McGuire's candidacy. The mayor, for his part, was committed to stumping the whole state. There was only one minor flaw in the plan. McGuire was only thirty-two years old and Article II, Section 1 of the U.S. Constitution required that the president and vice president must be thirty-five years old. Nothing less than a constitutional amendment would be required for the plan to get off the ground.[184]

While the Democrats dreamt of national office, the Republicans were concentrating on weakening McGuire in the event he decided to seek a fourth term.[185] In addition to pushing the deficiencies into the election-year budget, the Republicans in the state legislature devised another way to drive up the city's tax rate. Senator White proposed amending the city charter to create a sinking fund that would require that one-third of the fees the city collected from licenses and other miscellaneous sources, other than taxes, be included in the fund to pay down the city's bonded indebtedness. McGuire characterized the proposal as a "sinker around the necks of the people of Syracuse."[186]

While the talk of a vice presidential nod appeared to be cooling, talk of a possible gubernatorial bid by the mayor began to heat up. The *Niagara Falls Journal* touted him for governor.

McGuire offered his own assessment of the upcoming election to the *Buffalo Courier* in which he predicted that Bryan would be renominated for president and that the Democrats would be victorious. In the same interview he described Roosevelt as representing the "dangerous military spirit" that would make America "an imitation of imperialist Great Britain."

Privately, McGuire was less sanguine about the party's chances of success. He told his closest confidants that he would not be a candidate for governor that year because McKinley was sure to sweep the state, damaging his chances for a future successful run for the office.[187]

The issue of the city's deficiencies continued to heat up as the New York State Assembly created a special committee to probe the city's finances. The chairman of the committee contended that the only purpose the committee had was to determine how the deficiencies originated.[188]

At the end of April McGuire traveled to Ireland for "private business" in Dublin.[189] Unlike almost all the mayor's other trips, which were well covered by the press, no details of this time in Ireland were disclosed or reported. The *Catholic Sun* dutifully reported the day of his departure, April 27,[190] and the date of his return, May 19,[191] but McGuire sent them no dispatches concerning his activities as he usually did. The secrecy should not be surprising since, at some point, he had joined Clan-na-Gael, the secret organization that was involved in all aspects of the fight for Irish independence, including the raising of an army to liberate the island.[192]

In early May the "Report of the Special Legislative Investigation Committee," which reported on Syracuse's finances, went to Governor Roosevelt. If there was any question about whether the committee had acted politically in its recommendations or whether this was another attempt by Hendricks to put an end to McGuire's career in politics, it was surely dispelled by Hendricks's and John S. Kenyon's lobbying the governor in private at the executive chamber in Albany.[193] Unsurprisingly, Roosevelt, who may have had concerns about McGuire as an opponent given Croker's analysis of the outcome of the last election and his low regard for the Irish,[194] directed the empaneling of a special grand jury. At the same time he designated supreme court justice Wilbur F. Smith of Patchogue in Suffolk County to preside over the matter. Before accepting the appointment, the judge and Roosevelt had a long conference followed by lunch together.[195] Only the most partisan or myopic could have had any doubt about what the future held.

When McGuire returned from Ireland on May 18, some details about his trip were made public. He had spent five days in Ireland and additional time in London and Paris. While in Paris, McGuire was taken into custody by French police following a fight with a trolley conductor. Fortunately for the mayor, there was an American at the station house who interpreted for him and was able to clear up the confusion without charges being lodged.[196]

Once home, McGuire was visited by a delegation of politicians from Buffalo promoting William Jennings Bryan's candidacy at the state convention. They informed him that they would support him for governor if their own candidate, Senator Mackey, could not secure the nomination. McGuire adhered to his position that he was not a candidate.[197]

The term of the extraordinary grand jury was barely a month old when word leaked that indictments had been returned against the mayor, Jacob Sehl, and fifteen aldermen. In a hearing before Justice Smith, testimony was elicited that Alderman Matty was the source of the rumor.[198] When Matty testified, he claimed that the source of the rumor was a dream that he had.[199]

If the legislative, civil service, and grand jury investigations were designed by Hendricks to end McGuire's political career, they had the opposite effect. In an interview with the *Herald* on June 24, McGuire announced that he would seek a fourth term as mayor the following year. Both supporters and opponents speculated that McGuire was seeking vindication by the people.[200]

In one of the most unusual episodes of his mayoralty, McGuire appeared in police court and sought to have an operator of a gambling den declared a public nuisance. In a written statement made in support of his complaint, the mayor described Peter O'Neill:

> This man O'Neill is the town pest. So vile, so shocking is his tongue that women shudder if they pass him on the street and decent men turn away in disgust. It is time that some restraint be placed on this vulgar, loathsome talking wretch in order that our men and women be protected from his vile attacks. No man is safe from that obscene tongue. He has vilely abused every public or professional man in this community. If he suffers from an attack of rabies he ought to be placed in one of the insane asylums, and if considered sane he ought to be placed in the Penitentiary, where his language will no longer afflict the public. He cannot harm me with his obscene remarks and billingsgate,[201] but I appear against him in the name of the community because he is a common nuisance. For twenty years he has been frothing like a mad dog, snapping without restraint because people are afraid of him. He is a worthless, lazy reprobate, too lazy to work and has been living for years off the charity of his worthy sister, who earns her own living . . . [202]

Shown the mayor's statement, O'Neill denied running a gambling den and vowed to sue for false imprisonment.

While McGuire was in Kansas City, Alderman Matty's dream came true. McGuire, the aldermen, and Jacob Sehl were named in multiple indictments by the extraordinary grand jury.[203] Upon returning to Syracuse, McGuire insisted on an early trial of the two indictments he was named in. The mayor's supporters felt the charges needed to be disposed of before he could be a candidate for governor.[204]

As if McGuire didn't have enough on his plate, he agreed to become chairman of the Executive Committee of the State Democratic Party, which meant he would have responsibility for the party's campaign efforts in the coming election. McGuire announced that he would spend three days each week in New York City and discharge his obligations as mayor in Syracuse the other three days of the work week.[205]

In the immediate postconvention period, at City Hall, in the midst of a speech in which he called Governor Roosevelt a "hypocrite" for appointing Francis Hendricks the state superintendent for insurance, McGuire fainted. He was taken to a hotel room, where he recovered and was driven home. His faint was attributed to a bout of vomiting. He was able to recover without medical attention.[206]

On Election Day, McKinley and Roosevelt handily carried New York, leading to the defeat of John B. Stanchfield for governor too. McGuire attributed the defeat to Bryan's insistence that the Free Silver plank be included in the platform at the convention in Kansas City the past July.[207] Despite the loss, McGuire's political fortunes continued to rise. By mid-November it was rumored that he would become the next chairman of the State Democratic Committee, and he traveled to New York to learn the operation of the Republican State Committee in anticipation of building a year-round organization.[208]

Upon returning to Syracuse, the mayor made two announcements. The first was that the city would construct a municipal golf course in Burnet Park on the city's west side.[209] The second was that he would not be a candidate for mayor the following year. McGuire declared that his need to bring financial security to his family trumped his political ambitions. He insisted that his decision was final.[210]

McGuire's announcement did not put an end to speculation about his political future. Observers of the political scene, particularly his supporters, fully expected that he would be a candidate for governor in the next election. Indeed his fortunes and their needs had grown to the point that they believed that a run for another term could jeopardize his chances of becoming governor in the unlikely event that he lost a mayoral election.[211] It was a far cry from the days when they insisted he forgo the nomination for lieutenant governor because of its lack of patronage. Now they were prepared to forgo the municipal patronage, betting on his success for the highest office in the state.

As the year drew to a close, McGuire and fourteen aldermen charged with conspiracy in voting for the overdrafts went on trial in New York State Supreme Court.[212] At the same time, former overseer of the poor, Jacob Sehl, was on trial for alleged misconduct in his office and chose to present no defense.[213] Sehl's jury, which was composed of ten Republicans, one Democrat, and one Independent, failed to agree on a verdict.[214] Unlike Sehl, the mayor and a number of aldermen testified and told the jury that they had no criminal intent in voting for the various resolutions that led to the overdrafts.[215] While Sehl's jury stood nine to three in favor of convicting him; the mayor's was nine to three in favor of acquittal. When the proceedings were over, McGuire was very vocal about the experience, complaining that Hiscock and Hendricks had orchestrated the prosecution because they were unable to defeat him at the polls.[216] Despite his obvious satisfaction with the result of the trial, McGuire refused to sanction a reception in the Fourth Ward for the purpose of celebrating the outcome.[217]

As the year 1901 opened, McGuire was faced with an ominous budget situation. The proposed budget would amount to over 1.6 million dollars and would require the city tax rate to rise to $17.65 per thousand.[218] There was, however, some very good news in the offing. On January 17, the mayor announced that, after repeatedly beseeching Andrew Carnegie, the millionaire industrialist had agreed to commit $200,000 to the construction of a new central library. The only conditions attached to the bequest were that the city must provide the location and agree to spend $30,000 annually for its maintenance.[219] McGuire was a big proponent of preserving the area's culture. In addition to soliciting money for the library, he had also been a supporter of establishing an art museum. In a letter to George Fisk Comfort, the founding director of the museum, dated March 17, 1899, McGuire had enthusiastically endorsed the efforts of the committee that had formed to establish the museum. He proclaimed the benefits such a museum would bring to the tourist economy of the city, drawing upon his visits to the Smithsonian Institution and the Museum of National Art in the nation's capital.[220]

McGuire received additional good news at the start of the year when Governor Odell directed the attorney general to discontinue the state's role in the prosecution of the city officials and turn the cases over to Jay B. Kline, the Onondaga County district attorney. McGuire, who detested the special prosecutor, Ceylon B. Lewis, could not resist crowing about this development publicly, claiming that he had signed affidavits from nine grand jurors who swore they did not intend to indict him.[221]

McGuire turned his attention to a more positive and popular project, the new proposed public library. He traveled to New York City to confer with Andrew Carnegie and upon returning shared his opinions about the industrialist, telling the *Herald*, "I did not talk details with Mr. Carnegie. I did not get a chance. He is the greatest man I ever saw to dispatch business. He seemed surprised that I should come to see him about a little matter like a library. He said that the letter which I had received told what he would do, and before I knew it, I was on my way out of the house." Turning to the actual construction of the library, the mayor laid out his plans to appoint a library board to oversee the construction of it.[222]

Although the budget process continued to drag on, the mayor made it clear that he would not let the lack of approval interfere with a proposed trip to California and New Mexico that he had planned because of his health.[223] Perhaps because he was in ill-health, McGuire reiterated his pledge that he would not be a candidate for reelection that year and urged that Public Works Commissioner James Meagher be the candidate of the Democratic Party.[224]

While the mayor and his wife were visiting the West, speculation about the fall campaign and his candidacy continued. One Democratic leader observed that McGuire would certainly be a candidate if only to prevail over Hendricks and his enemies in the deficit dispute.[225]

McGuire also wrote to his political allies insisting that he would not be a candidate for reelection, although they continued to insist that he would be persuaded to run, causing the *Herald* to observe that "the wish is father to the thought."[226] McGuire's position inspired supporters of the district attorney, Jay Kline, to begin promoting his candidacy for mayor; however, Kline was not viewed as being a favorite of the Hendricks faction of the Republican Party.[227]

As the mayor was working his way east and back to Syracuse, he met George McKeough, a partner in the McGuire and McKeough Insurance Agency, in Chicago. There the two men invested $5,000 in a company that would make automatic shovels or stokers for steamships and power companies. McGuire was elected president of the company and announced that its eastern headquarters would be in New York City.[228] Clearly McGuire was planning life after the mayoralty.

McGuire arrived back in Syracuse on May 1, after stopping to visit his sister Elizabeth, who was a college student at St. Mary's College, the sister school to Notre Dame University, in Indiana. He had been gone nine weeks. He proclaimed his health greatly improved and held forth on a variety of subjects. He immediately reaffirmed his position that he would not be a candidate for reelection that fall. He went on to pledge that if the Mackenzie Stoker Company, which he had formed in Chicago, was a success, then the plant could be moved to Syracuse.[229]

During this period, McGuire traveled to New York City to try to persuade another wealthy benefactor, Mrs. Russell Sage, to underwrite the cost of a Home for Aged and Indigent Men. Mrs. Sage had lived in Syracuse during her youth and, while sympathetic, stopped short of making a commitment.[230] The mayor's efforts drew some criticism concerning his seeking such assistance from a nonresident, leading him to challenge the local citizenry to come forward and undertake the project.[231]

While the political jockeying was taking place, the administration lost a court fight to keep the deficiency out of the current year's budget. On the heels of their court victory, Republican leaders began drafting a bill to include the deficiency amount of $400,000 in the current year's budget.[232]

If the political situation among the Republicans seemed muddled, the financial picture for the administration appeared bleak. The city comptroller, G. A. Manz, forecasted that with the deficiency items added into the budget, the tax rate would be $21.30 per thousand.[233] The mayor was quick to try to remind people that he was not responsible for $340,000 of the $400,000 figure,[234] but whether the voters would remember or even care remained to be seen.

McGuire certainly did not act like a candidate. On the day of the Democratic convention he left to join his family, who were on vacation in Skaneateles, and talk began to turn to the prospect of either G. A. Manz, the city comptroller, or E. F. Allen, the city treasurer, leading the ticket.[235]

In the meantime, the Republican Party held its convention and Jay B. Kline emerged as the Republican nominee. Observers of the political scene attributed his success to his persistence and his having sown support in all parts of the city organization.[236]

On the night of the Democratic convention, McGuire arrived at the Alhambra urging the selection of Meagher or Moffat and left as the nominee. He made no secret of the fact that he was unenthusiastic, telling the convention, "I am weary of the active turmoil of political strife . . . I want to rest. I want to give more of my attention to my personal affairs and to my family. Mrs. McGuire, before I left Skaneateles this afternoon, asked me for her sake, and the sake of our children, not to take up my time with this campaign and break myself down physically. I have never been entirely well since the last campaign." McGuire had no sooner taken his seat than he was nominated by acclamation for another term. He then returned to the platform and told the convention that he could not give them an answer that night.[237]

The following day an extraordinary interview, for its time, appeared in the *Herald* in which Frances McGuire made known her feelings about another campaign and public life in general. Speaking of her children, she told the reporter, "I'm glad they are not old enough to know anything about their father as Mayor of this city. I tremble to think of what would happen if they once had an inkling of the fact and understood anything about what is meant. The number and the kind of questions they would ask would be something appalling." When asked if McGuire would accept the nomination, she replied,

I don't—I really don't want him to. He is not well enough to go through the wear and tear of another campaign to say nothing of two more years of office if elected. When I think of what the next three weeks will mean if he is a candidate, I feel like throwing every grain of influence I possess against it as I have for two years. And besides he can do just as much for his Party outside city hall as he can in it.

There are days at a time when he never thinks of coming home from morning until night and when he does, he is so completely tired out that he scarcely knows where he is.

Why on earth would any wife want her husband to be in a position that would injure his health and take him entirely away from his home life? The children are growing old enough now so that it is their father's duty to be more to them than a scarcely familiar figure that comes and goes occasionally. I may be selfish in feeling as I do but I can't help it.[238]

By the end of the interview, however, she reluctantly gave her blessing to his accepting the nomination and McGuire was, once again, a candidate for mayor of Syracuse.

Voters were registering in record numbers for the fall election. The rolls were swelled to 27,840, 1,383 more than in the previous municipal election.[239]

McGuire, as expected, found himself having to defend the record high tax rate by insisting that the deficiencies included in the city budget were, for the most part, the previous administrations' and the state legislature's, asking, "If a Mayor can't get his vetoes sustained, and the Legislature passes bills over his vetoes, is it not manifestly unfair to blame the Mayor for the harm done by such resolutions and bills?"[240]

The *Herald* offered to sponsor a debate between the candidates at the Alhambra. McGuire was quick to accept, agreeing to debate Kline or any surrogate of his choosing. Kline declined the challenge.[241] Perhaps emboldened by Kline's reluctance to meet him in debate, McGuire offered a second challenge to debate the budget, but predicted that Kline would duck his challenge.[242] His prediction would prove to be an accurate one.

The campaign took another new downward spiral when one of Kline's surrogates charged that the mayor had been enriched by being in office.[243] McGuire then went on the attack concerning Kline's competence by suggesting that Hendricks sought a special prosecutor from the governor at a time when Kline was district attorney.[244]

Early betting on the results of the election favored McGuire. One building contractor, Thomas Marnell, offered 2 to 1 odds that McGuire would be elected and was willing to wager $5,000. W. B. Kirk offered $100 to $75 on the same outcome.[245]

If the campaign of two years ago was class warfare, the current one was taking on all of the characteristics of a street fight—sometimes with knives. McGuire went further on the attack, accusing Kline of holding up seventeen hundred indictments in cases involving serious crimes. He was graphic in his description of the cases, telling his audience, "I can show you affidavits which would make the women in this audience sob over the circumstances attending the violation of little children of 9 and 10 and 12 years." He concluded by telling his audience, "Two years ago there was no occasion for personalities. Mr. Hancock was a man whose record at Albany was such that it could not be assailed. There was not a flaw in it; and I merely defended my own. Then I said I was entitled to votes on my record. Now, I say that I am entitled to votes on my record and against the record of my opponent."[246]

As the rhetoric continued to heat up, tempers began to flare. At an outdoor rally, Kline was repeatedly interrupted by hecklers, and a crowd of young men and boys carrying McGuire banners flaunted them in front of his face. Police were called and had some difficulty getting them to disperse. Kline continued to pound on the payroll padding issue in red-hot language.[247]

In the closing days of the campaign the betting odds tightened, although they still favored the mayor. McGuire could be bet at $100 to $90.[248] Both candidates kept up a frenetic level of campaigning as the race went into the final forty-eight hours, crisscrossing the city, speaking to as many crowds as possible. The *Herald* reported that Kline's audiences grew steadily in size but that McGuire's were larger still. The mayor remained the favorite in the betting.[249] McGuire's criticism of Kline's handling of one case, known as the "Sanford" case, led to the highly unusual step of having Judge Ross, the Onondaga County court judge, come to the defense of the district attorney. On that uplifting note, the 1901 campaign for mayor came to an end.

On Election Day the voting was heavy, with more than half of the votes being cast before noon. The *Herald* reported that the Democrats seemed better financed than the Republicans and the "floaters" were voting early.[250] When it was over and the votes were counted, Kline had won by a margin of 1,425 votes. McGuire, as expected, carried the wards on the north side of the canal by a margin of 808 votes, but Kline had carried those on the south side by 2,233. The Republicans had swept every contested office in the election.

During McGuire's lame duck period, he sent a "confidential" letter to Dean Comfort at Syracuse University concerning the planned art museum, advising him, "I hear that the next administration intends to 'cut out' the Art Museum appropriation. I would advise you to get after Kline et al. with the aid of Mr. Hyde, Clark and your other friends."[251] McGuire's commitment to the arts and culture would be missed by some segments of the community.

The surprising defeat of McGuire may have been the result of a number of factors. One was the overwhelming party registration the Republican enjoyed, despite McGuire's successes of the past three elections. Another may have been the combination of McGuire's health and lack of enthusiasm for the campaign and another term, which were reported and clearly evident to the public. Some who have commented on the race always cite Hendricks's success in getting the deficiency amount into the 1901 budget and the inflated tax rate that resulted.[252] Finally, there is that simple desire on the part of the electorate to want change. McGuire had, by his own account, served longer than any previous mayor, and he may simply fallen victim to what modern pundits would call "McGuire fatigue." Whatever the reason was, one thing was clear. The era of the "Boy Mayor" was over.

5

The "Wilderness" Years

Unlike defeated politicians in the modern age, McGuire would not have the luxury of spending any years in the "political wilderness." He had a young family to support. He and Frances had three young children and their fourth, Rosalind, would arrive on January 16, 1902.[1] He had a number of business interests that needed his attention, and he still had his duties as chairman of the Executive Committee of the State Democratic Party. In this latter capacity he was editing a three-volume history of the party.[2]

As the year progressed, McGuire visited David Hill to begin the organization of the upcoming campaign for governor. Despite his loss the previous November, McGuire was still regarded as an attractive statewide candidate who could have a place on the ticket that fall. McGuire denied any interest in being a candidate.[3] Once again, he was being touted as a candidate on the statewide ticket, this time for comptroller. The former mayor rebuffed the suggestion but did commit to making speeches during the campaign as well as to taking charge of the campaign in Onondaga County. He had also committed to making five speeches for the Democratic candidate for governor of Pennsylvania. He would be replaced by former comptroller Bird S. Coler, who took the position in anticipation of becoming the Democratic candidate for governor that fall.[4]

On August 2, Mayor Kline managed to achieve a new low for pettiness as the Carnegie Library was dedicated in Syracuse. Despite the fact that McGuire had obtained the financing for the library from the industrialist, Kline and the library trustees kept him waiting

96

for the ceremony and did not undertake the laying of the cornerstone until after he had left. Observers believed that McGuire had been denied any part or mention in the program because the Republicans did not want him to have any favorable publicity whatsoever.[5]

At the convention in Saratoga, Bird Coler was nominated for governor.[6] McGuire played a more subtle role, albeit one that would have significant repercussions in the campaign. Throughout 1902, the nation was in the midst of a coal miners' strike that occupied much of the Roosevelt administration's time and effort in trying to bring about a resolution.[7] In the midst of this controversy, McGuire proposed adding a plank to the state party platform calling upon the president to nationalize the mines and coal industry. When the plank was first proposed, it was considered so radical that former senator David Hill was reported to have told McGuire, "It's worse than anything that Bryan ever wrote. Don't you think that you are jumping a century in a night?"

McGuire's plank was not some abstract concept that he had interjected into the campaign without considerable forethought. He likened it to the Government Printing Office and envisioned the mines' being run by a cabinet-level office: the Department of Mines.[8] It was an idea that would generate much discussion and that he would talk more about during the course of the campaign. In his opening speech at home in Syracuse, he defended the plank against the charge that it was Socialist.[9] Governor Odell, campaigning for reelection, charged that "the whole democratic platform appeals to passion rather than reason," and was "encouraged by those who desired to see conflict between labor and capital."[10]

After traveling on business for two weeks and having time to reflect on his situation, McGuire announced his retirement from politics. He was not, however, willing to assume responsibility for the most recent defeat. In his statement he explained that the reason the Republicans had prevailed was because Governor Odell was the better candidate. He offered to step down from party leadership but would not tolerate his friends being sacrificed.[11]

It was to be a short-lived retirement. While McGuire would be absent from the city for significant periods of time in 1903, as events unfolded it would become clear that he was still in charge of the local Democratic Party.

McGuire's business interests were continuing to prosper as the year unfolded. McGuire was employed by John Mack, an asphalt baron whose empire expanded dramatically as he and his partners acquired some seventy different asphalt companies in receivership. He had been doing some work for the lead and zinc trusts and would be obliged to discontinue that work with the expansion of Mack's asphalt business.[12] Despite his best efforts, McGuire could not seem to successfully extricate himself from local Democratic politics. As 1904 opened, he announced his intention to resign his party leadership positions. He had signed a long-term contract with the General Asphalt Company, located in Philadelphia, which already required him to travel extensively, and he anticipated that he would be required to travel more extensively throughout the United States and Europe on its behalf. As such, he would have little time nor be in central New York to be involved in local politics.[13]

On April 20, 1904, McGuire formally submitted his letter of resignation from all local party positions to Chairman Cummins. McGuire then left on a trip to the Pacific coast that would last six weeks.

On Election Day, Roosevelt was reelected president and carried Onondaga County by 12,482 votes, a new record.[14] In the wake of this debacle, Cummins resigned the position of party chairman.[15] McGuire had moved his family to New York City for the upcoming winter. He had vowed to return in the spring to aid his friends in regaining control of the organization. Now, beseeched by the reorganizers to return in the spring and restore some measure of control, he declined, noting, "they must stew in their own juice."[16]

True to his word, McGuire did refrain from any involvement in local politics throughout 1905. In late January, however, he dispelled the speculation that he would be moving his family permanently out of Syracuse, telling a *Herald* reporter that his family would be returning to Green Street in mid-April, that his move to New York City for the winter was only because it was more convenient for business travel, and that he would retain his voting residence in the city.

McGuire reaffirmed his belief that he considered William Jennings Bryan to be the leader of the Democratic Party nationally.[17]

Although his role in local politics and the municipal campaign was to be limited, 1905 saw the publication of the three-volume history of the New York State Democratic Party, titled *Democratic Party of the State of New York*, which McGuire edited.[18] The work contained a comprehensive history of the Democratic Party triumphs and pitfalls by the men who in some instances lived them, as well as a number of biographical sketches of party leaders and candidates.

McGuire was busy representing the interests of his employer and was seen in Albany lobbying against four bills that would have been detrimental to the asphalt industry. In this endeavor he found himself on the side of an old antagonist, Senator Horace White. White opposed the bills, contending that the bills were opposed by the mayor of New York and that they would only require the asphalt companies to pay tribute to Tammany Hall.[19] While McGuire remained keenly interested in issues, he was becoming increasingly disenchanted with politics and politicians, observing, "The more I see of Congressman, Mayors, Governors, Councilmen etc. the less interest and sentiment I have in politics . . . One-fourth of all the voters in Syracuse are bought and sold like so many sheep and cattle. I collected perhaps $200,000 in Syracuse for campaign purposes and to keep our men in power, and as I look over the victories as well as the defeats I am ashamed of them all."[20] He went on decry the belief that the moneyed interests would defeat President Roosevelt's attempts to regulate the railroads and that Mayor Alan Cutler Fobes would be handily reelected if the Democrats and Independents did not unite and wage a campaign on a nonpartisan municipal ownership of the utilities.

Nineteen six would prove to be the last year that McGuire tried to exercise his considerable influence in local politics. It would be the year that his friendship with his friend and closest confidante in politics, M. Z. Haven, would be irreparably damaged. The genesis of these unlikely developments came from a most unexpected source: William Randolph Hearst.

The year had barely begun when M. Z. Haven and the McGuire allies found themselves again embroiled in the ongoing internecine fight with the "reorganizers." The reorganizers claimed that Haven had abandoned his patron, the reform-minded David Hill, and had switched his allegiance to Tammany Hall boss Charles Murphy.[21] The McGuire supporters, anonymously, did not dispute this assertion and conceded that they might make common cause with Tammany leaders in support of former comptroller Bird S. Coler's potential candidacy for governor again. They viewed themselves as opponents of the Wall Street wing of the party whose allegiance was to former gubernatorial candidates Alton Parker and D. Cady Herrick, and to former leaders Hill and William Sheehan. Into this breach stepped William Randolph Hearst, the newspaper magnate, former congressman, and unsuccessful candidate of the Municipal Ownership League for mayor of New York City the previous year.

Five years older than McGuire, Hearst was the only son of U.S. Senator George Hearst of California, who had founded the *San Francisco Examiner* as an organ for the Democratic Party in California. After being expelled from Harvard, Hearst had returned to California, where he took over the newspaper and, after spending millions of dollars of his parents' money on contests and promotions to increase circulation, had built it into the most widely read paper in the state. In 1895 Hearst moved to New York City, where he bought the *New York Journal* and promptly began a circulation war with Joseph Pulitzer's *New York World*. In addition the contests and promotions that had worked so well in California, Hearst used the *Journal* to bring yellow journalism to either a new height or a new low, depending on the viewpoint of the reader. His efforts are widely considered to have culminated in his bringing about the Spanish-American War in 1898, which the *Journal* covered with relish.

Hearst had given all-out support to William Jennings Bryan in both of his presidential bids in 1896 and 1900. Following Bryan's defeat in the latter campaign, Hearst reached the inevitable conclusion that the only man who could or should be president was him. To that end, he embarked on a path he believed would take him to the

White House. In 1902 he sought the support of Charles S. Murphy and Tammany Hall to secure the nomination for the congressional seat in the Eleventh District in Manhattan. He was elected to Congress that fall. The following year he threw the support of the *Journal* behind the successful mayoral campaign of George McClellan Jr., son of the Union Civil War general and Democratic presidential opponent of Abraham Lincoln in 1864. His loyalty to McClellan and the Democratic Party earned him praise from State Senator Patrick McCarren, the political boss of Kings County and Brooklyn. This loyalty was short-lived, however, and Hearst and the *Journal* soon became McClellan's and Tammany Hall's harshest critic. In 1904 Hearst mounted an all-out campaign for the Democratic Party nomination for president. His rival for the nomination was New York Court of Appeals judge Alton Parker. Due to Hearst's attacks on McClellan and Tammany, Murphy backed Parker, and the New York delegation supported Parker at the party's national convention in St. Louis. At the convention Hearst asked William Jennings Bryan to nominate him for president. Bryan, however, refused and, while praising Hearst, instead seconded the nomination of Senator Francis Cockrell of Missouri. It was a betrayal that Hearst would not forget. Bitter and disappointed, Hearst returned to New York and, with Murphy's and Tammany's support, was reelected to Congress.

The following year Hearst renewed his attacks on McClellan and Murphy, calling the former a tool of Murphy and the latter the reincarnation of Boss Tweed. As the political calendar ripened, Hearst was casting about trying to find an opponent for McClellan. Ultimately he accepted the designation of the Municipal Ownership League and found himself in a three-way race against McClellan and Republican William Ivins. Hearst and the *Journal* all but ignored Ivins, as they launched attack after attack upon McClellan, Murphy, and Tammany Hall. When the votes were counted, McClellan had 228,651 votes, Hearst had 225,166 and Ivins 137,049. Hearst, crying fraud on the part of Murphy and Tammany, would not concede.[22] Despite having been defeated in this bid barely five months previously, Hearst was generating interest for his candidacy for governor.[23]

In mid-May, McGuire injected himself into a national controversy involving two of his old antagonists. Syracuse University Chancellor James Day castigated President Roosevelt for his antitrust policies involving Standard Oil and other monopolies and referred to Roosevelt as "that anarchist in the White House." There is probably no other ethnic group that is more devoted to and unalterably embraces the principle that "the enemy of my enemy is my friend" than the Irish. McGuire was no exception. No sooner had Chancellor Day leveled his criticism of the president, which was reported nationwide, than McGuire found himself at the White House conferring with Roosevelt. After meeting with the president, McGuire told the *Herald* that he informed Roosevelt that the chancellor had referred to him as an "anarchist" during his mayoral years and that he would refer to the chancellor as the "Bloodless Monster on the Hill." He went on to accuse Chancellor Day of seeking "tainted money from millionaires who earned their wealth from exploiting the working man." McGuire's criticism of the chancellor was echoed by the *New York Times*, the *Chicago News*, and other big-city newspapers.[24]

The Hearst bandwagon continued to roll across the state. McGuire dropped a political bombshell. He too was for Hearst. He reiterated that he would take no role in the battle for leadership of the local party and declared that he would not be able to participate in the primaries. He pledged $500 to the Hearst campaign and further declared that he would not contribute to anyone else. He was adamant that Hearst was the only candidate the Democrats could nominate that could win.[25]

Hearst's candidacy was not only proving divisive in the Democratic Party, where conservatives detested him in the same way they detested Bryan, but it was also having an impact in the Republican Party. At the beginning of the year it was generally believed that Governor Frank Higgins was so unpopular that for Republicans to hang on to the governor's mansion, it was necessary for Higgins to retire and be succeeded by Charles Evans Hughes. With the rise of Hearst and divisions widening in the Democratic Party, Higgins's candidacy for renomination took on new life.[26]

McGuire's embrace of Hearst, instead of being welcomed by the reorganizers, was greeted with suspicion. One of the early Hearst supporters expressed resentment that the support of McGuire and any other prominent Democrat associated with him would have the effect of eclipsing him at the end of a successful campaign.[27]

McGuire arrived back in Syracuse in mid-June after a long trip throughout the western states. On his first day home, he continued his assault on Chancellor Day, telling a *Herald* reporter,

> I have spent the last fourteen nights on a sleeping car between here and Mexico eating veal labeled canned chicken, eating dog's tails branded as Chicago sausages, eating rats, cats and beef, according to Upton Sinclair or the Roosevelt investigators, and wondering when the next minute of ptomaine poisoning would follow. But all of these fears ceased and the grief of the stomach was assuaged when the New Orleans sleeper of the Queen and Crescent railroad turned into Cincinnati yesterday and I read my eminent townsman's defense of the makers of canned meat.
>
> I must have another talk with President Roosevelt soon and ask the "terrible anarchist" in the White House to desist from the effort to give us travelers meat fit to eat, in order that some possible beneficiaries of Syracuse University among the beef barons might find it easier to give a few hundred thousand dollars of our money to the college. The country doesn't need good, clean, sanitary meats. We need more subsidized colleges and subsidized Bishops.
>
> Scarcely twelve decades have passed since the Bishop of France enriched by subsidies at the hand of the King and the head of a college, told King Louis that the mutterings of the people against the nobility were hysterical and nothing to be feared. Within a year both the heads of the King and the Bishop fell into the basket.
>
> Let me say for the information of the Chancellor that in the western states the people are simply horrified over his attempt to continue railroad extortions by attacking the President. Have we not seen within this very week, confessions of the Pennsylvania Railroad officers, the existence of the very evils the President endeavors to suppress?

Chancellor Day considers the country extremely happy as measured by the moneys received by the university and its own affluent condition. That man does not look beyond the green bills or the great safes of his capitalistic supporters. I have seen within three months the industrial side of the vaunted New South. In Alabama laborers live like animals in hovels near Birmingham and Bessemer. In South Carolina little stunted children, slaving in the cotton mills, anemic and emaciated girls who ought to be in schools, existing amid surroundings that make the heart shudder. If you ever had any doubts of the benefits of organized labor you should see the difference between the conditions of the union workers of Fall River and South Carolina's unorganized workers. Sympathy is wasted on the average man with millions. He does not need help, cynically, he can buy his way.[28]

One of the reasons that McGuire may have continued his assault upon the chancellor, besides the fact that he seemed to have an antipathy for him from their earlier history, may have been that the chancellor, in his initial criticism of Roosevelt, took a dismissive attitude toward Hearst. Day had characterized Roosevelt as a "dangerous" anarchist and Hearst a "harmless" one. In the end, however, McGuire's hostility toward the chancellor was likely the product of the simmering resentment that Irish immigrants and the sons of Irish immigrants held toward the wealthy, well-educated, white Anglo-Saxon Protestants who oozed entitlement and smug superiority whenever they were in their presence.

McGuire continued his advocacy for Hearst, while at the same time eschewing any role in local politics.[29] McGuire found himself occasionally having to justify his somewhat anomalous position in which he was a lobbyist for one of the largest trusts in the country while at the same time espousing very populist, if not radical, economic views. He acknowledged this contradiction in explaining his support for Hearst, saying,

I am for Hearst because he always takes the part of the weak against the strong, of the oppressed against the powerful, and fights for government by the people against the rule of money.

The *Herald* says that my position is inconsistent in that I am "a high salaried official of a rich trust." Is a man to have no solid convictions of his own because he is employed by a corporation?[30]

He went on to make an unconvincing case that the paving concerns he worked for were not a trust, before continuing,

I say that the predatory rich criminal is making it hard for every other corporation. As a man who wants to see the Democratic party become the victorious instrument of the people, I want to see Hearst nominated by that party because he is the only candidate who can win on that ticket. Narrow partisans say that he ought not to come into the Democratic convention at the head of an independent movement. What absurd objection that is in times like these when old party lines are going down in a crash everywhere.

McGuire's views should not have come as a surprise or been viewed as anomalous or inconsistent by anyone. As mayor, he had been steadfast in his unsuccessful advocacy of municipal ownership of the city's utilities and, when thwarted, would only grant franchises to companies that would agree to pay a percentage of their profits back to the city. If that were not enough of a harbinger, the "Coal Plank" of the State Democratic Party platform in 1904 should have enlightened the world to his way of thinking. McGuire continued his cheerleading for Hearst, mixing his message with criticism of the political parties that he contended were controlled by special interests whose mission was to gain financially.

Hearst was not blessed with any of the attributes of a natural politician. He had a high-pitched voice, spoke with a lisp, and had a weak handshake.[31] While he demonstrated a genius for having his finger on the pulse of the public as a newspaper publisher, as events past and future would prove, he was a narcissistic megalomaniac with atrocious political judgment. One of the many political blunders Hearst was to make that year was the challenge to the legitimacy of Mayor McClellan's victory over him in the mayoral race the previous year. Hearst brought the challenge to the state attorney general in April

1906 as his campaign for governor was taking shape, and the attorney general denied it in July.[32] Thus he was held up before the public as a poor loser at a time when he least needed such an image and made a confirmed enemy in the mayor of the state's largest city. Likewise, Hearst would not content himself with seeking the nomination of the Democratic Party. On August 1, it was announced that his organization, the Independence League, would hold a nominating convention in Carnegie Hall, before the Democratic caucuses and the state convention, to nominate Hearst for governor.[33] This action led a faction of the Democratic State Committee's self-proclaimed "regulars" to take the position that Hearst would have to be the candidate of the Independence League only.[34] Undaunted by this split in the party, the leaders of Hearst's Independence League let it be known that they would try to enlist McGuire to manage Hearst's effort in the local Democratic caucuses during the coming September.[35] McGuire, for his part, disclaimed any interest in being involved in the local caucuses but continued to defend his advocacy of Hearst.[36]

Despite his repeated declarations that his business interests would keep him from being involved in the local delegate selection, McGuire was back in Syracuse organizing for Hearst.[37] McGuire, who had been in New York City attending a reception honoring William Jennings Bryan, returned home to announce that he would publish a newspaper, called the *Citizen*, devoted to furthering Hearst's campaign.[38] It was a tactic that Hearst himself had employed on behalf of Bryan in his campaign against McKinley when he published the *Chicago American*.[39] McGuire went on to disclose that the *Citizen* would be an eight-page paper that would cost a penny and be published from the offices of the *Catholic Sun* each morning. He justified publishing it by noting that there was not another central New York paper friendly to Hearst.[40]

McGuire was reported to be working harder for Hearst than in any of his own campaigns.[41] Indeed, he introduced a new dimension to campaigning by touring the outlying county in an automobile referred to as a "gasoline wagon."[42]

On the day of the primary, the Hearst forces ran ads in the local papers urging Democrats to "Smash the Plunderbund." Among the candidates listed on a slate of candidates for contested delegate seats in the Thirteenth Ward in Syracuse was McGuire's younger brother George.[43] It would not be the only time they teamed up in politics.

When the votes were counted, McGuire and Hearst won a victory in the city beyond anyone's expectations. Out of 2,245 votes cast, the McGuire-Hearst faction won all but 198. Commenting on the victory, the *Herald* declared that McGuire had "recovered his grip upon the Democratic organization, and will again dominate it as completely as he did in his palmiest days."[44]

Ultimately, at 2:00 AM on September 27, Hearst was nominated for governor by the Democratic Convention.[45] The Republican Convention had met in Saratoga the previous day and nominated Charles Evans Hughes as its standard-bearer.[46]

McGuire had one more surprise for everyone. Despite his repeated disclaimers that he was through seeking office, the *New York Times* reported, on October 9, that he would be the candidate for Congress against Congressman Michael E. Driscoll in the Thirty-ninth District encompassing Onondaga County.[47] It would prove to be a very short-lived candidacy and the reasons behind it would not be readily apparent until after Election Day.

On Election eve, McGuire traveled to New York City and returned home declining to make a prediction on the outcome of the race. He was quick to spike rumors that he would be a candidate for mayor the following year. Before commenting on the following day's election, he observed that the primary elections had consumed much of his time and money. He said that Hearst would not supply any money to buy votes on Election Day, although he believed that there would be almost 15,000 "floaters in the 5,000 election districts throughout the state." He went on to declare that Syracuse had 8,000 "purchasable" voters and more in the towns. While he would not predict the outcome, the enthusiasm he had witnessed in New York City left him optimistic.[48]

Immense crowds were turning out for Hughes too. On the eve of the election, the *New York Times* estimated that he had spoken to 12,000 citizens in a single night of touring New York City.[49]

McGuire's election prognosticators proved to be very short of their mark. Hearst carried New York City by a margin of only 71,644 votes. He lost Erie, Schenectady, and Monroe Counties, which he had counted on winning. New York had elected Charles Evans Hughes governor by a plurality of 63,383 votes. Hearst had run behind every other candidate on the Democratic ticket.[50]

Locally, Hughes carried Onondaga County by 8,600 votes with a plurality of 4,800 in the city.[51] W. W. Van Brocklin of Pompey, who had replaced McGuire as the candidate for Congress, was beaten handily by Congressman Michael E. Driscoll.[52] At the time McGuire had offered himself as a candidate against Driscoll, some political pundits suspected that it was a temporary ploy designed to attract other candidates to the ticket owing to Hearst's unpopularity.[53] They were undoubtedly correct.

Within days of the result, McGuire was offering an explanation for the defeat. Hearst had refused to buy votes. McGuire maintained that if Hearst had spent $150,000, amounting to $50 per election district, he would have won. Pledging his continued loyalty to Hearst, he chastised those in the party who had abandoned the candidate and declared that no one but Hughes could have defeated Hearst.[54]

Since the Democrats had won every statewide office except governor, there was ample patronage in Albany to be doled out. Oddly enough, despite his having championed the losing gubernatorial candidate, McGuire was the most sought-after patron from central New York to wield his influence. He made it clear that his ally State Committeeman William Rafferty was in control of all patronage for Onondaga County. He also commented on the philosophical divide in the party. He may still have been stung by Hearst's defeat and the desertion by the conservative party leaders, whom he labeled "moneyed men" and "Bourbons." He posed the interesting idea that those who were considered to be "radicals" in the Democratic and Republican parties should form a party of their own. He even went on to suggest that conservative Democrats should be purged from the party and that no conservative Democrat should be supported again.[55]

McGuire's reference to "moneyed men" and "Bourbons" as the conservative enemy was ironic given the campaign filings, which occurred later that month, reporting campaign expenditures. Hearst had outspent Hughes by a margin of $258,372.22 to $671.38. Indeed, he had spent more money than all other statewide candidates combined.[56]

Nineteen seven would prove to be one of the strangest years in local politics. It would lead to one of the most unpredictable, if not unimaginable, candidacies for mayor that the city would ever see.

Several candidates offered themselves to McGuire and other leaders in the local Democratic Party but none of them appealed to a consensus of the leadership. Into this vacuum stepped a candidate who could hardly be considered a "young blood," Alderman Frank Matty.[57] The Republicans had no such quandary. The party simply renominated Mayor Fobes and all its current citywide officeholders.[58]

Turning to the newly found Haven-Matty alliance, McGuire declared, "The last year that I served as Mayor, Alderman Matty was at Haven's throat every second and no name or epithet was too hard for him but because he is disgruntled he wants to make the Democratic party ridiculous by nominating candidates for mayor who from the time of their nomination would cause every burglar alarm in Syracuse to go off and keep ringing until the last ballot was in the box until election day."[59] The burglar alarm comment would reverberate more loudly than the alarms themselves right through Election Day.

Matty was nominated by a vote of 61 to 55. Upon his selection as the party's nominee, McGuire, in a show of unity, gave him $500 and promised to support him.[60]

During the last two weeks of October, the *Herald*, alarmed at the prospect that Matty might become mayor, ran a series of articles reviewing Matty's history on the council, questioning whether his votes were bought,[61] and whether he stuffed the ballot box during his election as council president.[62] The articles recounted the gambling scandal surrounding his saloon,[63] his ties to the Rapid Transit Railway

Company,[64] and whether he had received free electricity at his place of business.[65] They recounted how he had leaked grand jury indictments,[66] and whether he had paid all the taxes he owed.[67] The *Herald* also ran stories recounting how McGuire had Matty's saloon raided for illegal gambling in 1897,[68] and quoted extensively from Matty's divorce proceedings, which involved testimony by his second wife concerning his use of marked cards.[69] As damaging as all of this coverage was, the *Herald* determined that the most effective campaigner against Matty was McGuire, and it ran articles extensively quoting McGuire's attack on Matty during the March 27, 1896, council meeting.[70] McGuire himself fed into these attacks by first announcing that he would not be home to vote in the election,[71] and then by announcing that he would not be able to find time in his schedule to come home and speak on Matty's behalf.[72] One of McGuire's friends, discussing the former mayor's earlier commitment to come home and campaign, sounded a note reminiscent of Elihu Root's disposal of Hearst, telling the *Herald*, "He will probably make good his promise to deliver a speech during the closing week of the campaign, but he cannot be expected to say anything about Matty. He gave his opinion of Matty in the Common Council in 1896 and it hasn't changed."

The *Herald* seemed unable to write about McGuire and Matty without repeating this observation, as well as McGuire's suggestion that if Matty were nominated "all the burglar alarms in the city would start ringing until the last ballot was counted on election day." One prominent Democrat only made matters worse by remarking, "I could not picture McGuire speaking for Matty. McGuire probably figured that if he attempted to speak for Matty his voice would be drowned out by the ringing of the burglar alarms."[73]

McGuire, for his part, tried to ameliorate the situation by writing Democratic Party Secretary John Scanlon to explain that his failure to fulfill his commitment and his failure to register to vote should not be construed as a lack of support for Matty. The damage, however, was done.

On Election Day Fobes beat Matty by 2,326 votes. If there was an interesting dimension to the election, it was that Matty ran substantially ahead of all the other Democratic candidates despite the fact that they had the support of the Independence League and he did not.[74]

The former alderman and mayoral candidate declared that McGuire would have to answer for his lack of support during the preceding mayoral campaign. Some of McGuire's supporters thought Matty's criticism was unfair and inaccurate, pointing out that McGuire gave Matty $500 on the night that he was nominated.[75]

McGuire, as expected, was not the least bit cowed by Matty's charge or challenge; responding from one of his offices, located in Philadelphia, he not only rose to the challenge but dropped a bombshell. Before he would see Matty run again, he would be a candidate himself:

> Matty is sore because I said the town's burglar alarms would go off as soon as he was nominated for Mayor. And ring they did, as the election returns show . . . Any Democrat but Matty would have beaten Fobes . . . I see that he says he is to be a candidate again. He won't get the nomination by default next time. If there is no opposing candidate against him in the primaries, I intend to so arrange my affairs as to contest the primaries with him as a candidate for Mayor myself and I am confident that I can defeat him when I make a thorough canvass of the city.[76]

He confirmed that he would play no role in the local primaries that year but would defer to Rafferty in those matters.

Matty, for reasons best known to himself, insisted on keeping the "burglar alarms" reference before the public by replying to McGuire, "What does he mean by 'burglar alarm?' He keeps springing that every time he feels like talking. If he refers that to me I'll answer him."[77]

The following year, McGuire announced that after he spent a few days in Syracuse in mid-June, he would travel to Lincoln, Nebraska, to confer with Bryan about the party's platform in the upcoming national campaign. Informed that W. B. Kirk favored Governor Johnson of Minnesota as the party's standard-bearer, he declined to criticize Kirk and observed that "Mr. Kirk has a better opportunity to judge local sentiment than I and he may be entirely right as to home sentiment."[78]

McGuire could not be persuaded to abandon Bryan, ignoring letters sent to him by Democrats living throughout central New York and the pleas of some of his supporters in the local party.[79] He was not shy about expressing his views on what should be in the party's platform, and if observers thought the "Coal Plank" in 1904 had been radical, they hadn't seen anything yet. McGuire pointed out that Bryan's platform in 1896, considered radical at the time, had been largely enacted under President Roosevelt. He felt it was unfair for Taft to reap the benefit of what Bryan had advocated and Roosevelt had adopted. He then dropped the twin bombshells that Bryan should campaign on a platform advocating a graduated income tax and an inheritance tax![80]

In Denver for the convention, McGuire worked hard, albeit unsuccessfully, to bring a unanimous vote for Bryan from the New York delegation. Commenting on Bryan's views, he remarked, "I'm a radical and, of course I am for everything that Mr. Bryan wants."[81]

McGuire's feelings were not mirrored by many Democrats locally. After Bryan had been nominated, local Democrats expressed their loyalty to the party's nominee, but their enthusiasm waned.[82] McGuire was convinced that Bryan would make big gains because of his having won the support of conservative politicians and publishers that he did not have in the past, but he stopped short of predicting victory. His principal concern was a well-founded one; it involved the loss of the support of William Randolph Hearst. Once Bryan had been nominated in Denver, all eyes turned to Chicago, where the Independence League was holding its national convention. McGuire noted that while Bryan had emissaries at the convention trying to secure the nomination, it was doubtful that Hearst was of a mind to enter into a fusion ticket.[83] While he would not make time to campaign locally, McGuire donated $1,000 to the Bryan campaign and committed four weeks between the New York and Chicago conventions to campaigning for Bryan at his own expense.

There was no mollifying Hearst, who believed that Bryan had betrayed his loyalty by failing to support him at the 1904 convention in St. Louis. The Independence League nominated Thomas Hisgen for president. Hisgen, a successful Massachusetts businessman, had polled more than 100,000 votes for governor of that state as the Independence League candidate in the 1906 election.[84] Hisgen set out on a campaign swing through California in an effort to wrest the state from Bryan. McGuire tried to tamp down any criticism of the newspaper magnate, while at the same time extending an olive branch to him.[85]

In addition to his concern about Hearst's rival Independence League campaign, McGuire was keeping a close eye on the campaign of Eugene Debs, who was running for president as a Socialist. Commenting on Debs, McGuire remarked, "Debs is addressing some wonderful meetings throughout the country, which effect is causing the political managers of all parties to sit up and take notice. His candidacy is likely to prove a factor in the general result. The people flock to his meetings and pay to hear him in most places, which last is a curious political phenomena [sic] to us, for it indicates earnestness rather than idle curiosity."[86]

McGuire soon found himself under attack for contributions he had made in the amount of $1,500 to Bryan's campaign. Critics of Bryan charged that these contributions were monies from the Asphalt Trust. McGuire was quick to respond, declaring, "I have always contributed towards the Bryan fund, long before I was connected with corporations. . . . My corporation connections have nothing to do with my personal contributions. I have a good income, and I like Bryan, and as I cannot give the time to campaign speeches, I give as generously to the cause as my means will permit."[87]

President Roosevelt's efforts on behalf of Taft provided McGuire with the opportunity to revisit an issue that, in the past, had unfairly tarred him: the Coal Plank. Commenting on the president's position, he observed that Roosevelt was taking credit for asserting federal ownership of the coal mines. He recalled that when he had advocated such a position in 1902, he had been roundly criticized by the mine owners and the press. He went on to ruminate about what those critics now thought of the president's action.[88]

McGuire's concerns about Hearst and the Independence League campaign proved to be prescient. In the summer months, before Labor Day, the Hearst newspapers savaged Bryan in articles, cartoons, and editorials. During October, Hearst took to the campaign trail himself, concentrating his efforts in the South where the Democratic Party was strongest, heaping invective on Bryan. In New York, the Democratic Party candidate for governor, Lieutenant Governor Lewis Stuyvesant Chanler, who had been Hearst's running mate in the 1906 election, fared no better. Hearst launched bitter attacks against him for his perceived betrayal.[89]

On Election Day, Taft won a landslide victory over Bryan and Hughes was reelected governor. Out of 18 million votes cast, Hearst's candidate, Thomas Hisgen, drew only 83,000, less than he had polled in his race for governor of Massachusetts.[90] Given the size of Taft's victory, however, one can only wonder at how badly Hearst's attacks on Bryan contributed to the outcome.

McGuire returned to Syracuse and offered his assessment of the outcome of the election. He offered something of a mea culpa for his support of Bryan, acknowledging that those local leaders who had tried to convince him that Bryan could not win were right. McGuire also paid tribute to Roosevelt's overt support of Taft as a significant factor in the outcome of the race. Perhaps most telling, however, was his analysis of Hearst's role in the defeat of both Bryan and Chanler. At long last, it appeared that McGuire finally saw Hearst for the petty, arrogant, narcissist megalomaniac that he was, and the days of either lionizing him or apologizing for him were finally over.

As 1909 opened, attention, as expected, became focused on the mayoral election that would be held that November. Unlike in the previous mayoral election, McGuire returned to Syracuse, registered to vote, and stumped for George Driscoll, the Democratic candidate for mayor. In a speech in the Fifth Ward, he reminisced about his political career, telling the audience,

> I want to say right here and now, as the last Democratic Mayor of Syracuse, that while there was some evil in the McGuire Administration, much good too, came out of it. . . .
>
> Now, I'm not trying to make out that my long administration as Mayor was perfect by any means; far from it. We made many

grievous mistakes. We put altogether too many men to work especially the last year that I was in office. I think I grew somewhat
indolent and tired of the office the last year that I held it, occasioned
chiefly by my mind being diverted to State and national politics.

High political ambition was the dangerous political disease
with which I was afflicted. When I was a boy down here in the
old Fourth ward the lads would gather around Paddy Hayes's hall,
and Hugh Mulherin, John Welch, Kelley Hopkins, O'Brien, Corey
and the others would listen to me with amusement when I would
boast that I was determined to be Mayor of Syracuse before I was
30 years old and Governor of the State before I was 35, and I actually believed the boyish dream would come true until the night
the returns came in that announced my first defeat. Time has long
since dispelled those dreams and I have long since ceased to think
of political honors.

The young men of this ward nominated me for School Commissioner and Member of the Assembly before I was of age, and, it
was the splendid support in the primaries, when I was nominated
in the primaries, when I was nominated and elected Mayor the first
time, when I was scarcely 26, and it was this ward that passed the
first resolution declaring me for Governor, and there has not been a
day, beginning with those boyish dreams in Lodi street, twenty-five
years ago, up to the present hour, that the Democrats of this ward
have not given me practically their solid vote in every primary contest and election that has taken place in this locality. And, strange
as it may appear, the realization of that boyish dream seemed to be
approaching in 1898, when I was a candidate for Governor.

The nomination for Governor was controlled by Richard Croker, and Mr. Croker has since stated to the present chairman of the
Democratic State committee of New York that he had made up his
mind to throw the New York city delegates to my support, thus
nominating me, only that at the last hour he was dissuaded from
that purpose by the appeals of the Kings County leaders to nominate a Brooklyn man, Judge Van Wyck, and Mr. Croker has said
several times that he has regretted not nominating me that year, to

have contested the State with Roosevelt. Van Wyck was only beaten that year by 16,000, and many of my friends have thought that was the one year when I might have won, through the aid of the big vote that I had been in the habit of getting in this city, and it seemed the right time for an up-State man, but whether all that is so or not, the point that I want to emphasize is the neglect of the Mayor's office occasioned by my insatiable ambition of that day to become Governor of the State. . . . From there I drifted into national politics, with the result of further neglecting the Mayor's office. I believe that Driscoll will let State politics alone and give the city his attention, and a businessman's sound administration and keep expenses down to a reasonable figure.[91]

He closed on a valedictory note, telling his supporters,

It has been falsely charged against me that I did not care to have any Democratic candidate elected for Mayor, so that it could be said for years and years, that I was the only Democrat who could be elected to that office. My friends the time has come when the political conditions are favorable to us, and when I can say to you that the day has come when by presenting a united ticket you will be led to a victory as glorious as in the days when I led you.

The following day the *Syracuse Evening Herald* offered its editorial judgment of McGuire's speech and how the race should be decided, telling its reader that McGuire was "frank" in admitting that his ultimate defeat was owing to his efforts to build a political machine and that was the reason the Hendricks machine should be defeated in this election.[92]

The following year, McGuire made his break complete with the local party and the city he led and loved. He announced that he would make New York City his voting residence and take no further role in local politics.[93] He had been both the party boss and its most successful candidate for office throughout his lifetime in Syracuse. His role as the political leader had come at some cost to his relationships. While he had vanquished some Lilliputians in his own party, like Matty, he had also sacrificed some relationships with talented and loyal confidantes. In some of these instances he had wielded power in a heavy and ham-handed fashion. The next chapter of his life, in both the national and international arenas, would be characterized by a different, more reticent style. Still, it was the end of a most interesting era.

True to his word, McGuire played no role in local politics during the next municipal campaign. Nineteen twelve, however, would both be a presidential year and see the election of a governor. What role McGuire played in the selection of the Democratic presidential nominee is not clear. He had been a delegate to every national convention that he desired, but there is no indication that he attended the 1912 convention in Baltimore, where the strange remarriage of Tammany boss Charles Murphy and his nemesis William Randolph Hearst would occur.

Hearst, once again, had visions of himself in the White House as 1912 dawned. This time, however, he saw earlier than usual that he could not be nominated and decided to throw his support behind the Speaker of the House of Representatives, Champ Clark of Missouri. Murphy, who had been excoriated in the Hearst newspapers the previous year during the New York City mayoral race, was backing Governor Judson Harmon of Ohio, whose candidacy was failing to catch fire. As the convention opened, Hearst and Murphy agreed to support the 1904 Democratic nominee, Alton Parker, for chairman of the convention, and the New York delegation would vote for Clark rather than the governor of New Jersey, Woodrow Wilson. In the end, Wilson was nominated on the forty-sixth ballot and Hearst, Murphy, and the New York delegation had earned the undying enmity of the future president of the United States.[94]

McGuire proved to be somewhat prescient in predicting who the gubernatorial nominee for the Democratic party would be that year. On October 3, at the state convention in Syracuse, the delegates selected Congressman William Sulzer as their nominee. McGuire had made the speech nominating Sulzer for governor at the state party convention in Buffalo in 1896. Sulzer proclaimed that he had no enemies within the party and that he would be able to work cooperatively with Tammany boss Charles Murphy.[95] He also met with McGuire's younger brother George, who appeared to be exercising whatever influence the McGuires had in the local party. The meeting would have dire consequences for both men.

Sulzer was apparently correct in his prediction that he had no enemies and would have the support of a unified party, as he was elected handily with a 215,000-vote margin over his Republican opponent, Job Hedges, on Election Day. The Democrats also won control of both houses of the legislature.[96]

Sulzer's honeymoon with Murphy would come to an end barely three months into his term. The breach occurred when Murphy sought to have one of his friends, Jim Gaffney, appointed as state commissioner of highways and Sulzer refused to make the appointment. Despite Gaffney's protests that he did not seek the office, the rift became so public that Murphy and the governor ignored one another at the annual St. Patrick's Day dinner in New York City. Astute observers of the situation predicted that the rebuff to Murphy would involve a bitter fight with both houses of the legislature.[97] In the days following the dispute over Gaffney, Sulzer appointed John A. Hennessy as a special commissioner to investigate corruption in the awarding of the contracts for the construction and maintenance of the state highways. Hennessy announced his intention to conduct closed hearings with sworn testimony and, where appropriate, to refer matters for criminal prosecution.[98]

As predicted, the legislature conducted hearings into certain matters involving Sulzer's campaign for governor that resulted in articles of impeachment being filed against the governor.[99] Following a trial before the Court of Appeals, at which Sulzer did not testify, the judges and the state senate found him guilty of four of the eight articles of impeachment and removed him from office.[100] The corruption probes, however, were far from over.

On October 31, New York County District Attorney Charles Whitman announced that he would conduct a "John Doe Proceeding" into allegations of corruption made by Sulzer's corruption investigator, John Hennessy, in speeches Hennessy made on behalf of the Fusion ticket in the New York City mayoral campaign then being waged. The proceeding would involve sworn public testimony before the New York City Court's Chief Magistrate William McAdoo. Hennessy had apparently provided the district attorney with approximately fifty names concerning campaign contributions that were never reported.[101] Whitman, a Republican, was not afraid to involve himself in partisan politics and had been sought out by the Republican Party in Syracuse that fall to stump for its candidate in the municipal election.[102] He would not be the last Republican district attorney from New York City to harbor greater political aspirations.

Hennessy became Whitman's first witness before McAdoo in the "John Doe Proceeding" and promptly named George McGuire as the source of his information about a long list of contractors from whom political contributions had been demanded in exchange for state highway work. George McGuire denied he was the source of the information but claimed he had met with Hennessy at Sulzer's request in Utica, New York, the previous September. George had been appointed by Sulzer to a commission to draft recommendations for road building. Expecting to be called as a witness in the proceeding, he traveled to New Rochelle to stay with his older brother James, who had relocated there after the previous mayoral race involving Matty.[103]

On November 6, Hennessy and George McGuire contradicted each other in sworn testimony before McAdoo. Under oath, George testified that he gave Sulzer a $500 campaign contribution in a meeting in Syracuse the day after Sulzer's nomination as governor. He denied, however, that an additional $2,500 he gave Hennessy was to help underwrite the cost of his corruption probe, but claimed it was a gift to Sulzer, who was experiencing personal financial problems. According to Hennessy, George McGuire did not want to appear to be disloyal to the local organization, which was aligned with Murphy, the subject of Hennessy's probe. George went on to deny that he provided Hennessy a list of contractors being extorted for campaign contributions by Tammany Hall. While being questioned by Whitman on this subject, George admitted to receiving money from seven contractors that went unreported. Hennessy then produced a telegram he had received the week before the "John Doe Proceeding," on the eve of a speech he was to deliver in Syracuse, in which the sender claimed Onondaga Democratic Party Chair William Kelley was involved in shaking down contractors. The telegram was signed M. and Hennessy testified he believed the sender was George McGuire. Recalled to testify by Whitman, George denied he was the sender.[104]

George McGuire's situation became more precarious the next day when former governor Sulzer testified that he had supplied Hennessy with most of the information he received from George McGuire concerning graft paid by the highway contractors and that the $2,500 was volunteered by him to underwrite the expense of Hennessy's probe. Following the appearances of the three men, Whitman and his assistants traveled to Syracuse to subpoena the stenographers in McGuire's office and to examine the typewriters there.[105]

When the proceedings resumed several days later, George McGuire, fearing that he was about to be indicted for perjury, admitted that he sent the telegram signed M. and vowed to provide Whitman with all that he knew concerning the graft that was being probed. Upon publicly making his admission concerning the telegram, he collapsed on the witness stand and had to be excused. Reports that he attempted suicide in his hotel room were denied by his lawyer.[106] Following George McGuire's admission that he authored the telegram signed M., Whitman indicted Everett Fowler, alleged to be a Tammany "bagman," who was named in the telegram as having obtained contributions with William Kelley from upstate contractors.[107]

In the wake of George McGuire's disclosures, Whitman blanketed the state with subpoenas for contractors who may have been victims of extortion. At the same time, Governor Martin Glynn, who had succeeded Sulzer, appointed James Osborne to succeed Hennessy as his corruption prober.[108]

As George McGuire's health improved, Whitman began publicly to send him signals that he must fully cooperate and be truthful once he returned to testify. Among the subjects that Whitman was now interested in was whether former governor John Alden Dix, Sulzer's predecessor, was instrumental in setting the political graft machinery in motion as George McGuire claimed. He was also interested in James K.'s travels to South America on behalf of Barber Asphalt and in the nature of certain commissions that George testified about, for the sales of all Barber Asphalt products to the state and other contractors.[109] As George McGuire served notice that he would not waive immunity before any grand jury, Whitman claimed to have information that the McGuire brothers had met with Governor Sulzer and State Highway Commissioner John N. Carlisle on the previous July 5, where it was agreed that Barber Asphalt products would be used exclusively on state projects. One of Barber's competitors, C. B. Warner of the Warner-Quinlan Company, claimed that its products were rejected following this meeting and that they were forced to sue.[110]

Whitman next developed a lead to a target that proved irresistible, Tammany boss Charles Murphy. In the course of his debriefings by Whitman and his staff, George had informed them that his bonding company, which furnished the bonds to all contractors on state jobs, had formed a partnership with Charles F. Murphy Jr., the nephew of the Tammany boss. As part of the arrangement, George's bonding company would forgo opening an office in New York City and refer the business there to Murphy in exchange for half the commission. Additionally, he was questioned about seeking a $5,000 contribution from Fillmore Condit of Union Oil Company and a one-cent-per-gallon commission for himself and James K. on their products that he could sell to the state before Union could do business with the state. George contended that neither the contribution nor the commission was received or implemented.[111]

Two days later Whitman dropped a real bombshell. A grand jury had indicted James K. McGuire for illegally soliciting a campaign contribution from a corporation, namely Fillmore Condit of Union Oil Company. Despite the fact that the charge was only a misdemeanor, the district attorney obtained a warrant for McGuire's arrest.[112] Despite the widely reported fact that McGuire was out of the country on business, Whitman placed guards around McGuire's home in New Rochelle on the chance that he might return.[113] McGuire was not only in no hurry to turn himself in, he seemed to enjoy tweaking Whitman from afar, sending him a cable from San Juan, Puerto Rico, that said, "I am sailing for home to-morrow. My indictment is an incident of the fight between the asphalt companies. I will answer effectively. Please agitate for reduced cable rates."[114]

He was next rumored to be arriving on the ship *Brazos*; however when it docked in Brooklyn, he was not aboard, although one of its passengers, a Major J. M. Hamilton of Kingston, New York, who knew McGuire, said he was "anxious to face the charges against him."[115] He next turned up in Havana, Cuba, where he gave an interview in which he accused Condit of lying. He went on to assert that he was anxious to return and face the charges and had not fled but was merely pursuing opportunities in Santo Domingo.[116] He was reported to be the "life of the ship," with fellow passengers recounting his regaling them with stories about his meeting with the Dominican president despite the police "shadowing him on Whitman's orders."[117]

On December 8 he surrendered to Whitman on the indictment and was arraigned in New York County Supreme Court. He entered a Not Guilty plea and the court released him on $1,500 bail. The case was adjourned until December 22, to allow McGuire to either change his plea or to make any motion he desired. McGuire then proceeded to hold forth on two subjects. The first was his brother George, and he pulled no punches:

> The mania possessed by my brother George H. McGuire, that he represented many lines of big business has led to glaring errors in his statement. He stated that he represented many cement companies; he never represented any cement company and never sold a barrel of cement. Most of his statements about contractors are irresponsible and indicate a weakened mental condition.
>
> I have no fear that injustice will prevail, for I have wronged no man and never injured the Commonwealth.[118]

In an interview with the *Herald*, he was somewhat sanguine about the fact he had been indicted, noting that it was not the first time. "You know I have been indicted before," he said, recalling the time when he was indicted for malfeasance in office.[119]

9A and 9B. James K. McGuire surrendering to the New York County District Attorney's Office on December 8, 1913, Library of Congress, George Grantham Bain Collection.

Interviewed about the famous telegram that George had signed M., he denied any knowledge of it and said,

> I cannot be held responsible for the mistake that my brother made in the municipal campaign as I advised him on my way to California to help Mr. Dolan in every way possible. I had him contribute $500 to the city committee and no one in the country was more amazed or startled than I on reading the "M" telegram.
>
> George McGuire is broken in health and looks now as though it would be a long time before he is well and I have no heart to discuss the subject further.[120]

While McGuire was doing his best to discredit his brother George, he did find time to write a letter to Secretary of State William Jennings Bryan, exonerating the U.S. minister to the Dominican Republic of any suspicion concerning McGuire's business dealings there.[121]

George McGuire was proving to be a much sought-after, albeit elusive, witness for the corruption probers. Governor Glynn's corruption investigator, James W. Osborne, sought his presence unsuccessfully at a hearing in Albany. George was rumored "to be in a sanatorium somewhere, suffering from shattered nerves."[122] At the same time, District Attorney Whitman and Osborne were jousting with each other about who would probe graft and corruption outside of New York City. Whitman sought to be deputized by Osborne in order to obtain statewide authority, only to be rebuffed by Osborne and the governor.[123] Despite having rebuffed Whitman, Osborne took the unusual step of allowing the attorney for Warner-Quinlan, Barber Asphalt's competitor and McGuire's principal accuser in the criminal case, to question James K. in a hearing held before him in Albany. When McGuire objected to the arrangement, Osborne ruled that the attorney, Henry A. Rubino, represented him. McGuire went on to use the forum to attack Warner-Quinlan for procuring his indictment and to establish an alibi for the meeting that allegedly took place in Cooperstown the previous July.[124] McGuire characterized a meeting with the state commissioner of highways in Syracuse as a chance occurrence in which he invited the latter to visit his office at McGuire &

Company to view an autographed picture that President Wilson had sent him. When the company attorney asked him about a conversation he had with Edward Joy, one of the company's stockholders, McGuire replied, "Joy said that Quinlan was making a fool of himself at Albany and he wanted to know why we couldn't get together on the Albany work, as we were in Syracuse. C. M. Warner tried twice to get me to take Quinlan's place in Albany, for he said Quinlan was destroying the business." McGuire again accused the company and Rubino of threatening him with indictment if he did not use his influence in Albany to get them some of the asphalt business.[125]

All in all, McGuire, quite effectively, was using his appearances before Osborne to cast doubt on the legitimacy of his indictment and to lay out his alibi for some of the events that were alleged in the criminal case.

As 1913 turned into 1914, Whitman was forced to dismiss an indictment against one of the targets of his probe after determining that his accuser had an ulterior motive to lie about him. At the same time, Whitman revealed that he expected McGuire to stand trial that fall.[126]

Whitman next announced his intention to call former governor Sulzer and Tammany boss Charles F. Murphy to testify in the "John Doe Proceeding."[127] Sulzer's testimony proved to be a bombshell as the former governor accused Murphy ally James S. Gaffney of trying to exact $150,000 from a wealthy contractor as the price of obtaining work on the Barge Canal. Sulzer also contended that Murphy had orchestrated his impeachment by the legislature in retaliation for Sulzer's refusal to discontinue his investigation into graft and corruption. Sulzer testified that State Senator James A. O'Gorman had cautioned him not to appoint Gaffney as state highway commissioner because he was Murphy's "bagman," and that he had requested the State Canal Board to refrain from awarding the contract in question based upon information contained in a telegram sent to him by George McGuire. Sulzer further contradicted McGuire's claim that he solicited $2,500 from him and testified that McGuire gave the money to John Hennessy to underwrite the cost of his investigation. He likewise denied being at any meeting in Cooperstown to discuss Barber Asphalt's business. At the conclusion of Sulzer's testimony, Whitman declared the former governor to be "a valuable and important witness" and arranged for him to appear before the grand jury.[128]

Whitman's observations about Sulzer's testimony and credibility would certainly seem to be of value to James K. McGuire, since they not only undermined his brother George's version of his dealings with the former governor but bolstered James K.'s repeated assertion that he was never at any meeting in Cooperstown conspiring on behalf of his company, Barber Asphalt.

The district attorney had requested that Sulzer provide him with the telegram sent by George McGuire concerning the barge canal bids, but Sulzer's former secretary, Chester C. Platt, later reported that he could not find the telegram from George McGuire among Sulzer's papers.[129]

On February 1, the district attorney suggested that James K. McGuire's trial could be held in the next two weeks.[130]

The year 1914 would end without a trial or any other resolution of McGuire's criminal charges. Whitman, however, would become the Republican candidate for governor and ride the graft and corruption issue into the governor's mansion.[131]

6

The King, the Kaiser, and the President

While McGuire's criminal case was pending in New York County Supreme Court, he turned his attention to Ireland and its struggle for freedom. He had been a "high-ranking" member of the secret society Clan-na-Gael, which was dedicated to securing Ireland's independence.[1] He also was a frequent visitor to Ireland.[2]

Irish American sentiment and Clan-na-Gael had always been in favor of a free and independent Ireland. In Ireland John Redmond, chairman of the Irish Parliamentary Party, had been advocating for "Home Rule" in the British Parliament. Until 1910 the issue fell on deaf ears because of the Liberal Party's overwhelming majorities in Parliament. In the 1910 election, however, the Liberal Party's seats were drastically reduced and Redmond's party became a much sought-after partner. In 1912 Home Rule became a central issue in Parliament.[3]

The issue of Home Rule would prove to be a complicated one. The first complication was that Ulster leaders Sir Edward Carson and Bonar Law wanted the six counties in the north of Ireland excluded from Home Rule. So that the world would understand that there would be more than nominal resistance to Home Rule, the Ulster Volunteers were formed and armed, composed of 100,000 militiamen. In response, Redmond organized the Irish Volunteers, a force consisting of 160,000 men. The command structure consisted of a mix of Redmond followers and the Irish Republican Brotherhood, a secret society that favored complete independence. In mid-June 1914, the Irish Volunteers managed to purchase 1,500 rifles in Hamburg, Germany, and on July 26, during an armed parade by the Volunteers, the police shot and killed thirty people in Bachelor's Walk in Dublin. Calls by Redmond for a full inquiry into the massacre fell on deaf ears.

Almost simultaneously, events in Europe were rapidly unfolding that would plunge the continent into war. On June 28, 1914, Archduke Ferdinand was assassinated; because of various treaty commitments, Britain would be dragged into the war alongside France. Irish republicans, both at home and in the United States, would view "England's necessity as Ireland's opportunity." But Redmond's dream of Home Rule would have to be shattered first. As the war clouds continued to build, Parliament, with Redmond's acquiescence, excluded Ulster from the Home Rule measure and suspended the effective date of Home Rule until the end of the war.[4] Redmond didn't know it, but he was well on his way to being fully discredited as a leader.

In the United States, Irish American republicans would use the U.S. status as a neutral country to advocate for support for Germany in the war against Britain. While much of the activity was overt, covert activities abounded. McGuire would author two books advocating American support for Germany. The first was *The King, the Kaiser and Irish Freedom*, published in 1915.[5] The second was *What Could Germany Do for Ireland?*, published the following year.[6] Lest there be any doubt about the intent of the books, the first one contained a picture of the author inscribed by his "friend" Kaiser Wilhelm.

Ireland was a bleak and depressing place during this period. As Redmond's biographer described it,

> Dublin desperately needed some prosperity. Ireland's largest city and former capital ranked as the greatest urban disgrace in the United Kingdom. The census of 1911 listed Dublin's population at slightly more than 300,000. The working class made up nearly two-thirds of this number. A government report on Dublin housing conditions showed that 45 percent of the working class lived in tenement housing. Dwellings built for one family often housed several, usually

with one family to a room. Dublin had more than twenty thousand one-room tenement dwellings, the highest percentage of any city in Britain or Ireland. A large number of these places held as many as seven or eight people to a room. The most egregious example of overcrowding showed ninety-eight people living in a single house.

The report further found that "life in tenement houses in the city are [*sic*] both physically and morally bad" and that the local clergy observed "much immorality" resulting from these conditions and feared its effect on the city's children.[7]

McGuire visited Ireland in 1914 to do research for his intended books. Ironically, his dispatches to the *Catholic Sun* described the conditions he found in England as it prepared for war but no account of what he saw in Ireland.[8] Apparently these were saved to be detailed in his upcoming books.

In *The King, the Kaiser and Irish Freedom*, McGuire recounted his observation of Dublin: "The writer has visited all of the cities of America and many foreign cities. Of the large town seen, beyond a doubt the capital of Ireland is the poorest, the most squalid and miserable. The only interesting things about Dublin are the ruins of its former greatness, the cemeteries, parks and decaying structures. The monuments to the dead are notable. There is scarcely a ripple in the Liffey aside from some boats from a brewery. Fifty years more will see Dublin altogether an English city."

McGuire's description of the city of Sligo was equally depressing. He described it as having "10,000 inhabitants old and poor, the remnants of a stricken race. Sligo has nothing to show at the end of 900 years but the melancholy ruins of a once flourishing town, her aged men and women and their rags. Long since most of the stalwart youth have departed for foreign shores."

The book made a forceful case, using facts and figures, about how Britain had exploited Ireland economically for its own benefit and to Ireland's detriment. He expressed a bitter view of conscription of soldiers in Ireland to fight on behalf of England, observing, "Ireland having inherited nothing from England except sorrow and misery, is always asked to furnish her the best blood for her exploiters whenever their empire is in danger."

Nor did he express any admiration for those Irishmen who had distinguished themselves in the British army in the past, declaring,

> We take no pride in the constant allusions by England to her great military commanders who are born in Ireland. They are Tories and all opposed to the freedom of their own country. No patriotic Irishmen rejoiced in Lord Kitchner, Lord Roberts, Rear Admiral Callaghan or the military genius of the Duke of Wellington. These men fought for England alone and never for Ireland. They were given their reward by England and no shrine is visited in Ireland which venerates their names. In bitterness of feelings toward nationalist Ireland, these Irish saviors of England have outdone the descendants of Cromwell. (20–21)

McGuire made no pretense about the way in which his views would conflict with the Wilson administration as he noted, "We have waited patiently for six months before launching this much needed book, which represents a vast and growing American public opinion, and much as we regret to have the appearance of disregarding the plea of our President for neutrality, to all fair minded men the facts contained in this work are very necessary to offset the unneutral propaganda."

On the subject of a German victory in World War I, McGuire minced no words, arguing,

> Freedom for Ireland—an Irish Republic—is by no means an idle or wild dream should war terminate in Germany's favor. Then the distribution of power in Europe, Asia and Africa would be rearranged. The maps of the world have been changed by the outcome of the wars. The opportunity for the creation of the present United States of America presented itself when England was exhausted by the long war with France. The British Empire like the Roman Empire, Carthage and all world-wide dominions must perish in the fulness and mutability of time. The old myth of British supremacy passes away with the defeat of England, overpopulated and with vast numbers

of her ill-fed families living within single rooms in crowded cities. Liberty for Ireland can only be won through the triumphs of Germany-Austria. Then and only then, will the Republic of Ireland be a glorious reality and the flag of green and gold wave on the seas and over the Emerald Isle. *God bless Germany ! God save Ireland*. (285)

He made no apologies for his pro-German views, declaring,

Sinn Fein has ever been and ever will be pro-Irish and pro-nothing else. While Irishmen have a country denied its national, its political and its economic liberties, no other nation right or wrong can have claim to their exertions. But if to defend the remnants of Irish manhood from being hurried to destruction in this war, planned by England, provoked by England and intended to serve only England; and if to vindicate from the monstrous calumnies that Ireland's continued calumniator and oppressor is pouring out upon a great nation and a noble people, is to be pro-German than we accept the title as one of honor and worthy of an Irishman to wear.[9]

The book received considerable attention as noted in an advertisement in the *Syracuse Post-Standard*, which claimed that "it breaks all records for war book sales."[10]

The following year he published the second book on this subject, entitled *What Could Germany Do for Ireland?*. This work was far more incendiary and condemnatory, particularly as America was about to enter the war. In the preface, McGuire told the reader,

The historic wrongs of Ireland find little space in this volume. They are too well known to be described at this time. Ireland is the natural strategic entrance to Europe, while her children tonight are at the parting of the ways. There are nearly 20,000,000 of them in various lands and only 4,000,000 in Ireland. Their kin across the seas, having lived under the sun of freedom, have a right to protest against the sacrifice of the remaining remnants, deceived by the representations of the ruthless foe of centuries. At present Ireland is only food-producing and recruiting ground for England. What earthly hope is there for her people as a race and a nation until the sun shall set on the British Empire?

In this second work he continued his assault on Irish conscription, writing,

> On October 22, 1915, King George of England appealed to his subjects in these words: "War has been declared in order that another may not inherit the free empire which my ancestors have built. There is no end in sight. More men and yet more men are wanted to keep my armies in the field and through them secure victory."
>
> Sensible Celts who would preserve their race must acknowledge that having no part of a "free empire" to lose, their ancestors having been enslaved and their country impoverished and its institutions destroyed by ruthless conquerors, the plain duty of the people of Ireland is to live and defend their country. There is not a single page in the last 700 years of Erin's melancholy history which can possibly inspire a true Celt to give up his life to help save the tottering government of the persecutors and oppressors of the land. (46–47)

He made no secret of how he hoped the war would end or how the outcome might affect the world at large, observing, "One thing seems certain at this writing—Germany will not lose the war and will either triumph or force a peace which may recast the map of Europe and perhaps Asia" (54).

He defended his economic analysis of Britain's economic exploitation of Ireland that had appeared in his first book, declaring, "In the first volume of this work . . . the writer proved the case by official facts and figures of the destructive effect of British control of the industries and resources of Ireland. In all the storms of criticism which the appearance of the book invoked in many quarters there is no denial of the changes in history that England deliberately destroyed Irish commerce and industries for the enrichment of English capitalists and the removal of a formidable and dangerous competitor" (65–66).

He alluded to what would later be revealed as Irish and Irish American secret contacts to enlist German aid in the Irish "Rising" to take place the following year, when he wrote, "Our friends in Berlin are giving serious consideration to the plan of assisting in the liberation of Ireland, thus insuring her future on the other side of the Atlantic Ocean, and the guarantees of her friendship have been given to the representatives (now in Germany) of Ireland as a nation" (70).

In this book, McGuire compared the standard of living in Berlin with that of Dublin. After reciting the average earnings of a family in Dublin, which was less than $7 per week, he noted,

> In Berlin, for every one man in this condition there are sixty-four in Dublin, and the number of single-room family dwellings in German cities is negligible. These "homes" of the Irish have no closets, and are foul, dark and extremely unhealthy. In Germany the government has taken in hand the building of artisans' dwellings. The writer has looked over the tenement areas in other cities and found the most unsanitary conditions in Dublin. Nowhere have I seen so many broken down and infirm people trying to live. The earnings do not admit to fire except in the severest weather, and the shivering, emaciated, poorly fed and clothed children wring the heartstrings of the visitor.[11]

If one reads the writings of the old Fenians who participated in the 1867 Rising, it quickly dawns upon the reader that these men who lived through the Potato Famine did not view it as a natural calamity that befell Ireland but rather as genocide by the British government to starve the Irish into leaving their country. These men almost uniformly make the case that Ireland had more than enough crops to sustain its population, but that the British exported all but the diseased potatoes, which they left for the Irish population to subsist on.[12] While McGuire did not apparently subscribe to this view, he did have harsh words about Britain's conduct during this episode in history, as he observed,

> The signal failure of England to starve Germany ought to be a lesson that would draw on the memory of the children of the Irish emigrants wherever found. They should contrast the neglect, and

worse, of the British Government of 1846 with the German Government of 1915.

The Irish famine is the black curse that haunts the memory of our old people and sends over to America shiploads of weakly peasants and boys from the potato fields of Ireland who dread joining the British army. We are told that we have bitter memories and in the light of the famine contributions we should forgive and forget British misgovernment in Ireland, for there may come a better day. We will merely say, then, that the government was incompetent to prepare for the famine. In 1841 the population of Ireland was 8,175,124, and probably close to 9,000,000 in 1845, all under "efficient" agricultural rule of England—nearly dependent on one vegetable, the potato. The potato crop in America in 1844 suffered the blight, but no warning came from the British Government officials. The officers dallied, postponed putting forth measures of relief, delayed the plans to divide the crops, although the crop of the year before was a failure, muddling as usual, and in July 1845, the blight on Ireland, and the most fearful horror that can scourge a people—grim, universal starvation—clutched the country in its horrible embrace. One fourth of all the people were swept from the country; a million died of hunger; a million more were expatriated, starving, dying in the holds of sailing ships; the bones of thousands lay along the reaches of the St. Lawrence, the bodies of children fed to the fishes, thrown overboard from the famine-fevered ships hurrying away from the blighted land. The absentee English landlords refused to visit Ireland, although to some of them the famine spelled ruin. Relief workers organized by an inefficient government in London came too late—the wretched people were doomed. In the late summer of 1846 mourners or coffins or shrouds were not to be had for the funerals. Horses and carts gathered up the dead for internment in "famine pits." (77)

He went on to assail England for not doing more to foster business and commerce in Ireland and provided an interesting observation concerning the Irish involvement in the police forces and politics in America, opining, "A race of businessman is not made in a single generation. The Irish immigrants turn to the police force, politics and those pursuits we see them in the oftenest because they and their fathers were never furnished with the opportunity in Ireland to learn modern business" (113).

He continued his analysis of the economic conditions in Ireland as part of his indictment of British rule and his argument that Ireland would be better served by a German victory, contending, "Ireland at present exports the raw material, timber, and subsequently imports its manufacturing products. A truly wasteful and uneconomic procedure! It is inconceivable that Ireland, under any other form of government than that under which she groans today, would continue conducting her economic affairs along such destructive lines" (163). He continued,

> The principal cause of all Irish industrial ills and the present decay in all branches of human endeavor within Ireland is *British Rule in Ireland*. It is a fixed, immovable principle of the English direction of Irish affairs that the country should not be permitted to become a formidable competitor of England. This has ever been the attitude of the conqueror toward the conquered. History holds no record of a subject race prospering exceedingly under foreign domination. England's view is that so long as Ireland exists she must hold her in subjection, to enable her to retain and maintain her supremacy of the seas. A truly prosperous Ireland could not be long held in subjection; she would soon assert her right to direct her own affairs, internal and external, and, as all who have given some thought to naval affairs know, this for England would inevitably mean the passing of the Trident out of Britannia's hands *for all time*. (203–4)

He seemed to revel in the criticism his first book had evoked in England as he wrote, "The writer was ridiculed in London last fall for stating that Germany would finance the war within her borders and that England would be driven to ask for outside aid; that the German people, in the mass, were more prosperous, thrifty, capable and healthy than the English people crowded in cities" (247).

He seemed to take even greater delight in appraising the British cabinet, observing,

The British system of "muddling through" makes a coalition cabinet of discordant politicians a composite picture of the people, lacking in training and special knowledge. Mr. Lloyd George has many of the political qualities found in our own William J. Bryan. The best friends of the Commoner would not suggest him for Secretary of the Treasury. Lloyd George had to give way to McKenna, another politician without expert financial experience. Churchill, a politician without naval training, injuring the prestige of his country by naval breaks resulting in sea disasters, is forced out by a clamor and replaced by Balfour, a Tory politician. Lloyd George is now in charge of munition factories instead of some great business expert in that line. (248)

The book was a far more strident call for action than that advocated in *The King, the Kaiser and Irish Freedom*, as McGuire told the Irish, the Irish American community, and the world that "the test of a government is not in its forms or name, but in the condition of its people" (98), and that "when the writer was in Dublin in the year 1900, returning army officers were counting on increasing the number of troops to keep Ireland in order, as many of the people of Ireland were active sympathizers and supporters of the Boers" (264), and ultimately that "this is not Ireland's war, and the pity is that any Irishman should have to die to save England" (82).[13] The message of resistance was unmistakable.

Events would prove that McGuire's calls for resistance and Irish independence were not mere lip service. He would more than demonstrate that he was willing to walk the talk.

In Ireland, Redmond's stock continued to decline through missteps of his own making. In the wake of the massacre at Bachelor's Walk, Redmond urged the British government to remove its troops from Ireland, vowing that the country would be defended by the Irish Volunteers and further pledging their loyalty to Britain during the war. This pledge, however, paled in comparison to his advocacy of conscription of Irish young men in Ireland by the British army for the war. The reaction to Redmond's advocacy of Irish conscription was swift. In America his popularity tanked.[14] McGuire, who had been an admirer of Redmond and a member of the New York branch of the United Irish League, resigned from the organization.[15]

As Britain became bogged down in the war and America continued to remain neutral, efforts were being undertaken both in Ireland and America to organize an insurrection or a "Rising" in Ireland. Risings were nothing new to Anglo-Irish history, with one occurring almost every half-century. The leaders of the Fenian Brotherhood, which staged the last major Rising in Ireland in 1867,[16] were imprisoned in England and Australia and then deported to the United States. Among those released and deported were John Devoy and Jeremiah O'Donovan Rossa.

Devoy had been born in County Kildare on September 3, 1842. He weathered the Potato Famine but by the age of eighteen had tired of life in Ireland and traveled to France, where he joined the French Foreign Legion. After a brief posting to the Algerian desert, he was discharged and returned to Dublin, where he joined the Irish Republican Brotherhood (IRB), a forerunner of the Irish Republican Army. He had already joined the Fenian Brotherhood before his stint in the French Foreign Legion. By 1863 the IRB was approaching an enlistment of 50,000 men. At the same time, it was estimated that there were approximately 150,000 Irish members of the British army, some of whom were garrisoned in Ireland. Devoy was given the assignment to infiltrate those troops to determine how many might have Fenian sympathies and to recruit them if possible. On February 22, 1866, Devoy was arrested by British authorities, who had learned of an imminent Rising and had suspended the *Habeas Corpus Act* five days earlier. Almost one year later he pled guilty in a Dublin court and was sentenced to Mountjoy Prison. On March 5, 1867, the long-planned Rising occurred and was crushed in one day.

Jeremiah O'Donovan Rossa was already a legend in the Irish resistance movement by the time Devoy encountered him in Millbank Prison.[17] Rossa had been born in County Cork on September 4, 1831.

By the time he was arrested in November 1865 for treason, he had already been convicted once for sedition in 1858. Found guilty of treason, he was sentenced to life imprisonment. In 1869, while still in prison, he was elected to Parliament from County Tipperary.[18] In Millbank Prison he became a leader in the resistance to the harsh British prison conditions, which forbade contact with the outside world. Repeatedly he managed to get notes smuggled out in which he detailed the prisoners' conditions of confinement. In retaliation, his jailers confined him to a bread-and-water diet until he appeared to be "a walking skeleton." When that failed to curtail his messages, they handcuffed him behind his back for a period of twenty-eight days, forcing him to eat, sleep, and relieve himself in this position. Still, he defied his captors. By 1870 Rossa's missives to the outside world had found their way to the press, which reported on the way the prisoners were being treated. Embarrassed by the press reports, the British government set up a Board of Inquiry to examine the conditions of confinement. Ultimately it led to Prime Minister William Gladstone's releasing the prisoners. Devoy, Rossa, and three others were put on a ship and deported to the United States.

In the United States, Devoy and Rossa settled in New York City. Devoy rented a room in a "flop house" that Rossa purchased in the notorious Five-Points District in the city, home to both immigrants and criminals alike. Devoy found a job as a $700-per-year clerk for a sugar trader on Wall Street.[19] Rossa, only months after his arrival in America, found himself becoming the Republican state senate candidate from New York's Fourth District against the renowned Tammany Hall boss William Magear Tweed. On Election Day, Tweed, as expected, triumphed. Both Devoy and Rossa remained deeply involved in the Fenian movement.

Devoy joined the Clan-na-Gael and, in time, successfully forged an alliance between that secret organization and the Irish Republican Brotherhood. Rossa, more publicly, advocated a bombing campaign against England and set up a "skirmishing fund" to raise money to support such an activity.[20] Rossa's views were perhaps best embodied in a quote in which he said, "England has proclaimed war against me, and, so help me God, I will wage war against her until she is stricken to her knees or until I am stricken to my grave."[21]

From 1873 to 1876, Devoy undertook a mission that would make him the preeminent Fenian in America. He persuaded Clan-na-Gael to raise money and purchase a ship to rescue James Wilson and other British soldiers who had been tried for treason and sentenced to life imprisonment in Australia because of their allegiance to the IRB. On April 17, 1876, after three years of planning, the prisoners success-fully escaped. They arrived in New York City that fall for a parade organized by Tammany Hall. John Devoy's reputation in America was made.

By 1914 Devoy was publishing the *Gaelic American* and had become one of the most influential leaders of the Irish independence movement. The weekly newspaper, which was started in 1903, was the voice of Clan-na-Gael. Devoy regularly used its pages to rail against his critics, enemies, and anyone whom he perceived as being insuffi-ciently supportive of the cause of Irish independence.[22]

On July 20, 1914, Sir Roger Casement landed in New York City, where he hoped to raise money to purchase arms for the Irish Volun-teers. Casement was retired from the British Foreign Office after being knighted for his service in uncovering atrocities in the Belgian Congo and against the Peruvian Amazon Company in the upper Amazon basin in Brazil. In retirement he turned his attention to the conditions in Ireland and became a proponent of Irish independence. Together with Erskine Childers, he arranged for a shipment of guns to be pur-chased in Hamburg, Germany, destined for the Irish coast at Howth. Before the guns were to be delivered on July 26, however, Casement visited the United States.[23] Upon arrival in New York, Casement vis-ited with Devoy about his proposed mission.[24] Following that meet-ing, Devoy and Casement traveled to Philadelphia on August 2 for a rally to protest the massacre at Bachelor's Walk. The decision to attend this rally, unbeknownst to Casement, would have lethal consequences. Casement and Devoy were photographed together by British Intel-ligence, making it impossible for Casement, whose face had not been well known, to escape detection in his subsequent trip to Germany.[25]

Almost immediately following the rally in Philadelphia, Casement and Devoy met with Joseph McGarrity, a very wealthy Irish-born American who would publish the *Irish Press*, a weekly newspaper started in 1918.[26] At this meeting, Casement proposed that he travel to Germany for the purpose of organizing an Irish Brigade among the Irish-born British prisoners of war being held by the Germans and to obtain arms for the Irish Volunteers.[27] While initially mistrustful of Casement, Devoy agreed to the plan and introduced Casement to his contacts in the German embassy in New York City.[28]

On October 13, 1914, in order to travel and avoid British detection, Casement was provided with the passport and identification of a New York City businessman, James R. Landy. The source of this disguise and the documents was McGuire.[29] McGuire was about to play an integral part in Casement's visit to Germany. According to an account of the meeting authored by McGarrity, "Landy left Sir R. his (Landy's) Sons of veterans badge. Said they (the Sons of veterans) had no regular meetings, but had three dinners each year, no grips or signs. Landy gave him his (Landy's) glasses and a number of letters including a letter from the Assistant Secretary of State. The Assistant Secretary was a friend of James K. McGuire, once Mayor of Syracuse, N.Y."[30]

The identity of the source of the letter is said to be a Philadelphia lawyer named Michael F. Ryan, who, like McGuire, was a friend of Wilson's secretary of state, William Jennings Bryan.[31] It would be interesting to know what the content of the letter was since Wilson was a renowned Anglophile who viewed the Irish and Irish Americans with distaste. In any event, it is clear that although he was not actively involved in politics, McGuire was willing to use his political contacts and relationships to further the cause of Irish independence.

Casement's mission to Germany was a failure on both counts. He found very few Irish-born prisoners of war willing to join a brigade and take up arms against the British in Ireland. He also was unable to consummate an arms deal with the Germans that met the needs of the Irish Volunteers. His trip was further complicated by an attempt by the British Foreign Office, aware of his mission, to capture or kill him.[32] Recognizing the propaganda value that publicizing such a plot would have, Casement endeavored to get Devoy and his comrades in the United States to interest the mainstream media in the story but had limited success.

Casement's trip may have been further complicated by some paranoia on the part of Devoy concerning contact that Casement had with a man named Brogan, who was a friend of McGuire's. Exactly what Devoy feared from Brogan's contact with Casement in Germany was never made clear by Devoy but, upon learning that Brogan had gone to Germany after Casement, Devoy wrote to Casement in Germany, warning him to have no contact with "the New York man." Casement replied that he had met with the man, who had letters from McGuire and another Irish American, Dr. John Kelly of Massachusetts, and found him to be honorable.[33] Devoy's paranoia about Brogan and his resentment of McGuire's relationship with him would ultimately prove to be unfounded. Unbeknownst to anyone, the British had already recruited Casement's servant and lover, Adler Christiansen, to spy on Casement.[34]

As Casement's mission to Germany was unraveling, events in the United States and Ireland were also unfolding. On June 29, 1915, the legendary O'Donovan Rossa died at St. Vincent's Hospital at the age of 83.[35] The *Catholic Sun* reported that he had completed his memoirs the previous year and urged its readers to purchase them as he lay dying in New York City.[36] On August 1, a huge funeral service, attended by the Irish Volunteers, was held in Dublin. Pádraig Pearse, clad in a Volunteer uniform, told the crowd at the grave of the old Fenian,

> Life springs from death, and from the graves of patriot men and women spring living nations. The defenders of this realm have worked well in secret and in open. They think they have pacified Ireland. They think that they have purchased half of us and intimidated the other half. They think they have foreseen everything, they think that they have provided against everything; but the fools, the fools, the fools!—they have left us our Fenian dead, and while Ireland holds these graves, Ireland unfree shall never be at peace.[37]

The fuse for the Rising had been lit.

At the same time, a trans-Atlantic conspiracy had arisen involving the Irish Republican Brotherhood, the German government, and Devoy and the Irish American leadership concerning the Rising. Communication was fast and furious on the subject of arms sales and other support the German government could provide to the IRB for a Rising in Ireland. Devoy, by courier, sent money to the IRB for the purchase of arms, while being kept abreast of the plans for the Rising. He and his close friend and collaborator Daniel Cohalan, in turn, kept the German government informed of the IRB plans through contacts they had made in the German consulate in New York.[38]

Daniel Cohalan, a New York State Supreme Court justice, had been born in Middletown, New York, in 1865. He graduated from Manhattan College in 1885 and was admitted to the New York Bar in 1888. He moved to New York City the following year, where he joined Clan-na-Gael.[39] Cohalan was a member of Tammany Hall under Charles Murphy. On April 15, 1910, Hearst had accused New York City mayor William Gaynor of making a $48,000 payoff to Cohalan, a Tammany sachem, for Murphy. The mayor contended that Hearst's documentary proof was a forgery, and the incident became the subject of a libel action brought by Hearst in the New York courts.[40] This episode would seem quite minor compared with what was to come.

In February 1916, a courier brought Devoy a message from the IRB that the Rising was now scheduled for the upcoming Easter Sunday. Devoy passed the message along to his contacts in the German consulate—Wolf Von Igel, Franz Von Papen, and a military attaché—and to a German journalist, George von Skalfor, for transmission to Berlin.

While these events transpired underground, the Irish American community decided to hold an Irish Race Convention on March 4 and 5, 1916, at the Hotel Astor in New York City. Principal organizers were Devoy, Cohalan, McGarrity, and John T. Ryan, a lawyer from Buffalo, New York. The convention was attended by approximately 2,500 leaders of the Irish American community. At the conclusion of the convention a new organization was formed called the Friends of Irish Freedom. The organization was designed as a fund-raising vehicle to advance the cause of Irish independence and to influence the Wilson administration. Fifteen of its seventeen-member executive committee were members of Clan-na-Gael. Among its members were Cohalan; McGarrity; Dr. John T. Kelly; the attorney John T. Ryan of Buffalo; Jeremiah A. O'Leary, who would later be prosecuted by the Wilson administration for treason because of his aggressive anti-British advocacy;[41] and McGuire.[42] The committee met for the first time on March 15, 1916, to begin its fund-raising appeal.

On April 18, the U.S. Secret Service raided the German consulate and arrested Von Igel. In the search of the offices they discovered Devoy's communications with Berlin. They now knew the date and location where the arms were to be shipped to the IRB, as well as the date of the Easter Sunday Rising. Moreover, the British had broken the German codes much earlier and had been privy to Devoy's messages to Berlin during the month of February about the impending Rising. To make matters even worse, the IRB in Dublin was completely unaware of this breach.[43] Disaster loomed on the horizon.

7

Fellow Traveler

In Germany, Roger Casement had soured on his mission. The inability to organize an Irish brigade among the prisoners and the British plot to kill or capture him had taken an emotional and psychological toll on him. He had been admitted to a sanitarium.[1] Moreover, he had come to believe that German assistance to the insurrection in Ireland was becoming ineffectual. Having learned of the imminent launching of the Rising, Casement decided to travel to Ireland to try and stop it.[2]

On the night of April 20, two vessels arrived off the coast of Ireland. The *Aud*, a German freighter carrying arms to the IRB, was in Tralee Bay and a German submarine carrying Casement and two companions was off the coast of Cork. A British Royal Navy warship sank the *Aud*. While Casement and his companions were put ashore, Casement, alone, was captured the next day.[3] Nevertheless, events continued to unfold.

On Monday, April 24, after a series of miscommunications among the IRB about whether the Rising was to occur,[4] a force of only 1,500 uniformed Volunteers seized the general post office in central Dublin. Pádraig Pearse, who commanded the brigade, exited the building and read a proclamation to those passing by, declaring, "Irishmen and Irishwomen: in the name of God and of the dead generations from which she receives her old tradition of nationhood, Ireland, through us, summons her children to her flag and strikes for her freedom." Pearse went on to declare the establishment of the Republic of Ireland, a pronouncement that would have profound repercussions for the Irish and Americans who desired a country free from British rule.[5]

The proclamation was signed by Pearse and six other leaders of the insurrection. Thus was the Irish Republic born.

The Rising lasted five days. It ended on the following Saturday with the surrender of the Irish Volunteers in the post office and elsewhere around the city.[6] Among the Volunteers who surrendered his troops that had been holding the Lower Mount Street Bridge was a young school teacher named Éamon de Valera.[7] Although Pearse had claimed "the allegiance of every Irishman and Irishwoman," as the captive Volunteers were marched through the streets of Dublin it became clear that they had very little support or approval. Residents came out of their homes to offer tea and refreshments to the British soldiers guarding them.[8]

In America, reaction to the Rising mirrored that in Dublin. In the main, the newspapers and public officials condemned the Volunteers and supported the British response.[9] While Devoy put up a brave and combative front, most other leaders kept a low profile. During this period McGuire was silent. It is unlikely that he feared expressing his opinion about the current state of affairs, indictment or no indictment. He clearly had put himself on record concerning the British, the Germans, and Irish independence with his two books. The more likely explanation is that he was devoting his efforts to the fund-raising campaign that the Friends of Irish Freedom had committed to.

Pádraig Pearse, Devoy, and Cardinal Gibbons, the most respected Irish prelate in the United States, agreed on one issue. The execution of the leaders of the Rising would change public opinion. Pearse predicted as much in a letter to his mother the night before his execution.[10] Devoy did so in a most impolitic observation in which he declared that he would start with the execution of John Redmond.[11] The cardinal expressed his view in a letter to the British ambassador in which he warned against "manufacturing martyrs."[12] The British government, however, failed to pay heed to any of the warnings. In May 1916, General Robert Maxwell, the British commander in Ireland, undertook a series of court martials in which the leaders of the Rising were tried and sentenced to death.[13] The outcry and shift in public opinion were almost immediate.[14] The fate of the last of the fifteen, labor leader James Connolly, who had to be tied to a chair before the firing squad, resulted in 20,000 protestors gathering outside Carnegie Hall in New York City. The next man scheduled to be executed was Éamon de Valera.[15]

There are two theories concerning the reason that Éamon de Valera was not executed. Both may have some validity. The most popular theory is that the British knew de Valera was an American citizen, having been born in New York City, and did not wish to incur the wrath of the American public when they were hoping that the United States would become an ally in the war.[16] Support for this theory is found in a number of accounts of the post-Rising period in which it is reported that both de Valera's wife and his mother provided birth certificates to the British authorities proving that he had been born in the United States.[17] Another explanation, which appears to have equal plausibility, is that public reaction to the executions had ripened to the point that they were discontinued following the execution of Connolly when de Valera was scheduled to be next. In either case it can be said that de Valera literally dodged a bullet. His sentence was commuted and he was imprisoned with the remaining prisoners in England.[18]

The execution of the leaders of the Rising and the backlash of public opinion in America, and its effect on American-British relations in the runup to the war, is somewhat captured in the correspondence between Sir Edward Grey; Sir Horace Plunkett, an Irish nationalist and peer; and Colonel Edward House, Wilson's confidant and unofficial diplomat. Plunkett, commenting upon a resolution of the U.S. Senate condemning the executions, had written House that "the Irish situation has been mishandled in a way which beats even the record of British blundering in my unfortunate country." Grey, however, took the view that

> I hope the United States will make it clear that in all questions of international law taken up by them, it is the merits of the question and not the unpopularity of Great Britain or anti-British feeling that is the motivating force.

We are not favourably impressed by the action of the Senate in having passed a resolution about the Irish prisoners, though they have taken no notice of the outrages in Belgium and the massacre of Armenians. These latter were outrageous and unprovoked, whereas the only unprovoked thing in recent Irish affairs was the rising itself which for a few days was a formidable danger. I enclose a short summary that was drawn up here as relevant to the Senate resolution though we have not yet sent it to the President. The natural question on the action of the Senate is, "Why if humanity is their motive do they ignore the real outrages in Belgium, etc.?"[19]

One prisoner for whom clemency was not to be shown was Roger Casement. Casement had been imprisoned in the Tower of London and was charged with treason in the King's Bench Division of the High Court.[20] In America, despite his misgivings about Casement's judgment and suspicion about his sexual orientation, John Devoy used part of the proceeds from his inheritance from his brother's estate to hire an American lawyer, Michael Francis Doyle of Philadelphia, to defend Casement in the British court. According to Devoy's biographer, when Boyle showed Casement Devoy's check for $5,000, he broke down and cried.[21] The outcome of the trial was never in doubt. In June 1916, Casement was found guilty of treason. Allowed to make a statement before sentencing, Casement made a passionate case about the unfairness of his being tried before a British tribunal. He declared that he would readily accept his fate were he convicted in an Irish court and convicted by an Irish jury. Upon the completion of his statement, Casement was sentenced to death.

In America, Irish leaders mounted a furious campaign to have Casement's sentence commuted. His American lawyer, Michael Doyle, beseeched Wilson's secretary, Joseph Tumulty, another Irish American, to seek clemency for Casement. Tumulty's communication of these entreaties to the president, as well as those of Irish American members of Congress, fell on deaf ears. As the date of Casement's execution drew near, the U.S. Senate adopted a resolution requesting Wilson to communicate its request that Casement's life be spared. The

State Department and the U.S. embassy in Britain dragged their feet, however, and the British were not informed of the resolution until after Casement was hanged on August 3. This turn of events resulted in Devoy's unleashing his harshest attack on Wilson to date. In the weeks before the 1916 election, Devoy editorialized in the *Gaelic American*. He accused the president of being anti-Irish and declared that Wilson's father had been loyal to the Confederacy and proslavery during the American Civil War.[22]

Wilson's delaying of the communication of the senate resolution incensed Devoy in particular, because Devoy blamed Wilson for alerting the British to the impending Rising following the seizure of his correspondence from the German consulate in the days before it occurred. Devoy and Cohalan endorsed Wilson's opponent, Charles Evans Hughes.[23] It was the second time they opposed Wilson in a presidential campaign and Wilson would not forget it.[24] Notwithstanding Devoy's and Cohalan's organized opposition, Wilson was narrowly reelected and the two Irish American leaders now had an implacable foe in the White House. The Friends of Irish Freedom claimed credit for Hughes's margin of victory in the states he won.[25] McGuire, as in the 1912 campaign, was an unseen presence in the election.

As the second Wilson administration began to unfold, the Friends of Irish Freedom stepped up their efforts to keep the United States out of the war on the side of the British. On February 10, 1917, the organization sent the president a statement setting forth the reasons why America should remain neutral.[26] It was likewise endeavoring to align itself with other ethnic groups, particularly German ones, in this effort.[27] On April 6, the United States declared war on Germany.[28] The atmosphere surrounding the fight for Irish independence was about to change dramatically for those involved in the United States.

At first the direction appeared to take a positive turn; late in April both former presidents Roosevelt and Taft announced their support of Home Rule. Wilson's secretary Joseph Tumulty, in a letter printed in the *New York World*, committed the Wilson administration to supporting Home Rule. This overture was rejected strongly by John D. Moore, president of the Friends of Irish Freedom.

On June 18, twenty-six of the Rising veterans, including de Valera, were released by the British government. They immediately signed a statement calling for Irish independence. Patrick McCartan, who would become the Republic of Ireland envoy to the United States, traveled to America hoping to present the petition to President Wilson. Here he had conferences with Devoy, McGarrity, and Cohalan.[29] On July 29, McCartan, John D. Moore, and McGuire took the petition to the White House. Wilson refused to meet with McCartan but had his secretary Tumulty accept it.[30] Tumulty referred the petition to Frank L. Polk, counselor at the State Department, who advised him to file it without a reply.

In England, Prime Minister Lloyd George introduced Home Rule legislation that would have excluded the six counties of Ulster. Redmond rejected this arrangement. The prime minister then proposed that a convention be called to write a constitution for Ireland. Redmond rejected this idea too. In America this rejection was echoed by Cohalan. McGuire and others issued a statement in which they declared that such a convention was an "insidious pretense, impracticable in its operation, and because of its lack of democratic honesty, foredoomed to failure."

In Ireland, Redmond's Irish Party received a major setback when Sinn Fein candidates de Valera and William Cosgrave won two seats in special elections held after the deaths of two of its members.[31] Both abstained from taking their seats in Parliament.[32]

In September Wilson decided to exact his revenge on Devoy and Cohalan for their support of Charles Evans Hughes in the campaign the year before, and for Cohalan's opposition to his nomination as part of the Tammany Hall contingent to the Democratic convention in 1912.[33] In order to discredit them in the eyes of Americans, on September 23, Secretary of State Lansing authorized the publication of the documents seized from the German consulate in April 1916. Some of the documents suggested that Cohalan, as well as Devoy, had been seeking German aid in the Rising. Cohalan denied ever sending such a message but the New York City press was filled with calls for his impeachment.[34] Public support for Cohalan came from the

Ancient Order of Hibernians, the Irish National Committee, and the Friends of Irish Freedom. Devoy went on the attack in editorials in his newspaper the *Gaelic American*, resulting in the Wilson administration's releasing more documents suggesting that McGarrity, Jeremiah O'Leary, and one John T. Keating were receptive to engaging in sabotage in the United States. Keating had died six months before the alleged cables had been sent to Berlin, and McGarrity challenged the government to prosecute him, but the water would become hottest for O'Leary.[35]

O'Leary was indicted for conspiring to obstruct recruiting and to commit treason.[36] A lawyer, he had incurred Wilson's public wrath during the 1916 campaign as he agitated for the president to be more forceful on the issue of Irish independence or face losing Irish American voters. At one point in the campaign, Wilson, responding to O'Leary's threat, said, "Your telegram received. I would be deeply mortified to have you or anybody like you vote for me. Since you have access to many disloyal Americans and I have not, I will ask you to convey this message to them."[37]

Upon being indicted, O'Leary, in very unlawyerlike fashion, fled to the West Coast. Apprehended, he was transported to New York City. On October 8, 1917, his publication *Bull* was banned from the U.S. mail. After spending more than a year in the Tombs jail in New York City, he was tried and acquitted on four counts of a five-count indictment. The jury reportedly was nine to three for acquittal on the remaining count.[38]

Bull was not the only publication banned from the mail. In February 1918, the *Gaelic American* and the *Irish World* met the same fate.[39] As the war progressed, the Wilson administration banned more books and publications from the mail, as well as restricted their dissemination to the American troops overseas. Among them was *What Could Germany Do for Ireland?*[40]

Sentiment for Irish independence took a backseat to the kind of nationalism that American entry into the war had inspired. The Friends of Irish Freedom were anemic. McGuire, encouraged by Jeremiah O'Leary, had proposed holding an Irish Race Convention but Cohalan had vetoed the idea, fearing a backlash.[41] In a letter to McGuire from a vacation home in Westport, New York, Cohalan wrote,

> My Dear Mayor; I was astounded at hearing from Mr. Dalton of the latest plea from Jer. O'Leary and I told Mr. D. yesterday by phone that I would in no way be a party to anything beyond organizing those whose names have been gathered in order through Irish activities to help advance the cause we have at heart.
>
> This is one of the few quarters from which to expect annoyance and it should be made clear at once that no personal ambitions will be permitted to interfere with the great questions. As to the Convention, you asked my opinion . . . it would be folly and poor judgment to convene such a gathering.
>
> I hope before you go away, that you will take occasion in every way that you can to put an end to this latest plea for action from New York which would simply make certain the re-election of the present incumbent and the securing triumph of all he represents.[42]

Jeremiah O'Leary, not to be dissuaded, called upon McGuire to schedule an Irish Race Convention in a letter printed in Devoy's *Gaelic American*; castigating Wilson, he observed, "Of course, whatever the President does, right or wrong, carries tremendous weight with the American people, but no American President can do injustice to Ireland under the pretense of doing her justice and hold himself the respect of the Irish people either in Ireland or America." O'Leary went on to question the propriety of American naval ships blockading Ireland to prevent the shipment of arms to the Irish and to contend that if Irish Americans were to die in the war as allies of England, then they deserved to be heard on the question of Irish independence when it came time for it to be considered. Personally appealing to McGuire, he declared,

> Of course, it is hardly necessary to say to you, a man who has been so brave and heroic, so devoted too with your time, brains and money, that every citizen of Irish blood in America has the right,

under the Constitution, to freely express his opinion on all public questions, and, with his fellow citizens, to assemble in a public gathering for the purpose of petitioning the government for a redress of his grievances. As the right of free speech and public assemblage is guaranteed by the Constitution, a Race Convention would be amply protected against any lawless effort to disrupt it.[43]

O'Leary's and McGuire's position carried the day and a convention was scheduled; however, after having set the date for it in November 1917, it was cancelled. At the same time, a more militant Irish Progressive League came into existence and established a National Bureau in Washington, DC, to agitate for Irish independence as the Versailles peace talks began. Cohalan's fears, that focusing attention on the issue of Irish independence accompanied by pro-German sentiment would invite repression, may have been correct. No less a personage than former president Theodore Roosevelt advocated interning some of the Irish American leadership as "enemy aliens." In January 1918, John Kelly of the Massachusetts chapter of Friends of Irish Freedom called on McGuire to set a date for an Irish Race Convention. The convention was scheduled for May 18–19 at the Hotel Astor in New York City.[44]

In Ireland, the British introduced conscription on April 16, 1918. An immediate strike was called that paralyzed the country.[45] On May 17, seventy-three leaders, including de Valera, were arrested and imprisoned in England, charged with violating the Defense of the Realm Act.[46]

At the Irish Race Convention being held in New York City, attendance was far fewer than at previous conventions. Cohalan, still mindful about provoking repressive measure by the Wilson administration, counseled caution in the reaction to the Irish internments.[47]

Both the British and the American governments contended that they had information that the Irish leaders being interned, and their American counterparts, were engaged in a conspiracy with the Germans involving an insurrection in Ireland. While the British press was skeptical of the claims, the American press was not. Challenged by

the Sinn Fein leaders to release the documentary evidence of this conspiracy, the Wilson administration refused. Whether the claims of a
conspiracy were pretextual or real, British Prime Minister David Lloyd
George suspended civil liberties in Ireland. In September, de Valera
and other Sinn Fein leaders were court-martialed and sent to prison.
Among those not apprehended by the British was Michael Collins, who
remained at large. At the same time, in the United States, Jeremiah
O'Leary and John T. Ryan were indicted for espionage and treason.[48]

On November 11, 1918, World War I ended. As the postwar Versailles peace conference was about to get under way, the issue of Irish
self-determination came to the fore.

Cohalan's fears about provoking repressive measures by the Wilson administration would prove to be more than a passing bout of
paranoia. Unbeknownst to McGuire, he had been the subject of an
investigation by the Department of Justice's Bureau of Investigation,
the forerunner of the FBI, which had been intermittently unfolding
for the past three years. On June 16, 1916, A. Bruce Bielaski, the chief
of the bureau, wrote Roland Ford, an agent in the bureau office in
Albany, New York, to commence the investigation. He related that

> I am informed through the Department of State, that one James K.
> McGuire, of 117 Market Street, Syracuse, New York, has been active
> recently in connection with the Irish movement in this country to
> support the rebellion in Ireland, and that he has been correspond-
> ing with people in Germany and with the Austrian Consul-general
> in New York.
>
> Please make prompt and thorough investigation of this man and
> his activities and connections. I suggest that among other things
> you secure his mail.[49]

Ford reported back to Bielaski three days later. He informed the
chief that he had traveled to Syracuse on June 16 to conduct the investigation. While there, he had learned that McGuire was the former
mayor of the city and that when he concluded his term, "he was broke
but, now, he is apparently a well-to-do man." He discovered that the

Market Street address was the printing plant and office of the *Catholic Sun*. He related that McGuire had written *The King, the Kaiser and Irish Freedom* and *"What Germany Can Do for Ireland"* and "is devoting a great deal of his time to speech making for the Irish colores." He interviewed the postmaster in Syracuse, who told him that McGuire received very little mail in Syracuse. He then turned to an interview he conducted with an anonymous "State Official" in Syracuse who told him that McGuire "is honest but the general impression is that he 'never gives unless he gets.' Whether he is doing this agitating and publishing these books for the amount which he receives for returns on the sales of the books, or for something higher up is a question. If Mr. McGuire has certain motives for his work, it would require very tactful work to fix anything on him, as he is a very clever man."[50] Interestingly, Agent Ford misstated the title of McGuire's second book, an error that would be repeated throughout many of the bureau's subsequent reports about the work.

Bielaski forwarded the investigative report to Leland Harrison, an attorney for the U.S. State Department, with the observation that it indicates "that McGuire has been very active in spreading German-Irish propaganda."[51]

The government's investigative interest in McGuire appeared to wane, according to the bureau's file, until December 1917, when he came to the attention of the War Department. In a memorandum from one Captain H. G. Pratt to Captain Henry Taylor, McGuire caught the former's attention based upon information supplied by an unnamed informant who related that McGuire was involved in lobbying efforts for "several large contractors who are interested in putting up the government building at 7th and B Streets" in the nation's capital. It went on to state,

> This man is the author of the book entitled "The King, The Kaiser Kaiser Country [*sic*]." He has been very active in Syracuse and New York City endeavoring to combine the Irish and German sympathizers. He is a personal friend of Judge Cohallan [*sic*] of New York, who is under charges of impeachment preferred by Governor Whitman;

also connected with a man named Burke, who is an intimate of Count Bernstoff. Subject is now living at the Raleigh Hotel, Washington, D.C. has entrance to all government departments and the informant states that from his knowledge of affairs engaged in by this man that he is a very dangerous man to be at large.[52]

The government clearly was surveilling McGuire during this period as evidenced by a report from one F. T. Walters, a bureau agent, to Captain Taylor dated five days later, which repeated some of the information in the Pratt memorandum and reported that "Subject left the Raleigh Hotel on December 29, 1917, but did not leave any forwarding address according to Hotel records. He has been making this hotel his Headquarters when in Washington for a number of years and usually before arriving is in the habit of sending a telegram to the hotel informing the manager when he is to arrive making for reservations. The next time he intends to visit Washington agent will be informed of his arrival."[53]

Walters would continue his investigation of McGuire into the next year and in a lengthy memorandum to Captain Taylor reported on his interview with the U.S. Marshal Service in which he learned the following:

Subject tried to hold meetings in Syracuse, New York in which he tried to join the IRISH and GERMAN residents of that city in protest against the selling of arms and munitions to the Allies but was stopped by the present mayor, Louis Hill. Subject even went so far as to have posters posted in re. above but the Mayor got wind of it when a few of them were posted and ordered them down. Subject had close relations with VON BERNSTOFF in New York city in a BAZZAR business to raise money to send to Germany for wives and orphans and create sympathy in this country. Mayor Hill made it so hot for subject that he does not have any activities in his home town any more making trips to and from his home in the night.

The agent went on to provide a less than flattering description of McGuire, whom he described as follows: "Features very ugly. (reported at one time to be the ugliest man in his home town) age believed to be between 55 and 60 years, height about 5'11" weight about 180, the mouth face, bull dog jaws with deep brown hair. Generally wears green soft hat, dark suit of clothes, long dark overcoat with belt."[54]

The War Department's report of its investigation of McGuire was forwarded to Chief Bielaski by its chief of military intelligence with a request that the bureau "submit a full history of this man's disloyal acts."[55] Four days later, Bielaski wrote the solicitor of the post office, William Lamar, to inquire whether McGuire's book *The King, the Kaiser and Irish Freedom*, which he described as "calculated to arouse the Irish people in the United States against the British," had come to the postal authorities' attention.[56] He also replied to the War Department's intelligence chief, Colonel Van Daman, on February 15, 1918, assuring him that the bureau would initiate a new investigation of McGuire since the existing bureau reports were outdated.[57]

Three days later, Bielaski wrote the bureau's agent in Syracuse, James C. Tormey, ordering the investigation and directing that "all information possible be secured as to his personal history and any acts disloyal to the United States."[58] Bielaski's selection of Tormey to conduct the investigation would prove to be fateful to McGuire.

A native Syracusan, Tormey was twenty years younger than McGuire. He had graduated from Christian Brothers Academy and Dean Prep School, where he had been a standout athlete in baseball and basketball. He was selected as the All–New England Center and would play professional basketball as the player coach of the Syracuse Stars. He obtained his law degree from Georgetown University in 1915 and became an agent for the Bureau of Investigation from 1917 until he entered private practice in Syracuse in 1919.[59]

Tormey was held in high regard by his superiors as evidenced by their seeking his deferment from military service in World War I. In a letter urging his deferment, his superior, Arthur Barkey, the special agent in charge of the Buffalo, New York, office wrote, "He is a lawyer and a man of judgment and tact. He is well connected in Syracuse and liked by all . . . I believe it would be rather difficult at this time to obtain the services of a man to be as efficient in Syracuse as Mr.

Tormey."[60] Bielaski also submitted an affidavit in support of the deferment request, echoing Barkey's praise of Tormey, noting, "He is in charge of the work at Syracuse and it would take considerable time for another man to learn to do the work there as well as Mr. Tormey does. He is devoting all of his time to war matters."[61]

On February 26, 1918, Tormey reported on his findings. Despite the indications in the bureau's previous communications that implied McGuire was "dangerous" and had engaged in "disloyal acts," and that the "investigation of McGuire [should] be along the lines suggested by the War Department," Tormey did a completely impartial inquiry that turned out quite favorably for McGuire. At the beginning of his report, Tormey declared that "personally I know the general reputation of James K. McGuire, who was at one time the Mayor of this city, is of the best. He is generally spoken of as a man of the highest type regarding his character."

Discussing McGuire's writings, he observed they "are construed by many to be pro-German to the extent they are opposed to England, but that is accounted for by the fact that he is a loyal Irishman and is sincere in his statements relative to the future of Ireland. However it is generally thought that McGuire, being a most intelligent man and with the finest associations, both business and social, in this Country, and being a man of great character is absolutely and unqualifiedly loyal to the United States."

Tormey then proceeded to outline the mechanics of his investigation: "Knowing the general reputation as I do, I concluded it would be better for me to interview men of the highest standing in the community who are not of the same religious or political faith as Mr. McGuire." He named New York State Supreme Court justice William Ross, businessman Isaac Rosenbloom, and T. Frank Dolan, a childhood friend of McGuire's. All three vouched for McGuire's character and loyalty. He concluded the report by stating, "I am not personally acquainted with Mr. McGuire but I heard him speak on one occasion and am familiar with his two books and I may state that I have always had the greatest respect for the gentleman because of his reputation in this community and from hearing people speak of him and observing the man whenever opportunity afforded it and it is my opinion that a man of his type would not consider his feelings toward other Countries at a time when his country is at war." He closed, noting, "I also understand that Mr. McGuire recalled his books from the market at or before the entry of the United States into the war, at a great financial sacrifice and loss to him, although I could not verify this statement."[62]

On the same day that Tormey submitted his report, the post office advised Bielaski that it had not obtained a copy of *The King, the Kaiser and Irish Freedom*.[63] On March 6, Bielaski submitted Tormey's report to the War Department, and it was returned to him the same day.

Throughout the investigative file on McGuire there are a number of letters of complaint by citizens from various parts of the country about the contents of McGuire's books. Whether the inclusion of these letters in the file was pretextual, in order to justify the investigation, or raised valid concerns on the part of the government is open to conjecture. In either case, Bielaski, at the end of May 1918, directed his agent in New York City, Charles DeWoody, to obtain a copy of *The King, the Kaiser and Irish Freedom*.[64] Bringing DeWoody into the investigation could have put McGuire at great peril, for few men were as zealous about hunting down opponents of the war effort as DeWoody. Indeed, during a three-day period in September 1918, DeWoody conducted what he termed a "slacker raid," in which more than 60,000 men were detained for allegedly failing to register for the draft.[65] Fortunately for McGuire, DeWoody limited his role to obtaining a copy of the book from the Devin-Adair Company in New York City.

Once the bureau had obtained the work, it assigned A. J. Robinson in Battle Creek, Michigan, to read and report on its contents. Why Robinson was chosen for this task remains a mystery.

On June 6, Robinson submitted a four-page report containing his analysis of the book's content. If there was any doubt about the government's view of the book, it was laid to rest by the notation "Seditious Matters" in its title and on each page. Robinson's analysis involved his quoting passages from the book and his opinion commentary about each one. Among the agent's observations were the following:

"The author seems to have acquired the German characteristic of disparaging the United States save when it may be complimented upon emulating the German example."

"To a certain class of readers this outspoken support of the German methods coupled with the derogatory inference anent the 'unhappy republicanism' of America would be excellent German propaganda."

"Excellent food for the propagandist, especially when in print."

"What better material for the I.W.W.[66] or soap box socialist?"

"The psychological effect of this statement on the little orator is such undoubtedly that he will vindicate the Hun in his wars of conquest and aggrandizement for identical reasons."

Robinson concluded his analysis by declaring,

Taking into account that this work was published in 1915 about six or seven months after the beginning of the war we cannot presume any malicious intent with regard to America on the part of the author but the whole trend of the work is such as to influence that large portion of our population who are seeking the means to argue themselves out of service. It is conducive to the organization of parties which injure our military efficiency by detrimental debate and contrary policy; it is particularly adapted to the fomenting of dissension among our multitudinous Irish population and it is intensely anti-British that in its nature it is pro-German to a certain extent. The author has adhered in most cases strictly to the debating of ways and means for the freeing of the Irish in so far as he is concerned with their present relations to the British but he has in his work succeeded in interspersing sufficient matter of an undesirable nature to make it unquestionably hurtful to our government in this crisis. Granting that the Author is beyond a shadow of a doubt Pro-American we can only conclude that in his enthusiasm over the subject of Irish freedom he has overly lauded the German characteristic and unjustly disparaged the American.[67]

The Bureau of Investigation also acquired a copy of McGuire's second book, *What Could Germany Do for Ireland?* during the month of July 1918. Assistant Division Superintendent Norman Gifford of the Boston, Massachusetts, office assigned Agent Samuel C. Endicott to read and analyze this work. The assignment was conducted at the request of Division Superintendent Kelleher, whose view of the book carried some particularly chilling implications for McGuire. Gifford reported that Kelleher requested the analysis because, in his view, the book was "decidedly pro-German and very likely a violation of the Espionage and Trading with the Enemy Acts."[68] The prospect of being prosecuted under this law was not something to be taken lightly. Pulitzer Prize–winning author Tim Weir, in his history of the FBI entitled *Enemies*, noted that in 1917, 1,055 people had been prosecuted and sentenced to lengthy prison terms because of their speeches and written criticism of the war. Among them were 165 union leaders including the 1912 presidential candidate Eugene Debs.[69]

The following month Assistant Division Chief Gifford also ordered a review of *The King, the Kaiser and Irish Freedom* by Agent Endicott, who had volunteered to perform the first analysis of *What Could Germany Do for Ireland?*. Apparently neither Gifford nor Endicott was aware that this book had already been read and analyzed earlier by Robinson in the Battle Creek, Michigan, office. Endicott's six-page report cited twenty-one passages from the first book to illuminate his superior's understanding of its content. An interesting feature of this analysis was Endicott's preoccupation with McGuire's focus on Sir Roger Casement's views concerning England's subjugation of the Irish.[70]

McGuire continued to draw the attention of the various government agencies involved in the war effort. On September 28, 1918, the director of naval intelligence, Hugo Johnstone, informed Bielaski that McGuire's second book, *What Could Germany Do for Ireland?*, had been barred from camp libraries. He went on to inform him that McGuire was associated with the chairman of the Democratic Congressional Committee and had previously rented Madison Square Garden to hold a rally "for the Irish and Germans to protest against the United States entering the war."[71]

Two weeks later he again came to the attention of Division Superintendent DeWoody, and this time would become the subject of a full-blown investigative surveillance. DeWoody wrote Bielaski that

> while Agent Bischoff was at Washington, he learned incidentally that James K. McGuire . . . was making visits to Washington on an average of about three times a week, and that he stayed at the Raleigh Hotel. McGuire, who is a rank Sinn Feiner and one of the promoters of the O'Leary crowd,[72] was reported by agent Vander Poel of this office under date of August 28th. In a statement made to Special Assistant to the United States Attorney, Alfred Becker, on Sept. 13th, McGuire acknowledged the receipt of $26,000 from Dr. Albert to further circulation of his two books, which were nothing more than propaganda. It was learned that the house detective in the Raleigh Hotel could not be relied upon. Therefore I suggest that a careful cover be placed on the movements of the above.[73]

At the end of October, McGuire returned to Washington and stayed at the Raleigh Hotel. Bureau of Investigation reports reveal that he was surveilled by a number of agents from the bureau. The surveillance was not without its comic aspects. On October 30, Agent E. J. Wells reported that he commenced following McGuire that morning from his hotel to the postmaster-general's office and

> lost subject by missing the elevator, and went back to the Raleigh Hotel and waited until 4:15 when the subject turned up again. I continued to shadow him in the hotel lobby until 5:45 at which time he, in the company with two other gentlemen took a taxi-cab, license number 19241. I followed them in another taxi-cab to the Trinity College, where they stopped twenty minutes. From there they proceeded to Catholic University where they stopped for a few minutes, after which they apparently became wise that they were being shadowed and proceeded up a blind street, where it was necessary to discontinue shadowing them for the evening.[74]

During the next several weeks, McGuire was followed by a number of agents who reported on his visits to various government offices, his meetings with unidentified individuals, and his eating meals in different restaurants. They obtained copies of the telephone messages left for him but appeared to learn very little about his activities.

On November 28, 1918, an all-out effort was made to locate McGuire so that he could be interviewed by Bielaski. Agents were sent to his home in New Rochelle and his office in New York City. Ultimately they found him in Pennsylvania Station in New York City, about to board the train for Washington, DC. He readily agreed to accompany them to the Bureau of Investigation office to meet with Bielaski. There he was questioned by the bureau chief.[75]

The files contain no record or notes that reveal the topics that Bielaski questioned McGuire about, nor what information McGuire supplied during the questioning. Whatever transpired during the interview, it appeared to end the bureau's interest in prosecuting McGuire for his writings and advocacy, since the file ends with this report.

What led Bielaski to decide that the bureau and the Justice Department should forgo prosecuting McGuire? While there is no clear record illuminating this decision, one factor must have been Agent Tormey's report endorsing McGuire's loyalty and attesting to his good character and patriotism. Tormey had included in his report that "McGuire had sold more Liberty Bonds in the Second liberty Loan, in the city of Washington than any other individual" and that "Mr. McGuire stated that his son, who is now a student at Georgetown University will enlist in the United States Army, when he reaches his majority, and that Mr. McGuire will gladly make this sacrifice for his country."[76] The inclusion of such information must have been a factor that weighed on Bielaski's decision.

The investigation of McGuire is also interesting for what it failed to uncover. Despite the bureau's focus on McGuire's attachment to Roger Casement's views, it apparently never discovered that McGuire procured Casement's false travel documents and identity from his contacts in the U.S. State Department, which allowed Casement to travel to Germany during 1915 in his ill-fated attempt to organize an Irish brigade from the British prisoners of war for the 1916 Rising. Likewise, although the bureau had identified McGuire as a "rank Sinn

Feiner," it never learned that he was the head of Clan-na-Gael nor is the organization mentioned anywhere in its file.

One other fact uncovered in the investigation is worth considering. On November 26, 1918, Agent C. P. McCarver reported that during their efforts to locate McGuire for Bielaski, they discovered that McGuire was the president of the Wolfe Tone Company, Inc., the publisher of the McGuire's second book, *What Could Germany Do for Ireland?*[77] The fact that McGuire had to self-publish this work suggests that at the time he was seeking to market it, it was considered too incendiary by the mainstream publishing world, particularly as the United States was nearing entry into the war.

Bielaski's decision to forgo prosecution of McGuire did not, however, assuage the Wilson administration's thirst to punish him and the others who questioned its allegiance to Britain at a time when Ireland was trying to free itself from its colonial status. In exacting its revenge, the administration chose at its public forum a subcommittee hearing conducted by the U.S. Senate Judiciary Committee investigating "brewing and liquor interests and German Propaganda," held on December 8, 1918.

Bielaski was dispatched to the hearing by the attorney general to give testimony about collaboration between the German government and Irish American leaders to spread pro-German and anti-British propaganda prior to America's entry into World War I. During the course of the hearing, Bielaski testified that the Irish American group that was alleged to have been collaborating with the German consulate officials in America was known as the "McGuire group, of which Mr. James K. McGuire, former mayor of Syracuse, was the man in charge."[78] Asked whether they were Sinn Feiners, Bielaski went on to characterize them as the "leading agitators for independent Ireland and for revolution in Ireland and so on." Bielaski then read into the record portions of the government's files on McGuire:

James K. McGuire, who organized this Irish Press and News Service for the Germans, was also the author of two books, "The King, The Kaiser, And Irish Freedom," whose publication he was financially assisted by Dr. Albert's[79] office and he was also the author of "What Germany Could Do for Ireland?" Both these books were circulated by the press bureau as propaganda books. He also made arrangements for the printing of these books in Austria and Germany.

McGuire is the owner of the following newspapers and publishing companies: The Syracuse Printing & Publishing Co.; the Wolff-Tones Publishing Co., New York; the National Catholic, New York; the Light, Albany; the Truth, Scranton; the Sun, Syracuse. He also furnished Irish news to a number of other Catholic papers.

He sent out through this news service bulletins two or three times a week to 18 or 20 papers in which he had been interested, and to the daily newspapers. The number of copies he sent out varied according to the importance of the subject matter. He would send out 50 or 60, sometimes, and sometimes two or three hundred. Copies of everything sent out were also sent to Dr. Fuehr.

Dr. Albert paid to Mr. McGuire in June 1915, $14,800, and other amounts were paid to him of which we have knowledge, and there may have been money that we have no knowledge of, which brings the total up to the neighborhood of $22,000. These payments cover money for books which have been mentioned, for the operation of the press service, and as part of this work he sent to Ireland one or two persons to gather information, and their expenses were also paid by the Germans.

Mr. McGuire was chairman of the executive committee of the Friends of Irish Freedom. He seems to have sincerely believed that Germany would win the war and that Ireland's hope lay with Germany, and so he cooperated with Germany's representatives here as best he could. He maintains that at the break in diplomatic relations he withdrew all his books from the market, prevented their further circulation, and has rendered patriotic service to this country ever since we entered the war.[80]

Asked about McGuire's views concerning Britain as an ally, the government agent conceded, "I take it he has simply been silent on that. At least he told me he has been. I do not suppose that his real feelings have undergone any change but he has so far as we know done nothing which might be classed as damaging to the cause of this country or its allies since we entered the war."

Bielaski was also asked about the timing of the pro-German articles that McGuire had been furnishing to Catholic newspapers. He told the committee, "He had been furnishing material for these papers before the war in Europe broke out. That was part of his regular business. He continued to do it, only thereafter the work was paid for by the German Government, and much of the information being furnished him by Dr. Fuehr,[81] and of course, it was exceedingly pro-German."

Bielaski further testified that McGuire's second book, *What Could Germany Do for Ireland?*, was preferred over some other similar works by the German government and that the government tried to circulate it on a large scale. He went on to allege activity by McGuire beyond advancing propaganda, claiming,

> The boat *Gladstone*, which was believed to be bearing supplies for the German boats in the south Atlantic, was held up a bit at Norfolk, and under date of December 18, 1914, Mr. McGuire wrote the following in a letter:
>
> > "I have reason to believe that our friends will have no trouble hereafter, of a like nature at this port (Norfolk) etc."
> >
> > This was addressed to Dr. Albert, I am satisfied. It does not show however;
> >
> > "There should be a special consul; or agent stationed there.
> > Yours truly; James K. McGuire
> > P.S. the British have an alert and powerful man there."
>
> Enclosed in that letter was a clipping showing that the collector, Mr. Hamilton, granted the former *Gladstone*, whose name had been changed to the *Marina Quezada*, a clearance. And enclosed with that card was a card of the collector, Mr. Norman R. Hamilton. It is my understanding that Mr. McGuire said that he had some relatives or something of the sort at Norfolk who was connected with Mr. Hamilton or something of the sort.

Mr. Albert, in discussing some other matters, also made a reference to McGuire helping him in labor matters. There was a very considerable propaganda among the labor element in this country, which I hope to take up in a short time. The reference to McGuire in the other work is very brief. It says:

"One of these Irish gentlemen, McGuire has written a very readable book, on the war, whose circulation in the United States was furthered by excellency Dernburg.[82] Under the guise of pushing this book further Mr. McGuire is now giving us assistance in suitable fashion in labor questions, to which I, in agreement with the Ambassador and Mr. von Papen,[83] am giving my special attention."

Bielaski went on to read a list of names of prominent academics, public officials, publishers, and editors who were in favor of Germany, including William Randolph Hearst.

Since the war had ended a month earlier and, as Bielaski conceded, McGuire's support for Germany ended upon the United States' entering the war on the British side, it is hard to fathom any purpose for these hearings and disclosures other than Wilson's desire to punish his enemies and perhaps neutralize them politically in the event he decided to seek a third term in 1920. This conclusion seemed to be buttressed by the fact that academics studying World War I propaganda viewed McGuire's efforts as being wholly ineffectual. In a study published by H. G. Peterson in 1939, the author declared, "The leading newspapers which were friendly to the Central Powers were German American and reached only the German reading public. To these should be added the group of unimportant Irish American papers owned by James K. McGuire. These backed the Germans because McGuire believed that Ireland's only hope lay in a German victory. As far as influencing Americans was concerned, however, they can be completely discounted. Their editors wasted their ammunition on captured forts."[84]

Unlike Cohalan, who was frantic over the disclosures made concerning his and Devoy's following of the earlier raid on the German consulate, McGuire shrugged off Bielaski's charges without any noticeable concern.[85] In a letter to the *Post-Standard*, he defended his actions and patriotism, declaring that he should be judged by his actions after the United States declared war on Germany rather than before. Not only did he acknowledge receiving the sums that Bielaski testified had been provided him by the German government but went on to disclose,

> The German records quoted simply show the payment of moneys for books that I had written and published, the circulation of them in the United States and Europe and the contributions to the press service which was owned by the publishing companies that I control outside Syracuse.
>
> I am inclined to think that the amounts contributed were larger than the figures quoted, but as the period covered before the war I cannot recall the exact sums. The Syracuse papers mentioned in 1915 the fact that the German official agency had bought my books and in various advertisements of the same announcement was quoted as an excellent reason why the books should be read.[86]

Turning to his visit to Ireland in 1914, he said,

> In the summer of 1914, I gathered the data in Ireland for my first book, and the object was to plant the seed in America and the continent for the young men of Sinn Fein. I stood on the platform in Dublin at the outbreak of the war, with fourteen young heroes of a seemingly hopeless cause.
>
> Of those fourteen, six have been executed and eight are in prison, and I have lived to see the entire eight elected without opposition last week as members of Parliament from Ireland. The elections in the next few days in Ireland will justify my claim that the Sinn Fein . . . will sweep the country and demonstrate the authenticity of the news which I furnished the American public even tho part of the cost was borne by the German official bureau.

Returning to the subject of his own conduct and loyalty, he went on to observe,

> The senate Committee has acknowledged that my patriotic record as an American since the break with Germany is without flaw. The

postmaster-general of the United States has stated that I have been of very great service to the American government and other members of the cabinet say likewise.

I have held the complete confidence of the administration during the war. There is not a Syracusan visiting Washington in the last two years but will confirm the statement that I have tried in every way possible to be of assistance to my old neighbors. I have served on several important war committees and I think in proportion to my means have contributed as largely as any one to all the war loans and relief funds.

In closing, he made it crystal clear that he was unrepentant and unapologetic for his advocacy for Irish freedom, declaring, "We may not have changed our views during the war as to the unrighteousness of an alien nation occupying Ireland by force of arms, but we kept silent on the Irish question when the fate of America was threatened and the boys at the front might be affected. However we might hold the fate at the heart in the cause of an Irish nation we could not be disloyal to America if we tried to be."

In December a mass meeting sponsored by the Friends of Irish Freedom was held in Madison Square Garden at which Boston's Cardinal William O'Connell made an impassioned plea for the leaders at the upcoming peace conference to honor the principle of self-determination for Ireland. Although he was a member of the Executive Committee, there is no mention of McGuire's role in this event. The reason might be because the cardinal was introduced by McGuire's nemesis and now governor, Charles S. Whitman.[87]

On December 14, elections for Parliament were held across the United Kingdom. In Ireland, Sinn Fein won 73 of 105 seats.[88] Forty-seven of the victorious candidates were in jail. Twenty-four of the thirty-two counties in Ireland elected exclusively Sinn Fein candidates.[89] It was a breathtaking breakthrough for the cause of Irish independence. During this same period the issue was being taken up in hearings in Congress. Correspondence between John Devoy, Judge Cohalan, and McGuire reveal tension between Devoy and Joseph McGarrity concerning the strategy for the hearing. In a letter from Devoy to Cohalan, the old Irish Fenian complains about McGarrity's attempt to get McGuire to try and have the hearing postponed, recounting,

> Coming back on the train on Saturday James K. told me he went to Philadelphia with Phelan. On Tuesday afternoon Joe got him to call Flood[90] and tell him to postpone the hearing. J. K. believed that Joe was acting for all of us, called Flood and F. agreed to postpone. Fortunately Gallagher[91] was in the room with Flood and got on the telephone when he heard what was up. He told J. K. that it would play the devil and explained the situation. J. K. realized the mistake and turned to Joe and said simply, "It can't be done." While Joe is in this mood he is likely to get us into a bad scrape. If Gallagher didn't happen to be in the room with Flood, we'd have all gone there and there would have been no hearing. Joe sent nobody: left the field clear for McL[;][92] the Doctor came Friday alone. The effect in Washington, J. K. found next day, has been very good. The committee will report favorably.[93]

Devoy went on to comment in more detail about a proposal by McGarrity to hire a "big name lawyer" to "state our case," declaring, "That proposition about making Elihu Root, our deadly enemy, our advocate is worthy of a lunatic asylum. I heard of that from Connor in Washington. These butters-in can do us little harm if they don't get a hold of some impulsive man like Joe, who will rush in at a critical moment and upset everything."

The suggestion of hiring a "big name lawyer" to present the case before Congress may not have originated with McGarrity but rather with McGuire. In a handwritten postscript to part of an undated letter from McGuire to Cohalan, McGuire inquires, "Could some international lawyer, for a moderate fee, like Harris Taylor, be secured to argue the Mason Bill?[94] This hearing should be along altogether difficult lines from the other Americans brought in. Also the men from the other side Fawsitt[95] etc. should explain trade & McCartan[96] should be present too I should say for this."[97]

This particular communication is interesting because McGuire discusses the importance of selecting someone to take charge of the information bureau being established by the Friends of Irish Freedom for the benefit of those representing the Republic of Ireland and advocating for Irish independence. It further reveals the low opinion McGuire had of the Irish American members of Congress, as he advised Cohalan that

under the shadow of the Capitol there are said to exist not less than 200 propaganda bureaus. Nine-tenths of their matter finds its way into the waste basket, without being read and only the most able, tactful and disinterested leaders of public opinion can make any headway with our cause.

Hence the vital importance of selecting for this post if he can possibly be secured, a man from active practical political conditions; one whose environment will not excite distrust and suspicion. We have not only to retain the confidence of the Irish race in America, but to win the support of the native American stock, who are in such overwhelming majority in the Senate and House. I need not remind you that the men of Irish blood sent to Congress are inferior in ability, industry and qualities necessary for leadership in Congress.

Their feebleness has a bad effect among the other elements in this field. Due to the world war, Washington has become the news center of America and one of the great publicity centers of the world.

The field of opportunities for this bureau are [*sic*] growing wider by the day. The effort to study the resources of Ireland, what can be done to make her pay her way, the movement to create American-Irish shipping and trade for mutual interests, the educational expansion of the Irish nation cause, make the head of this bureau the most important functionary in the entire movement on this side of the ocean.

I was agreeably surprised at Portsmouth, Norfolk and Richmond the past few days to meet many persons talking over Irish subjects, in spite of the pressing weight of our severe domestic problems.

McGuire, in a letter to Cohalan on December 22 from Atlantic City, New Jersey, confirmed his belief that the hearing was a success and reported on the status of a forthcoming publication in support of Ireland's brief. Writing the judge, he told him,

Mrs. McGuire has been sick here for three weeks but is better and I think will be able to return home in a few days. The editing additions and eliminations to the hearings at Washington are completed. The book will be large but the matter all excellent and few repetitions and extraneous data. I decided best to cut out letters from so many clergymen as they were beginning to come in letters from some Protestant bodies and ministers attacking the Roman Catholic Church which sinister appeal is still very dangerous in parts of the South and West. Some left in imposing list of names of organizations favorable and the few unfavorable as every phase of our case is fully covered in the addresses and "leaves to print" of the speakers at the three sessions. The report of the hearings of which 5000 copies have been ordered by the committee will make the most valuable work on Irish Nationality ever seen in America and promises to become historic.

It was too bad your illness prevented you from coming. Mr. Devoy and myself did not speak but our written thoughts are added here and there to various speeches and notes . . . Mr. Lynch[98] is not much of a speaker and got flustered over some of the committees questions but re-wrote his remarks and will read well in the minutes.

Mr. Lynch is a hard worker and well informed and he done most of the work ably preparing the minutes and every way deserving of great praise. I gave him the services of an efficient stenographer.

Congressman Tom Gallagher of Chicago is the finest Irish-American in Congress. He has been at his office with Lynch and his own secretary every day and until midnight has read over carefully all of the papers . . .

Katherine Hughes was the star for facts and figures and created a profound impression. She must live in libraries, whenever challenged she could fly to Hausards, Childers, Froude old and new histories, reports etc. and when the books were brought down from the Congressional Library she was correct.

Dalton held her to 30 or 40 minutes, if left to herself she would talk 10 hours. She was very helpful in compiling the record but how she does love to talk. I can see why no man has married her. He would get words for soup. But she is a credit to the race.[99]

Turning to the strategy for the future, he advised,

> From now on great tact and strategy must be used and not appear to have the R.C. clergy too strong behind it. The rousing of widespread opposition would be fatal and England knows how to work that game.
>
> All our Bishops should cease attacking the Russian Soviet gov't in their appeals for Ireland. The only government in the world to declare for Irish Freedom has been the Russian Soviets and they may yet get a place at the peace conference and bring up the Irish question. Besides our clergy needlessly offend the Socialist Party. The N.Y. Call for nearly two years was the only daily paper in the U.S. supporting Sinn Fein. Hillquist was the only Mayoralty candidate speaking out for Ireland, likewise London and Berger who won by 7,000 in Wisconsin. In our eagerness to win new friends let us not drive the ones away who stood true in darkest day especially when they are being lied about and oppressed by our common enemy.

As the year 1919 opened, the Irish American leaders planned another Irish Race Convention. At the same time, in Dublin, the victorious Sinn Fein Party set up an independent Irish Parliament called Dáil Éireann. It declared its independence and adopted a constitution. In one of its first acts it designated de Valera, Count Plunkett, and the father of the Sinn Fein movement Arthur Griffith as representatives to the Versailles Peace Conference. The only problem was that they were all imprisoned by the British.[100] De Valera's imprisonment would come to a sudden end on February 3, 1919, when Michael Collins and Harry Boland engineered his escape from Lincoln Prison in Manchester, England.[101] De Valera was ultimately smuggled back into

Dublin, where he spent some time as the elected chairman of the Dáil. In June, however, he decided to travel to America to champion the cause of Irish freedom.[102] His time in the United States would open an irreparable schism in the Irish American leadership as they formed both pro– and anti–de Valera factions.

8

Campaign Manager

On February 24, 1919, at the closing session of the Irish Race Convention held in Philadelphia, Cardinal James Gibbons of Baltimore presented to the convention a resolution calling upon the peace conference at Versailles to allow Ireland self-determination of its own status and inclusion in any League of Nations. The resolution declared that a state of war existed between Britain and Ireland, which brought it within the purview of the peace conference. The convention also pledged to raise $1,000,000 for Ireland within six months. A committee of twenty-four was designated to convey the resolutions to President Wilson. Among the members were Justice Daniel Cohalan and McGuire.[1] The committee went to Washington and the White House to present the resolutions to Wilson but he refused to see them for four days. The president's increasing resistance to meet with the Irish American leaders or to address their concerns caused public opinion to build against him and the League of Nations in the Irish American communities throughout America, and led to the White House's being deluged with telegrams in protest. On March 1, Wilson agreed to meet the committee to hear its requests after a speech he was to deliver in New York City the following week.[2] On March 4, Wilson met with the committee at the Metropolitan Opera House in New York but only after it agreed to exclude Judge Cohalan from the meeting.[3] According to Cohalan's biographer, Wilson's animus toward the judge was a mixture of his resentment at Tammany Hall's opposition to his nomination in 1912 at the Democratic Convention of which Cohalan was a delegate, and his mistaken belief that Cohalan could have curtailed Devoy's editorial attacks on him in the *Gaelic American*.[4]

On March 28, Cohalan announced that three prominent Irish Americans—Frank P. Walsh of New York, Michael J. Ryan of Philadelphia, and former governor of Illinois Edward F. Dunne—would travel to the Versailles peace conference to press the cause of Irish self-determination on behalf of the delegates to the Philadelphia Irish Race Convention.[5] McGuire commented on their selection in a letter to Cohalan two days later from his company office at Norfolk, Virginia, observing,

> The selections you have announced for the Irish Mission will be well received by the country. All are high types of the Irish Race, with creditable records. With a man like Walsh at the head, who in any cause he is interested in is a man of great energy and determination, we may be sure everything that can be done will be done by the three delegates. Greatly do I regret, in common with many others, the political situation in this country which seems to have prevented your acting as a member of this important commission. This I say in a wholly impersonal sense, as is my custom in such matters. But your superior knowledge of the conditions in Ireland and the study you have made of the international problems, with the great knowledge you have of Irish history and the relations of Ireland with England, together with the time spent by you in Ireland in recent years made you logically fitted for the post.
>
> The criticism that I hear of the personnel of the Commission is that all three men are active and ambitious Democrats, and that no Republicans or Protestants were selected and that all three are Roman Catholics. This is the view of some eight or ten Republicans and Protestants whom I have heard comment on the selections. One Republican of considerable standing and a friend of ours complained on the ground that the next Congress is Republican and the treaties must be passed by a Republican congress. However I argued that all this has doubtless been gone into most carefully and that there were cogent and strategic reasons for the selection of these three active

Democratic politicians and Roman Catholics. I presume that you found that the men selected were the best for the job of impressing the President of the United States, and every other consideration should be whistled in the winds, if they can make any headway.

I am leaving for Lillington and Fayetteville, North Carolina where I have some work going on that I am interested in.[6]

During this time, McGuire found himself fielding a request from his old political comrade-in-arms in Syracuse, T. Frank Dolan, for an appearance by Cohalan to speak on the Irish question. In a letter addressed to "My Dear McGuire," Dolan pledged a "subscription of $2,000" for the appearance.[7]

McGuire immediately passed the request along to Cohalan, writing him, "I know you are wanted in a thousand places but there are special reasons why a visit to Syracuse anytime within a month would be very helpful. What a great work you are doing in leading the Irish race in America. There are some fears that you may be sacrificing your health with such tremendous efforts."[8]

In the same letter, McGuire brought the judge up to date on the efforts of the Friends of Irish Freedom to become a presence in the nation's capital, informing him, "I had Miss Hughes change her plans & get into a modern office bldg. in Washington. She will speak at Norfolk tomorrow night where they have a good meeting arranged for her. Enclosed find an interesting letter from a Methodist minister near our work at Lilington, N.C."

Whether the appearance by Cohalan ever occurred is unknown and may well have been subsumed into the excitement caused by de Valera's unexpected arrival in America shortly afterward.

The correspondence between McGuire and Cohalan up to the time of de Valera's arrival reveals a cordial, if not warm, personal relationship, dating back a number of years even prior to Cohalan's elevation to the New York State Supreme Court bench. As early as 1902, McGuire found himself having to beg off a request by Cohalan that he speak to a group in Brooklyn on the Irish issues, explaining that

I should like very much to oblige our friends in Brooklyn, but I am compelled to decline the invitation to speak in Brooklyn on March 9th, owing to the fact that I expect to be absent from this part of the country during the month of March. I have one lung which is not too well and usually I leave for the south or southwest about the latter part of February so as to escape the March wind which is extremely severe in this section of the State. The March winds sweep through these valleys at a terrific rate and I am sure to take a bad cold, which I fear may sometime run into pneumonia, therefore I am compelled to forego the pleasure of speaking to our Brooklyn brothers and comrades.[9]

Moreover, their correspondence touched upon such subjects as referendums conducted on college campuses concerning student opinions on current events. McGuire expressed a dim view of the intelligence of the students, observing, "We talked with some of the boys last night. They are chiefly interested in girls, movies, sports, etc., etc. Might as well, for intelligence, ask a lot of bell boys to vote."[10]

In one letter from Watkins, New York, McGuire gave the judge, a Tammany Hall loyalist, an appraisal of Al Smith's electoral chances in the 1918 gubernatorial election, informing him, "I saw Al Smith here, his campaign has been broken up by the epidemic & he has had no meetings up state. Around here many independents & some Reps have declared for him, but the women are surprisingly independent and, as a rule dry. There seems to be very little interest in politics."[11]

Indeed, the subjects of sickness and health seemed to be a common and recurrent theme in their correspondence. In the same letter, McGuire told him, "Caught a severe cold in Cleveland which fortunately has not turned into influenza & think I will leave here Tuesday for Washington & Norfolk. An old man was digging three graves in the little Catholic cemetery here this A.M. There is much sickness hereabouts. The poor food, substitutes, diets, congested hotels, cars and so many changes in living doubtless make the human system more susceptible to attack."

Three weeks later, in a letter from New Rochelle in which he complimented Cohalan for a eulogy he delivered, he reported, "One of my daughters is getting over grippe. Have lost one nephew and two cousins." This news was leavened somewhat in a postscript in which he returned to the subject of women voters that had been discussed in the October 18 letter, as he informed Cohalan, "P.S. With the servants family we have 5 women voters and myself, some change, all Democrats today."[12]

De Valera arrived in the New York City on June 11, 1919, having been smuggled into the country in the guise of a seaman. There he was met by Harry Boland and Joseph McGarrity. During the next eleven days he held clandestine meetings with various Irish American leaders, including John Devoy and Daniel Cohalan, and visited his mother, who was residing in Rochester, New York. On June 23 he made his first public appearance at a news conference at the Waldorf Astoria in New York.[13] McGuire, in his letter to the *Post-Standard* responding to Bielaski's charges, had intimated that de Valera was one of the "young heroes" he had met "on the platform in Dublin" in 1914 prior to the Rising and who while imprisoned had been elected to office. From the tenor of McGuire's later correspondence, it is likely that he was part of at least some of the meetings held during this initial period.

De Valera's mission had a number of objectives. First and foremost was to advocate for Irish independence, or at least Irish self-determination. The distinction in these positions was nuanced but would take on much significance later in the rift that would ultimately emerge among the leaders. At the time of de Valera's tour, Wilson's League of Nations proposal was before the world and the Dáil had already signaled its intent that it wished to be one of the nations included in the League.[14] Second was to conduct a bond drive to raise money for Ireland.[15] Since the Friends of Irish Freedom were in the process of raising money in the Irish Victory Fund, the prospects must have seemed limitless.[16] Lastly, de Valera was here to ensure that the United States was not wedded to the concept of Ireland's remaining a part of England in the event the League of Nations became a reality.[17]

McGuire took a very hands-on approach to the management of the Washington bureau of the Friends of Irish Freedom, as is reflected in a letter to Cohalan concerning an invitation that Miss Hughes had accepted for de Valera to be entertained by a member of the U.S. Senate, in which he recounted,

I was in Washington two days during this past week and Miss Katherine Hughes had informed me that she had requested Senator Phalen of California to entertain Eamon De Valera at his home while in Washington. I told Miss Hughes that manifestly it was an error of discretion on her part and as a member of the Committee of Twenty-five, that I thought she had made a serious mistake in requesting the Senator to entertain, without reference to the Committee, the leader of the Irish Nation. Miss Hughes showed me a letter from the Senator stating that he would be very glad to entertain Mr. De Valera at his home and would make the proper arrangements for the entertainment. Thereupon I directed Miss Hughes, and she has complied with my request to notify the Senator as tactfully as possibly, that she had been acting without knowledge or authority, that no fixed date had been determined for the occasion of De Valera's visit to Washington and that in all probability he would fine [*sic*] it necessary to maintain his headquarters at some of the leading downtown hotels, where he could be accessible and it would be convenient for visitors to find him, also I told her to thank Senator Phalen for his courtesy, etc. etc., but to withdraw the request. I am sure this action of mine will meet with your entire approval and I have asked Miss Hughes to write you directly on the subject. No doubt she is well meaning but rather carried away by the thought that the Senator has a beautiful home and by that side of Washington, I mean that the social side, whihc [*sic*] is of no interest to the world, and she thinks it is of exaggerated importance.[18]

An interesting feature of this letter is that, although it conveys McGuire's thoughts to Cohalan, initials at the bottom, "G.E.M." reveal that it was prepared by McGuire's daughter Gertrude, who at age twenty-three was beginning to assist her father in his activities.

McGuire continued to keep up a vigorous and spirited correspondence with various members of Congress on the Irish question. In a letter from Senator Charles Thomas of Colorado, the issue of Ireland's recognition was discussed, a discussion that appears to have been the seed of a future public relations disaster that would befall de Valera. In it, Thomas, replying to an argument raised by McGuire, writes,

> You state that you are amazed because I am unable to see that the peoples of the Allies as well as the peoples of the other Central Powers are entitled to have freedom.
>
> I see it clearly. That is not my viewpoint at all. My contention is, and has been, that as the Allies are now treating as a collective body of nations, with the Central Powers as another body of nations, the internal differences—racial or otherwise—should not be brought forward by one of them as against the others at this critical time.
>
> If England should insist, for example before the Peace Conference, that we recognize the distinct rights of Porto Rico or the Philippines to independence, and demand of the Peace Conference that their claims be considered, I am sure that you, as an American citizen, would resent it, whatever your opinion of the right of these peoples to independent government may be.[19]

In rationalizing this position, the senator expressed little sympathy for the Sinn Fein government, observing,

> One nation cannot take such a position toward its allies without expecting and encouraging similar procedure. The result must be a disintegration of the allied forces in the face of a conquered Germany, and you must permit me to say that this is especially true in the case of the so-called Irish Government, representing in a large degree at least, that element which during the war not only sympathized with, but refused to bear arms in behalf of a cause which had we lost it, would have committed Ireland with the rest of the world, to a permanent German domination.

He made it clear that political considerations would not alter his position, declaring, "If, to take this position means the disintegration of the

Democratic party, I am very sorry. If on the other hand, the condition is essential to the continuance of the Democratic party, I am unable to perceive that its days of usefulness are not over." He seemed to have little respect for de Valera and no sympathy for the Fenian movement, observing, "The Fenian revolution is entirely another question, as is the valor of De Valera during the turbulent times in Ireland. So also is the latter's ability or lack of it. I am quite willing to testify to my sympathy for the Irish people hereafter and heretofore when we get this treaty off our hands and the old pre-war relations between the nations constituting the allies shall have been established." He appeared to be stung by criticism contained in their earlier correspondence and closed with what appears to be a veiled criticism of McGuire and the other Irish American leaders, writing,

> The statement that I have turned from my many Irish friends in Colorado, is therefore, your own conclusion and not the fact. If the above statement is not clear, I am unable to make it so.
>
> As far as Germans are concerned, I know those among them who are my friends and who know my position, will continue to be my friends. On the other hand, every naturalized citizen—I care not what his race or nativity—who during the war aided and abetted the German cause by word or deed, should in my judgment be required to give some practical manifestation of his repentance before he is restored to the confidence of his late friends and neighbors. It is a comfort to reflect that although they can be numbered by the thousands, they are a comparatively small segment of the great body of naturalized Americans.

Miss Hughes continued to try McGuire's patience, as he wrote Cohalan,

> I stopped at the Washington headquarters yesterday on the way north, and a live, intelligent man is badly needed to assist Miss Hughes who flutters and flutters and I fear uses up three-quarters of her time in idle chatter, and I have told her so. I told her two weeks ago to cancel the clippings as they are coming in by the pounds

every day, are heaped up on the floor and there are thousands of duplications. With the Press Association taking up De Valera every paper in the country, almost is reporting the dispatches, and the cost, in the next few months will be enormous and without value. I am writing Lynch on the subject to-day and also about some other things down here.

I had a meeting with Mayor Grace,[20] who thinks his chances of re-election are very good.

Over the South there is a decided change for the better in public interest in Ireland, and a couple of good organizers would make considerable headway now in organizing branches of the Friends of Irish Freedom.

I hope that you will be able to get a well deserved rest this summer after the great and noble work of the past year.[21]

His correspondence with and criticism from Senator Thomas seemed to burden him, as he observed in a postscript, "Senator Thomas was a forward man twenty years ago. To-day he is old and evidently without any realization of the changes in the world."

Not long after de Valera's arrival, the decision was made to alter his title from that of chairman of the Dáil to president of Ireland. Two nationwide tours were planned so that de Valera could achieve his aims of raising money and influencing public opinion, which would consume much of the remainder of the year.[22]

McGuire's years of campaigning became invaluable to the success of these trips throughout America, as he threw himself into organizing de Valera's visits. He reported to Cohalan on de Valera's visit to San Francisco, informing him, "A relative of mine in California, sent me an article from the San Francisco Chronocle [sic] which states that De Valera spoke to 500,000 people. This is probably a considerable exaggeration as there is not enough in that vicinity to furnish such a number, but I would not be surprised if the total had actually reached 250,000."[23]

The relative in California was, most likely, his younger sister Elizabeth, who had moved there in 1914. Despite having to leave school prematurely to support the family, McGuire and his younger brother Charles had been successful enough to send their younger brother Edward to Notre Dame University and Elizabeth to its sister school, St. Mary's, in South Bend, Indiana, where they both graduated. Elizabeth had taught briefly in the Syracuse schools before marrying Rubin L. Young, an engineer, and moving across the country.

One of the stops on de Valera's upcoming itinerary that McGuire felt strongly should be included was a speech at the New York State Fair in Syracuse. In a letter to Diarmuid Lynch at the Friends of Irish Freedom office in New York, McGuire advised,

> This is the largest gathering of people in this commonwealth at any one time in the fall of the year. It is a state event where the Governor and many Members of the Legislature are present. I strongly urge Mr. Ryan's recommendation as the presence of our President there is equal to fifty meetings that could be held in New York State outside of New York City. All of the Press Associations are fully represented and doubtless the arrangements could include many notable men and women from all of the sixty counties of the Empire State. Will you please at once have this taken up with the Sub-Committee in charge of the movements of De Valera.[24]

Shortly thereafter Lynch advised McGuire that his request was being forwarded to Harry Boland, along with the committee that would be determining de Valera's itinerary.[25] De Valera's visit to Syracuse would come to pass. On August 28, 1919, he spoke to an audience in McGuire's hometown where he declared that Ireland would accept nothing less than complete independence from Britain.[26]

During this same period, McGuire reported to Cohalan on a perceived change of heart on the part of Senator Thomas, opining, "You notice that my old friend Senator Thomas is beginning to see light in certain directions. He told a friend of ours that my letters were bothering him considerably as he knew I was a Progressive Democrat."[27]

The delegates chosen to attend the peace conference in Versailles returned home after three months believing that it had put the issue of

Irish freedom squarely before the conference.[28] Frank Walsh, a member of the delegation, assailed the proposed treaty establishing the League of Nations during an Irish Victory Fund rally.[29]

In August, McGuire wrote Cohalan from Lake Placid and shared his impressions of de Valera, telling him,

> Pres. De Valera leaves here either Sunday night or early Monday a.m. for Baltimore where the Mayor gives him an official reception at 1 P.M. I talked with him last night for several hours and *more than ever* regard a visit by you as highly important. Have urged him to see you at Westport in his interim after Labor day Sep 1 to 5th or 6th and to make no interfering engagements. A gentle, brave, kindly, noble souled, determined idealist, like Desmonlius, St. Just and the guillotined Girondists who died to make a new World and succeeded but a most difficult man to fit in the most selfish, self centered, materialistic great country in the world—the greatest and most powerful of all nations because of its vastness, resources, *newness* etc. etc. China and India were probably just as good *thousands* of years ago while we marvel when we see *1703* the year of a building at Burlington, N.J. The Washington news dispatches are very encouraging.[30]

Within a week after his first news conference in America, de Valera undertook a month-long, coast-to-coast tour during July 1919, in which he made seventeen speeches.[31] McGuire received reports of its success that he passed on to Cohalan. In a letter from the Raleigh Hotel in Washington, DC, he wrote,

> The four local papers, as well as the Baltimore & Richmond papers of to-day, gave complete accounts of the hearing. Our foes countered by the statement of the President of the American Federation of Labor, the Governor of Maryland and the declaration of Senator Nelson of Minnesota, of whose obligation I warned last night.
>
> Rev. Father McCabe here with me some time this evening. Says De Valera made a truly wonderful speech at Chicago, (following the degree)[32] which appealed to the intellectuals. Several persons here from Richmond Va (Protestants) greatly impressed with De Valera.

Back fire started on Shields—county mass meetings being held demanding his resignation.

Talked with the old man at length today. Do not raise De Valera's hand high and hurt it when you shake hands with him or any other underfed man and speak to him not at him.[33]

In addition to the wildly successful speaking tour, August would bring the news that the Friends of Irish Freedom Victory Fund had brought in $1,005,080.83. This success would lead de Valera to propose a bond drive for Ireland in the amount of $10,000,000.[34] The proposed bond drive met with opposition from Cohalan, a foretaste of disagreement between him and de Valera. Cohalan believed it to be illegal since the United States did not recognize the Republic of Ireland. This issue was resolved, however, when a bond lawyer advised that "bond certificates" rather than bonds be sold. The lawyer was Franklin D. Roosevelt.[35] De Valera turned to Frank P. Walsh, who had served as a delegate to the peace conference, to head the drive. At the same time, an Irish banker named James O'Mara was imported from Ireland to do the actual fund-raising.[36]

As plans for de Valera's second nationwide tour were being made, McGuire found himself more and more involved in setting up the itinerary and events. In a letter from Harry Boland, "Secretary to the President" of Ireland, operating out of the offices of the "Irish Bond Sale Department of the American Commission on Irish Independence," the upcoming tour, the bond sale, and its importance to conditions in Ireland were presented to McGuire. Boland informed him,

I am in receipt of your letter of Sep, 10th. I have written Mr. McGarry of Chicago to the effect that the President only intends to remain two hours in Chicago. This no doubt will please McGarry.

I am sending out today a final notice to the different cities to be visited by the President and the start is fixed at Philadelphia, Tuesday Sept. 22nd. The President has made a change in the scheduled tour. He has decided not to spend so much time in the South and I am sending notices as far as Los Angeles. We can work our way home through the friendly cities of the South.

The details of the Bond Issue are not yet worked out satisfactorily. However, we are hastening slowly and I hope by the end of the week to have final details completed. We have had legal opinion on the Bond Issue and find that while it does not offend Federal law in its original form it might be stopped under the Blue Sky law of the Western States, so it has become necessary to slightly alter the prospectus. We hope to have this completed tomorrow.

You will have noticed within the past few days that the situation in Ireland is very intense. It is quite evident that the British Government hope [*sic*] to provoke us into open insurrection. If we are to prevent this attempt of theirs and hold the country solid as it stands today we will require the wholehearted support of the Irish in America and particularly we must make this Bond drive a huge success as it will give great heart to the people at home and help us to hold our present position until such time as the Republic of Ireland is recognized.

Convey my kindest regards to Mrs. McGuire and family.[37]

Boland's last observation about Britain's intention proved to be prophetic. The following day the British government ordered that Dáil Éireann be disbanded and its members arrested. The move resulted in the birth of the Irish Republican Army, and guerilla warfare broke out in Ireland.[38]

McGuire's organizational talent and energy came into increasing prominence during this period, as is reflected in his almost daily correspondence with Cohalan. On September 17, 1919, he wrote him from Washington, DC:

I spent some time yesterday and today at our headquarters here and they seem to be doing effective work. The book of the hearing has gone up to 25,000 copies, so great is the demand. O'Connell managed to get 20,000 copies printed free, but had to pay $600 for the extra 5,000. I think this money is well spent. The demand for literature is very great and I am inclined to suggest that all Irish literature be handled and sent out from the Washington headquarters. Let the New York headquarters confine itself entirely to the organization of the Friends of Irish Freedom. There could be 5000 branches organized over the United States, if operated intelligently.

The meetings of De Valera are most extraordinary everywhere, in spite of more or less poor management. The American people are largely in favor of Irish Independence and as President of the Irish Republic he is the symbol of the cause and everywhere the multitude gathers to see him. Advantage should be taken of these great demonstrations to organize new branches and special attention should be paid to women, who I notice form the greatest percentage of the visitors to our Washington headquarters.[39]

McGuire was watching the parade of the victorious troops in World War I that morning and shared his thoughts on war with Cohalan:

Pershing's legions are thundering past the hotel today in great invigorating weather. This is the last parade of the great war and let us hope that we should never live to see another. When Pershing reaches 17th Street he returns to the spot where General Grant, 54 years ago, reviewed the 80,000 victorious veterans of the Army of the Republic, which parade lasted two full days. Pershing's division alone lost half as many in casualties as the Union Army lost at the Battle of Gettysburg. Through the streets of Washington are 5-1/2 solid miles of death dealing implements of every conceivable description, from whence it is self-evident that science and chemistry are able to destroy pretty much of the human race if future wars prevail.

We hear that the President intends to discuss Ireland at his San Francisco meeting."

McGuire followed up with a brief note the following day from New Rochelle in which he praised a pamphlet titled "Indictment" being prepared by the Friends of Irish Freedom. He also praised a speech by de Valera criticizing the treaty being advanced by Wilson and approving that the southern portion of de Valera's upcoming tour had been reduced.[40]

In a letter of September 20, he replied to a letter from Cohalan and reported on a meeting with de Valera and others, informing the judge,

I have your letter of the 18th instant, and will see Mr. Gillen this morning at the Waldorf.

President De Valera asked me to see him as soon as possible as I returned from Washington, and I spent some time with him on Thursday. He wanted me to take charge of the Speakers Bureau which would have charge of his meetings, but I explained to him that my occupation kept me away from New York most of the time. He was very persistent however, stating that he was desirous of getting into the hands of the right people south and west, and thought I might be able to make the right connections for him. Finally I told him that I would allow my name to be used on condition that I would not do any clerical work, and that I wanted Moore[41] to help, and it was arranged to ask Mr. Wheeler to do the active work. The president then brought me to Col. P. H. Callahan at room 215, who is in charge of the Bond Drive. And he is probably as good a man as can be obtained, under the circumstances. He was at the head of the Knight's of Columbus War Drive, but through some kind of row he was eliminated before the end of the war, but he likes this sort of work, has been a successful business man at Louisville, does not know much about Ireland, but like many other converts is quite enthusiastic now. In view of the great difficulties confronting the Bond Drive, I think we are fortunate to have him.

The president wanted me to go over with him the subject of appointing a State Chairman in all the states to take charge of the drive. There were present, Callahan, Wals Shannon, McGarrity, Ryan, Martin, and a few others aside from De Valera and Boland.

We held another meeting yesterday, and I had John D. Moore come in as he has considerable knowledge of people over the country. Whether the men selected for the task will accept is another question. They are all being telegraphed and I await their replies with some interest.

The form of the subscription is harmless, it is practically a voluntary subscription; in the event of the British army being withdrawn and a nation established the bond will be paid.

The Brooklyn meeting was a huge success, the Brooklyn papers state the crowd was the largest ever gathered under one roof in the borough. Nothing was said by any of the speakers about the Bond Drive which was a mistake because it was a great audience to whom it would have been explained. We had a very good meeting at New Rochelle on Tuesday evening which I addressed and they have gone over the top here very well, but do not enthuse over the Bond Drive.

You have overworked yourself as I feared you would do and you must let up this fall or you will break down.[42]

Two days later, he again wrote the judge to report on his meeting with Gillen and other matters, informing him,

As you requested I spent some two hours with Martin Gillen of Racine Saturday. He looks like a down town broker or banker, a very alert, cool and decisive man. He is drafting a memo for Col. Callahan of the Bond Drive organization. He has been interested in the Mitchell Wagon and Automobile factories at Racine and what is known as the Gillen Municipal Drive was adopted by the U.S. government in cities for the 2nd Liberty Loan.

Col. Callahan has received a number of acceptances from various men as State chairmen for the drive.

I took hold actively of the Irish World meeting, and all your friends did everything possible to make it the huge success it proved to be. The old hall was crowded, and many were turned away. It was a typical hair-trigger Cooper Union audience, rapid volleying of cheers for four hours. I opened with a short speech, Judge Goff[43] followed for twenty minutes, then came Bourke Cochran,[44] whom I asked to speak for forty minutes and wonder of wonders, with my eyes riveted on him, he did not exceed the limit, which with all of your great influence with him is more than you are able to do, as nearly as I can re-call. I held Frank Walsh back till last, in order to hold the big crowd for De Valera who had three meetings in New Jersey afternoon and evening. Walsh spoke with special reference to labor and the Irish World and on that theme he is most effective.

We had some good singing from professional[s] and a pretty fair orchestra. De Valera got in some time after 11 P.M. and made a nice ten minute speech with one or two stories about Ireland. Boland closed towards midnight in a five minute reminiscent talk with a bit of humour and the band played the soldiers songs and with the audience singing the meeting closed with the Ford family in tears and I helped old Brandon Ford out of the hall, and reached home around 2 A.M.[45]

McGuire continued to defend de Valera and the Irish Republican movement against all critics. In one such instance he had written U.S. Circuit Court Judge Martin Manton of the Second Circuit Court of Appeals, located in New York City, following the judge's speech at Atlantic City, New Jersey, attacking de Valera. In the speech the judge referred to de Valera as a "half Spaniard." Manton wrote him in reply,

I fully appreciate the spirit of your letter. We, in common with so many others, hope for the same result as to the fortunes of Ireland. Our differences are only in the method pursued for its accomplishment. For months I have been unable to see any particular good in the speeches of Mr. De Valera and others in opposition to the League of Nations, and, indeed, I have thought much damage has been done to the cause of Ireland by this opposition. The difficulty is that the faith and hope and confidence of the Irish mind (I speak collectively) are aroused to a high pitch of expectancy by these promises and they are led to believe that there is no hope or solution for Ireland in the League of Nations. In the near future, the League of Nations will become a reality whether or not America becomes a member of the council, and it is my opinion that the one hope for Ireland lies in the presentation of its cause to the League of Nations. When the treaty is approved by the United States Senate, as it will be within the next few months, we can readily appreciate how quickly the Irish mind (I again speak collectively) will find despair—and hope gone. It is this condition that I intended to point out in my speech at Atlantic City. When the case is presented to the League of Nations, those who are now opposing the Treaty of Peace must take back what they have told the Irish mind, namely that there is no hope or consolation for

Ireland, and the difficulty of this position will be—it will be hard to convince the Irish mind that the same men are sincere, for they must take a position inconsistent with their former utterances . . . [46]

Needless to say, it can hardly be gainsaid that the Irish and Irish American leaders had received little encouragement from Wilson, Tumulty, and the others in his administration concerning the future hopes for Irish independence if the League were established. Nonetheless the depth of hostility arrayed against them was evident from the denial Manton next made in his letter: "Speaking of Mr. De Valera, I made no personal attack upon him, and it is untrue that I called him a half-Spaniard. What I said as to him was that he was born in Syracuse of a Spanish father and Irish mother and was educated in a college in Ireland; that it was a good thing to have him arouse sentiment in America for the Irish cause but that it was an unfortunate thing for him to misdirect his energies and misdirect his efforts in his opposition to the League of Nations."

Contrary to his denial, the *New York Times* reported on Manton's speech, and the content of his criticism was far worse than he had claimed. The *Times* reported that he referred to the president of Ireland as a "half Spaniard attempting to mislead the American people" and went on to tell them,

Isn't it a weird and strange spectacle for the well wishers of Ireland to see the course of conduct of the men of Irish birth and Irish extraction in the last few months? A former citizen of Syracuse, born of an Irish mother and a Spanish father, has been heralded as the President of the Republic. He has been permitted to land on our shores and by speech and by conduct make propaganda to arouse Irish sentiment.

What a misfortune it is that, with the privilege accorded him, his energies should be so poorly spent and misdirected. It is well enough to create sentiment for the Irish cause and to keep it going, but to base it on false doctrine is worse than never to have created it. [47]

Manton was wrong about the place of de Valera's birth, perhaps confusing it with McGuire's longest residence, as everyone, including the British, knew he had been born on October 14, 1882, in the Nursery and Child's Hospital in New York City.[48] In one respect, Manton's attack was surprising since he had been the law partner of U.S. congressman Bourke Cochran, a committed Irish Republican. Manton, however, owed his career to Woodrow Wilson, who appointed him to the federal bench in 1916.[49] Thus his attack on de Valera appears to be little more than another case of political loyalty trumping principle. Manton would ultimately resign from the bench in disgrace, be convicted of bribery while he was a judge, and spend nineteen months in a federal prison.

Undaunted by the defeat of the League of Nations treaty in the Senate, Wilson had embarked on a coast-to-coast, whistle-stop campaign during the month of September to rally the American people in support of it. The trip proved to be exhausting, and on the advice of his doctor, Wilson returned to Washington. On the night of October 2, he suffered a massive stroke, which would put an end to the treaty, if not his presidency.[50]

On the eve of de Valera's second tour, McGuire continued to remain deeply involved in making it a success, as well as in making the Friends of Irish Freedom more organizationally efficient.

De Valera was scheduled to speak in St. Louis, Missouri, on October 24, and McGuire was requested to change the date of the visit to the day before in order to accommodate Cardinal Mercier, who wished to be present.[51] Likewise he was to travel to Kansas City, Missouri, on October 26 and was asked to provide "lithographs, clippings or other matter you think would be of assistance in making this meeting a big success."[52] In a letter to Cohalan on October 3, he expressed concern about Diarmuid Lynch, the national secretary of the Friends of Irish Freedom. He opened the letter by sending the judge a corrected itinerary of de Valera's scheduled meeting from October 1 through the 21st and then advised,

> I spent considerable time today at the headquarters and I believe that all work outside of the Friends of Irish Freedom, should be lifted from the shoulders of Mr. Lynch who is overburdened and nervous.

I told Mr. Wheeler that he should take up his headquarters with Col. Callahan and that if he would attach himself to the sale of the bond certificates he would help in relieving Mr. Lynch of a great deal of pressure. The problem of extending the Friends of Irish Freedom is a big one. This is a work which will have to be carried on long after the other diversions have passed. Ireland is not to be free this year or next year, and like John Brown's soul the Irish cause will "go marching on" long after the grass has grown over your grave and mine.[53]

As the treaty embodying the League of Nations came closer for a vote in the U.S. Senate, McGuire stayed abreast of developments and used his considerable contacts to gather political intelligence. On October 6, 1919, he wrote Cohalan,

> At Hamilton where Elihu Root has a home and spends much time, I met some friends who tell me he has sent a letter there in which he says the League of Nations will go through by Nov. 15, without amendments but with some interpretations and reservations which will be accepted abroad and not require returning treaty. The upstate newspapers are nearly a unit for the ramification of the treaty. The circulation of Judge Howards able article would do some good.
>
> Sen. Reid had a very great meeting in Denver Sat. night.[54]

As the St. Louis and Kansas City visits for de Valera drew near, McGuire again turned his attention to the details he thought would maximize their success. This time, it was to make them more ecumenical, as he wrote Cohalan,

> Inclosed please find a letter from O'Neil Ryan.
>
> I have urged him strongly to secure several Protestants, officers or speakers at the St. Louis and Kansas City meetings. There is a great truth in the statement of Dr. Kane, namely, the activity of the clergy at the De Valera meetings make greatly for their success, but there is too much deference to the clerics, as presiding officers, which I know as a man who has traveled everywhere in the west and south, offers the occasion for exhibitions of bigotry and religious prejudices,

> Our own people ought to make a reasonable effort at every meeting of the tour to introduce, if possible, leading personages of every faith or no faith.[55]

In a handwritten postscript, he tried to reinforce this observation by reminding the judge of an incident involving a member of the Senate: "Let no one mistake the effect of Sen. Williams tirade in interior of South, outside of cities. The 'hillbillies' 'wool hats' mountain men, children of Confederates, love to hear the cry 'the Irish or no one else can beat us in a fight.'"

By late October, as the Senate moved toward a vote on the treaty, the intensity of the disagreements among the Irish American members of Congress grew, as was reflected in a letter from McGuire to Cohalan on October 24, 1919, in which he related,

> The common enemy greatly enjoyed the vicious battle between the "two Boston terriers" as I heard one Southern Congressman express it. The South mostly voted for Tague, likewise many others "horrified" over Lomasney disciplining a man over Ireland etc. etc.
>
> It is well the miserable thing is out of the way here as O'Connell[56] has been too much occupied with it and some think has mixed the cause with it. I realize I was his client & he had a duty to perform but the incident is unfortunate.
>
> Fawsitt had to hear a lot of it among some he met and the effect was not inspiring.
>
> O'Connell is doing well and will broaden out where he understands Irish national questions more. To make a man impersonal is difficult and takes time & age.[57]

Opposition to the League of Nations came from wider and more abstract reservations than simply those of the Irish American community. In the U.S. Senate the Republican majority was split into two camps. The "irreconcilables" were completely opposed to the concept out of a sense of historical isolationism, and were headed by Senator William Borah, Republican from Idaho, who also championed Irish self-determination. The second group had reservations but were not ideologically opposed to the concept of such an organization and were headed by the chairman of the Foreign Relations Committee, Senator Henry Cabot Lodge of Massachusetts.[58] On October 27, Senator Borah, in a letter to James McGurrin, the organizer of a rally in opposition to the treaty to be held in New York City, expressed his views on the League, writing,

> The League in its present form is a complete autocracy. At no place and at no time are the people given a voice in this scheme of world peace, and in no way and by no process are the subject people permitted to have a hearing. In addition to being an autocracy it is an autocracy so arranged in its machinery that it may be controlled by European powers and against the only real Republic in existence today.
>
> When this League is organized five dominant powers (an alliance) will dominate and control as subject peoples nearly one half of the inhabitants of the globe. There is not to be found in the covenant a single line or phrase giving these subject peoples a right to be heard as to their independence or their freedom. There is no machinery provided in the covenant by which these subject peoples can set up there [sic] own form of government or be permitted to live their own lives. So far as the terms of the League are concerned these people must live their lives in subjection for all time to come. And we agree to do our part in keeping them in subjection. Ireland, Egypt, Korea, India and all subject peoples alike can find no door or escape from this autocratic machine save that of war with all great powers combined against them.
>
> We were promised a democratic league, a league based upon self determination and the right of the people. But this scheme promulgated by President Wilson was shoved aside at Versailles and a soulless, unconscionable autocracy established. It is at war with every principle of the Magna Carta, the Bill of Rights, the Declaration of Independence, the Constitution of the United States and with the fundamental principles of justice, liberty and freedom. It is a challenge to the first principles of free government and an insult to

liberty loving people everywhere. Let's fight it now and fight it for all time as our fathers fought tyranny and autocracy before. Men who will compromise with such a scheme for the oppression of the masses and for the domination of the few have forgotten the first principles of representative, democratic government. We should raise the banner once and for all. No compromise now or hereafter until the last vestige of this new scheme of autocracy has been wiped out.[59]

On November 14, 1919, McGuire wrote Cohalan from Washington, DC, on a wide variety of subjects including a potential Irish backlash among the electorate. At the outset, he informed him,

In Lynchburg Wednesday, returned here yesterday. Saw M[60] last night. Some of his suggestions are good, others chimeral & to be disregarded. I told him what I would recommend here when I see you in a few days.

I heard in Lynchburg that Gov. Davis is opposed to the League of Nations and might appoint the right man Senator. If so, Virginia will split and may lead the way for a new alignment in the South.

The shipping programme for Queenstown is moving forward although the resignation of Director Rossiter is a loss as he was well informed, able and dependable. Have heard protests from British sources against Consul Fawcitt, but can secure no definite information, am to call at State Dept. again today with Turner.

Some people here are taking comfort from Mass. election as indicating "American feeling towards Irish domination" as one minister said here today. American Patriotic Assts. organizing to defeat Irish Catholics in many places, claiming to have been successful in many places.

In Syracuse all Catholics on Rep. ticket for School Board were defeated by 11,000 while remainder of Rep. ticket won by 6,000 to 10,000.

I notice some element is busy against De Valera in So. Calif.

As you know the important office of Secy. of Commerce is vacant. With the war over this is the most powerful place in the Cabinet and one, where the incumbent could do a vast amount of good to help encourage and develop Irish trade. If a broad farseeing New York or Boston friend could be named great good may follow.[61]

On November 19, the U.S. Senate rejected the League of Nations treaty.[62] With the defeat of the treaty, McGuire's attention turned to other issues. That same day he wrote Cohalan, "'The Freedom of the Seas' is a strong and powerful work and one of the best of your undertakings. A copy ought to be mailed at once to each representative, Senator and Governor *at his home address in his district* as the House has adjourned for ten days. Ask Secy Lynch to do this *now*. The American Merchant Marine legislation comes up next month, of great importance to U.S. & Ireland."[63]

Despite the defeat of the treaty, McGuire feared it was not dead. His fears were fueled by the political intelligence he was gathering, which he shared with Cohalan on November 21:

I met some press men at the Press Club in Washington who have a fairly good line on the leading members of the adm. & their views.

They figure they have 78 or 80 votes for a "mild reservationist treaty" and they will be embodied in an agreed document as soon as the political jockeying is ended and the partisan game is over. Evidently too there are some leading Democrats who, believing they are weak on all other issues, harbor the hope that the Reps support monied interest, press, pulpit, colleges etc. etc. may leave the Rep party & come to their salvation in 1920. They want the Treaty defeated and delayed until the campaign near at hand. This I think explains the statement of Sen. Underwood & of A. Mitchell Palmer,[64] Sen. Owens of Oklahoma wants the president to accept the reservations so as to secure the votes of Sen. Walsh of Mass., Shields and Smith of Geo. They will have the support of the new Va. Sen. Glass whose appointment by the Gov. was a surprise here and a grievous disappointment to the opponents of the League of Nations. Partisan politics and pride of opinion will succumb to powerful pressure. There are only 13 Reps and 2 Democrats, Reed & Gore with the courage to follow the advice and preserve the principles of Washington and Jefferson.

The enemy is checked severely but not routed and our friends are far outnumbered. What I want to urge is increasing vigilance and untiring activity at all points and not to rest in fancied security as a result of the success this week. I notice such disposition in Washington, our friends and press should be warned of the quick revival of all the enemy forces prepared now to know and to meet compromises but always keeping in mind their main objective as Borah & Reed show.

The speeches of Kellogg,[65] Edge[66] and Lenroot[67] are the idle words of political timeservers, the same sinister influences who delivered them into the Senate will hold them unless the fear of political destruction stops their shift.

Am sending you copies of the Manchester Guardian with some very interesting articles on Russia. If printed here the newspapers would be suppressed. There is far more freedom of speech & press in England to-day than in America.[68]

As the year 1919 drew to a close the Irish American and visiting Irish leaders began to look to the presidential election that would be held next November. They clearly viewed it as an opportunity to secure new leadership in the White House and more support in the Senate and House of Representatives. On December 19, McGuire wrote Cohalan two letters. The first involved the electoral prospects in South Dakota, which he analyzed for the judge: "This is the first state to hold primaries which will take place in March."[69]

He went on to recount the votes cast for president in 1916 and governor in 1918, where the Republicans won both races. He then continued, observing,

> With women voting next fall the total will possibly be around 150,000 votes of which more than one-half are normally Republican. There are few Democratic partisans in the state, but a large number of independent farmers who will join the Non-partisan league. I noted that Gerard proposes to attend this primary as an advocate for the League of Nations. There will probably not be more than 20,000 Democrats appear at the primaries, perhaps not

over 15,000 if winter weather interferes. Reed and some other westerners could probably defeat Gerard on the main issue and while the delegation is not important at the National Convention yet the first gun early in the year might reverberate over the country.

S. Dakota is less radical than N. Dakota but is influenced by its neighbor. In 1916 the vote of Wilson was 55, 206, Hughes 53, 147. Last fall Fraser non-partisan league received 54, 917 against Doyle, Democrat 36, 733 and many Republicans voted for Doyle because the non-partisan League had broken up the Republican Party.

The second letter was in response to one in which Cohalan had sent him for his review the results of a special congressional election held in North Carolina. Analyzing this race, he observed,

I thank you for the inclosures although I cannot see any gains. Mr. Moorehead utterly failed in the last week of the campaign in discussing the League of Nations issue on its merits.

It is true that members of the cabinet and Senators Underwood[70] and Overman[71] went into the District to save it, but from all accounts Moorehead relied on the $50,000 slush fund, protective tariff interest and the old reactionary set which once controlled the district and the state.

You must bear in mind that at special election, a relatively small vote is polled compared with a Presidential election. Webb was always from 1000 to 1500 votes stronger than his ticket. Inclosed find list of votes received for his Party for President and for U.S. Senator. You will notice that President Wilson's plurality was only 2800, Senator Overman's 2100. The normal Democratic plurality in the district runs from 1500 to 2000.[72]

Despite the overwhelming success they achieved in their unified effort of defeating Wilson's League of Nations, the next year would tragically be marred by irreparable infighting and political miscalculation on the part of all of the Irish and Irish American leaders.

9

The Mediator

Nineteen twenty was barely a month old when de Valera gave an interview to the British newspaper *Westminster Gazette* concerning Ireland's future relationship to England, in which he suggested that Ireland could enjoy the same status with England that Cuba did with the United States. In the interview he was quoted as saying, "Why doesn't Britain do with Ireland as the United States did with Cuba? Why doesn't Britain declare a Monroe Doctrine for her neighbouring islands? The people of Ireland, so far from objecting, would cooperate with their whole soul."[1]

There can be little doubt that this proposal implies that the question of Irish self-determination could be resolved by much less than independence, indeed, that the Irish people would be satisfied by dominion status within the British Empire. The proposal was not well received in Ireland or the United States.

De Valera sent the Irish envoy Patrick McCartan back to Ireland to calm the waters by explaining to the Irish cabinet that the interview was merely a ploy to initiate negotiations with Britain. While the explanation was not entirely well received, it was accepted, and the cabinet was willing to let the incident die without calling de Valera home. Interestingly in light of events to come, the two Irish Cabinet members that were willing to take de Valera's explanation at face value and end the controversy were Arthur Griffith and Michael Collins.[2]

Tension between de Valera and Cohalan and Devoy had been building throughout the previous year almost from the moment of de Valera's arrival. It had certainly been present from de Valera's announcement of a bond drive that Cohalan had not approved of. It had been fueled by McGarrity's successful motion to have the Friends of Irish Freedom pay $1,515 in expenses for a rally held the previous September to protest the British suppression of the Dáil.[3] Now, de Valera's apparent blunder gave Devoy an opportunity to wage open warfare on him. Unlike the Irish cabinet, there would be no private or quiet discussion of de Valera's ill-conceived interview with the *Westminster Gazette*. Devoy wrote a scathing editorial in the *Gaelic American* in which he pilloried de Valera, writing, "The effect of the publication can easily be foreseen. It opens the way for the discussion of a compromise or a change in objective, while England has her hands on Ireland's throat. It will be hailed in England as an offer of surrender . . . The Britishers will conduct their side of the controversy in the hope of creating cleavage among the Irish forces in Ireland and America. England's only hope of triumphing over Ireland now lies in the position of creating disunion in the Irish ranks."[4]

The editorial led to an exchange of letters between de Valera and Cohalan in which the former accused the latter of being behind Devoy's editorial attack. Cohalan replied that de Valera misconceived the nature of his relationship with Devoy, and while he admired and agreed with him, he did not control him.[5] Cohalan went further and laid out his view of their relationship, writing,

> May I venture to suggest that you labor under a serious misapprehension as to the relations which exist between you and me. I know no reason why you take the trouble to tell me that you can share your responsibility to the Irish people with no one. I would not let you share it with me if you sought to . . . What I have done for the cause of the Independence of the Irish people recently and for many years past, I have done as an American, whose only allegiance is to America, and as one whom the interest and security are ever to be preferred to those of any and all other lands . . . I have no appointment from you or any other spokesman for another country, nor would I under any circumstances accept one . . . Do you really think for a moment that American public opinion will permit any citizen

of another country to interfere as you suggest in American affairs? Do you think that any self-respecting American will permit himself to be used in such a manner by you? If so, I may assure you that you are woefully out of touch with the spirit of the country in which you are sojourning.[6]

One of the only leaders apparently not disturbed by the *Westminster Gazette* interview was McGuire. In a letter to Cohalan on February 8, two days after the interview, McGuire didn't even mention the controversy. Instead, he covered a variety of other topics, informing Cohalan,

Rec'd your good letter & mighty glad to hear of your improvement. Let us hope you will do no out of town work the remainder of this severe winter. You have had a most severe five years since 1914 and the nervous and physical strain added to your daily work is too much to endure. R.R. service is abominable since the war. Not one Pullman car has been built in 2 years. The rails, cars, engines etc., etc. all are badly worn down.

I was laid up 8 days but am out again. Yesterday Sat. I spent most of the day at 411–5th Ave. sending out tels, letters etc. I must confess I was wrong in estimating the results of the Bond Drive. I think I said to you $2,000,000. The writer had not gauged the true effort of the work done in the past few years and I fear missed somewhat the spirit of the people.

Can they but perfect an organization am sure the $10,000,000 can be secured.

One day in Washington I wrote 30 form letters to acquaintances over the country, most of Irish blood but not active, urging subscriptions to the Bond Drive. Was amazed to receive all replies and favorable. A Worcester friend (Marsden) sent me the enclosed a/c of the very wonderful reception to De Valera where 6,000 men marched thru the heavy storm, four meetings. There are 18 or 19 Dem Senators who will stick with the President and oppose Lodge, Gray which with the True Blues ought to block it.[7]

When McGuire did get around to commenting on the interview, he was genuinely unconcerned by it, informing Cohalan,

> I read over twice today the article given to the Westminster Gazette (N.Y. Globe). I can see no serious objections to it on this side and may do some good in Ireland and a little in England where, of course, the govt. will pay no attention to it.
>
> There are many people in U.S. who take Lloyd George's last speech seriously and believe that the control or possession of Ireland is vital to the existence of the Empire. I meet such people everywhere and they are not all of Anglo-Saxon stock.
>
> As I understand it from the enclosed (Springfield Republican) De Valera does not commit himself beyond the principle embodied in the Article from the Treaty of 1903 quoted.
>
> Bryan[8] is really responsible for the Paris Treaty. He swung enough Senators to saddle us with the Philippines and Porto Rico for 20 years.
>
> I was in Cuba in 1897 just before the war & often afterwards. This small state today is probably the wealthiest in the world. Americans claim great credit for saving it and I think people generally like to compare free Cuba with the possibilities of a free Ireland. It's my opinion that the article in question will do little harm and in some quarters good and forgotten in a week.
>
> The serious realities we have are the care, disposition and intelligent accounting and wise expenditure of the large sums of money collected. The whole Irish campaign is to be a protracted one and all hands will have to do some practical thinking along material lines. Very necessary that you talk with Fawcitt who has a critical yet a constructive mind, one of the few.[9]

Whether McGuire planted the seed of the Monroe Doctrine and Cuba analogy cited in the *Westminster Gazette* interview with de Valera may never be known. It does, however, bear some similarity to the analogy being argued in the McGuire–Senator Thomas correspondence of the previous year. In any case, McGarrity was suspicious that "someone had given De Valera the idea, and he not knowing better, and consulting no one, had sponsored it."[10]

Harry Boland confided to his diary that McGuire and others would "stand up with the Chief Out of evil cometh good 'we will clean the Augean stables yet.'"[11]

While the war of words between de Valera, Cohalan, and Devoy continued to escalate, McGuire concentrated on a wide variety of larger issues. On February 18, McGuire was back in Washington and wrote Cohalan,

> Several southern senators tell me in their opinion there is very little likelihood of coming to an agreement on the Treaty. There is much feeling over the summary dismissal of Lansing.[12] The Democratic Senators are in doubt whether the President will sustain them, even though they agree practically on the Lodge reservations.
>
> I called at the headquarters today and was sorry to learn that Capt. O'Connell had gone. He has rendered good service and will be difficult to replace.
>
> Fawcitt arrived this morning and I took him over to the Secretary of Agriculture to see what could be done toward getting the regulations rescinded, governing the importation of Irish Potatoes. For the past seven years, shipments of potatoes from Great Britain, Holland and some other foreign countries have been prohibited on the ground that they are infested with the potato wart. The quarantine is maintained all these years. Although the disease has run out in Ireland. Ordinarily the price of Irish potatoes would be too high to compete with the domestic vegetable, but the advantage to the exchange for an Irish exporter is so great as to render very profitable the sale of potatoes raised in Ireland. There are 6000 tons awaiting export now. The freight ships secured directly for Ireland, go over loaded with American goods, but usually return light and cannot be made to pay permanently unless there are return cargoes, although one ship is on the way, containing a full cargo of Irish dried mackerel, skins and woolens.

Have arranged for Fawcitt to appear next Wednesday at a special hearing of the Federal Horticultural Board, with the hope the quarantine may be lifted.

Every possible aid should be given to the resolution of Senator Jones forbidding the sale of German ships and requiring them to be reconditioned, at the expense of the Government. If the International Mercantile Marine secure a considerable part of this fleet for the Hamburg and Antwerp routes, they will not stop at Cork or Queenstown, but will make South Hampton and Liverpool the ports of call and there will be no passenger ships of American make to be ready for a long time, it will mean that Ireland will have no direct passenger service outside of the single small Cunarder, which will run once a month only, for New York via Londonderry to Glasgow.

I have prepared a memorandum for the Senate Commerce Committee on the great importance to America of direct shipping to Ireland, including passenger service.

Mr. Gillen informs me that the sale of the ships has been called off and the whole subject will be deferred for congressional action. Admiral Benson Retired succeeds Judge Payne, as Chairman of the Shipping Board. This is the Admiral who is said to have told Sims that he had better not let England pull the wool over his eyes; although born in Georgia he is a devout Roman Catholic and in Navy circles is reported to have been a critic of British methods.

The Democrats are exacting considerable comfort from the Missouri election. They claim that is the first district where the League of Nations issue was clearly defined. I think that the influence of Champ Clark was the greatest in holding the District.[13]

It was not until the last paragraph of the letter that he touched on the emerging rift between Cohalan and de Valera, and counseled him, "I hope and trust that you will have seen President De Valera by the time I get home, and have composed all differences. Most unfortunate from every point of view would be the manifestation of a public quarrel. The Catholic Clergy and the Catholic Press of the country would, almost with unanimity, take the side of De Valera. That is the information I get from my own men who have made inquiries. That is only one of a hundred reasons why sacrifices of opinion must be made for the good of Ireland."

On February 22, Boland recorded in his diary, "Spent Sunday with J. K. McGuire discussing the pros and cons of situation and deciding plan of action. The more I see of this scandalous affair the more disgusting it becomes . . . Cohalan an evil for Ireland."[14]

The following day, McGuire wrote Cohalan again, this time from New Rochelle. He dealt exclusively with the trade issues, informing him,

> I missed you Sat. being away, retd, from New Haven. We held a fair meeting here to organize the drive. Am going to Washington and Carney's Point, Del. this A.M. on my own affairs and will talk to Fawcitt before the Horticultural Com. I suspect the Farmers Organizations are behind the embargo on Irish potatoes.
>
> I see no present prospect of Irish passenger service . . . The chaotic conditions of the Shipping Board, divisions of opinion & other things affect our requests.
>
> Mr. Gillen expects to leave with Judge Payne, Major Cushing who succeeds Rossiter & was favorable has resigned. Scott has resigned also Taylor so we will have to begin all over again.
>
> In the meantime while we are drifting England is catching up & passing us in turning out new ships and re-establishing new trade routes, bldg. 40 large dieseled engine motor ships, we have not one and only a single one planned. Europe is dependent on the U.S. & Russia—England is planning for a big trade with Russia and her boats are on the Baltic now while we are "investigating" matters, our exports dropping and a severe period ahead.
>
> Consider the suggestion of having John D. Moore at Washington. Am aware this will excite the opposition. You know his qualities & faults fully. He possesses great energy. I believe would now advise & consult on all matters of policy and where now can you find a man of better equipment.

I shall [say] nothing to him about the suggestion but submit it for consideration. Am not all well yet but getting so—trust you & all are well.[15]

While McGuire was trying to heal the widening breach between de Valera and Cohalan, John Devoy was having none of it. De Valera's biographer described Devoy as a "difficult man,"[16] which seems more than an apt description. In reality, however, he and de Valera were two sides of the same coin. Both were austere, opinionated, and inflexible. Far from shying away from a disagreement with the president of Ireland, Devoy seemed to relish the fight. While McGuire was counseling reapproachment, he was throwing fuel on the fire, as evidenced by a letter to a colleague on February 26, 1920, in which he wrote,

I want no fight if we can avoid it but I would not sacrifice the fundamental principle of the movement even to avoid a fight with him because we'd be worse off in the end than if we fought it out now . . . I am also convinced that he meant to fight us all along and was only waiting for a good opportunity. He selected the wrong time and the wrong issue because his judgment is very poor, but he is filled with the idea (although he says differently) that the great ovations that he got here were for him personally and practically gave him a mandate to do whatever he pleases. His head is turned to a greater extent than any man I have met in more than half a century. Every move he has made or that has been made in his name, in my judgment shows a deliberate intention to attempt to sidetrack both the Clan and the Friends and to substitute for both an organization subject to his orders . . .

His persistent attempts to get us to stop the Victory Fund Drive to make way for the Bonds and Joe's[17] fight to get most of the money sent over was to my mind then, as much as it is to-day, for the purpose of depleting our resources for work here, where the real battle is being fought now, and to cripple us . . .

DV's letter shows how much he has been filled up with misinformation about us here. He has also been informed that [Cohalan]

directed the policy of the G.A.[18] so instead of dealing with me he writes to the man he has been told is my MASTER . . . We cannot deal on his terms WITH A MAN who undertakes to command us.[19]

During this same period McGuire gave Cohalan a glimpse of the toll the dispute was taking on de Valera as he again tried to bring it to a halt. In another letter, which began with a discussion of shipping and trade, he disclosed, "My daughter Gertrude does some work at 411-5th Ave. & takes Pres. De Valera's letters at times. She told her mother that he is very nervous, overworked and needs a rest. I told Fawsitt when he left here to urge him strongly to rest up now, that he is mentally & physically tired and I learned today that he is going away for as long as a week."[20]

With that observation, McGuire went on to plead for an end to the rift: "He should take a month and for the love of Unity as well as liberty let there be peace. All leaders will be damned eternally otherwise, few people will inquire into the causes of the break, they will be judged only by the results."

McGuire subtly tried to bring the combatants together in a common purpose as is revealed in a letter to Cohalan on March 8, from Norfolk, Virginia, in which he wrote,

I was in Baltimore Wednesday, Washington Friday & will be in Petersburg, Va. tomorrow. My son James had the influenza, recovered nearly and I sent him home from the college infirmary where he will get better care. There is much sickness in Washington including the college.[21]

President De Valera was at the Washington headquarters when I called. He is very anxious to have some steps taken to forward the advancement of an amended Mason resolution,[22] in accordance with the enclosed copy or something like it and wanted to suggest a legislative committee to come to Washington & organize for the passage of the same. He suggested the names of Devoy, yourself, Rooney, McGarrity, Kinkaid, Maloney the tobacco man, McGarry, the writer & one or two others. I said the personnel of the committee was ok but the wisest method of selection would be to have the

committee selected by the F.O.I.F Nat Committee. In this suggestion he finally concurred. He thinks a meeting ought to be called at
Washington of many persons interested. Mr. Mason has told us he
would press the resolution which Flood indicated he favored to you.
A Mr. Mulvihill of Pittsburg [*sic*], the Pres., a friend of Ch. Porter,
called on him to say he had seen Porter & that the book of minutes
had been ordered printed. Opinions as to Porters real attitude differ.
The Ulster Irish are numerous in Allegheny Co. and are reported
very active.

    If Pres. Wilson holds out the treaty is dead for this Congress
apparently and all hands can then center on the efforts made in
behalf of this resolution. Since O'Connell left our spacious Washington headquarters look deserted.[23]

De Valera's credibility in the aftermath of the *Westminster Gazette*
interview, perhaps fueled by Devoy's editorial onslaught, continued to
suffer. In addition to McGuire, Harry Boland, de Valera's aide, had to
come to his defense as revealed by a letter to one Lieut. Colonel A. E.
Anderson of New York City, in which Boland tried to put de Valera's
interview in context. Boland wrote the Colonel,

> Am I right in assuming that you honestly believe that President De
> Valera would be so base, that while he is conducting a campaign for
> official recognition and pledging the credit of the Irish people to a
> Bond-certificate Drive for the Irish Republic, that he is at the same
> time prepared to accept anything less than a Republic? It is very easy
> of course on that hypothesis to take sentences out of context and
> base an argument on them
>
>   I approach the question in this way, that English propaganda
> had created an opinion in the world that Ireland's subjection was
> essential to England's security, and this argument has so impressed
> itself on many Americans that they considered it quite reasonable
> of England to secure herself against Irish aggression. To clearly
> demonstrate to the world that it was not her national security that
> England wanted, but her domination, the President dealt with
> this argument in this now famous interview, but the fundamental

principle laid down by the President was that first the independence of Ireland must be acknowledged, and in that hypothesis he gave it as his opinion that the Irish people would not permit herself to be used as a base of attack by a foreign power on England.

I look upon this as an argument based on a hypothesis that is not likely to occur. I for one will be very happy when Ireland's independence is granted, and I confidently leave it in the hands of the Irish people to safeguard, firstly their national honour and, secondly, to enter into such treaties as may be necessary to safeguard her sovereign independence. . . .

I am convinced that the articles criticizing this attitude of the President were not leveled at him in a spirit of fair criticism, and developments since have shown clearly that the "Westminster Gazette" interview was simply an opportunity to show a frame of mind in our friends which I consider deplorable.[24]

Boland would later confide that he was surprised that no one privately came to de Valera in the spirit of friendship, and would try to point out the mistake he had made, rather than assail him publicly.[25]

McGuire grew very pessimistic, if not disgusted, concerning the priorities of the Democratic Party as the election year began to unfold. In a letter to Cohalan on March 11, from Washington, he poured out his frustration, observing,

On the boat coming up were a lot of Democratic politicians on the way to conferences that are being held here this week for the purpose of shaping up delegations from Southern states. One and all talked prohibition and the Volstead law, and nothing else. Most of them were anxious to see the Northern States send solid delegations and elect members to Congress to amend the law so that beer and wine could be sold—all admitting that the Democratic Party is broken to pieces on the Treaty, the League of Nations and the war, and their only hope is to appeal to the appetites of the people in the hope that the oppressions and blunders of the last five years may be forgotten.

I am reminded of a visit to the White House to see President Cleveland early in my first term as Mayor of Syracuse in behalf of a friend whom he appointed Surveyor. We were having some troubles at Syracuse over liquor selling and the President said— "Most people do their thinking through their stomachs and appetites rather than their heads." He referred to the fact that voters in 1888 were diverted from the Tariff and other national questions by the brewers who elected Hill and defeated him after a deal.

The Southern papers announce that Bourke Cockran is to lead the New York delegation to San Francisco where he is to use "his oratorical gifts against Bryan in behalf of the Liquor interests." Not a word about the League of Nations, the Treaty or the Irish Question, according to these veracious chroniclers. There is no doubt whatever but during the last month widespread hostility has been created against the Volstead law and the irritabilities surrounding its enforcement.

The National Committee politicians who are here to-day argue that the Irish, Germans, Italians and other European races want the return of liquor, and all these elements can be made to forget the grievances in the light of the proposed Democratic promise to gradually restore the use and sale of liquor.

The Irish are to forget the Freedom of Ireland; the Germans, the war; and the Italians, the Treaty; the Austrians—their unheeded appeals to prevent their dying from starvation—all in the name of King Booze.

Is it any wonder that Bryan suggests abandoning the Star as a Democratic emblem and substituting a beer barrel?[26]

Despite McGuire's best efforts to restore peace, harmony, and unity to the Irish and Irish American leadership, the conflict between de Valera and Cohalan and Devoy came to a head on March 19, in New York City, at what would come to be known as the "Trial of de Valera."[27] Exactly how the "trial" of de Valera came about is a matter of some dispute. According to Cohalan's biographer, the meeting of approximately one hundred Irish American leaders was called by Cohalan for the purpose of healing the rift.[28] Devoy's biographer has a somewhat different account, reporting that Cohalan and Devoy attempted to lure de Valera to a nonexistent meeting in Chicago so that they could have the group find him "guilty of arrogance and order him transported back to Ireland."[29] However the meeting was to come about, all agree that de Valera was present with Harry Boland and others, not only to defend himself but to point the finger at Cohalan and Devoy and accuse them of attempting to undermine his efforts on behalf of the Republic of Ireland in America. When de Valera threatened to produce a letter written by Devoy substantiating his claim, a call to end the proceedings was heeded. Accounts differ about whether de Valera and Cohalan shook hands at the conclusion of the meeting.[30] Whether McGuire was present at the meeting remains unknown, although given his prominence and involvement in all aspects of de Valera's efforts, it seems likely that he was one of the one hundred or so present. On the other hand, there is no mention of the proceedings in any of his later correspondence, although this could be a result of his relief that the dispute appeared to be resolved and a desire to get on to more substantive matters that would further the cause of Irish freedom. Harry Boland, however, noted in his diary that, in the midst of Devoy's attacks in the *Gaelic American*, McGuire was one of the people who came to de Valera's defense.[31] McGuire's siding with de Valera in his dispute with Devoy and Cohalan may explain the enmity against him that is evident in Devoy's memoir. Interestingly, McGuire's allegiance to de Valera in this dispute did not similarly poison his relationship with Cohalan, and McGuire continued to report and advise on strategy and events in the same warm and cordial manner as he had in the past.

While the Irish were busy fighting among themselves in America, the Irish Volunteers were waging their armed struggle against the British in Ireland. Michael Collins demonstrated an uncanny genius for guerrilla warfare and was systematically assassinating the political hierarchy of the British authorities in Ireland. Unlike Casement and Devoy, he managed to avoid being photographed by the British and was able to travel freely about the countryside directing his troops and squads against the British. The toll and terror became so great that the British government sent their own special forces known as the "Black and Tans" into Ireland.[32]

McGuire's attention was, once again, focused on the arena he knew best, politics. Those who were involved in the Irish independence movement cared not which party the presidential aspirants belonged to so long as they favored Irish independence. Thus Senator Hiram Johnson's victory in the Republican presidential primary in Michigan in early April produced this handwritten postscript to a letter from McGuire to Cohalan dealing with a rally in Carnegie Hall: "Read in Auburn today of Johnson's victory in Michigan. Wish LaFollette could win in Wisconsin now."[33]

Robert La Follette did not disappoint McGuire or the Irish, winning in Wisconsin on the Republican Party ticket and prompting an analysis by McGuire of the implications of his victory and others. In a letter to Cohalan on April 8, he informed him,

Rec'd telegram from Madison Wis. stating that LaFollette ticket has carried Wisconsin by 5,000 & all district candidates but two are elected. Jim Thompson who headed his ticket is to run for Senator against Lenroot next time (1922) and is partly Irish and a firm friend of Ireland. This is a great triumph for LaFollette.

Johnson has A 1 record on League of Nations but he voted for war, Espionage Bill etc. etc. whereas LaFollette was one of the "wilful 12" & fought in & out of the Senate the Espionage acts & sought their repeal faced imprisonment and expulsion from the Senate. Re-election of Socialist Mayor in Milwaukee is significant. The Republican delegates in Northern N.Y. are declaring for Wood. They were backed by groups of manufacturers. I suspect interests who want war with Mexico are behind him. Have sent a good man from our place in Norfolk down to Georgia to help Hoke Smith. Hoover vote extraordinary but result of skillful two year propaganda and distrust of both parties by many well-meaning people. I ran across a lot of farmers yesterday at Sempronious shouting for Hoover "to get rid of both crooked old parties."

Syracuse raised about $25,000 Irish Bond drive, not as much as they should have done in a city of 200,000 including suburbs.[34]

McGuire continued to report on the success of de Valera's speaking engagements around the country, writing Cohalan,

The first of the Southern meetings of De Valera held at Norfolk was a great success. We had delegations come in from Portsmouth, Hampton, Phoebus, Newport News from any shipyards & the Armory was full three-fourths Protestants. De Valera placing wreaths on Southern monuments, over graves of noted dead had good effect.

As you have perhaps heard Charleston, S.C. was a big affair. Mayor Grace turned out a special edition of his paper, the most important feat for Ireland of any daily I can ever recall. Must have cost him several thousand dollars.

Charlotte, N.C. was hostile as I wrote you it would be. Bigotry directed at Catholics runs high there. I have seen mill hands stone Catholic boys passing the mills.

The Southern press is giving much space to the "invasion." New Orleans Sunday next will do well although the French and Italians are far more numerous than Irish now.

I hope Bryan will defeat Hitchcock in Nebraska although the belief prevails here that Bryan will lose on the Prohibition issue.[35]

In Britain, the success of the bond drive and de Valera's triumphal tours of the United States began to raise concerns in the British Parliament. Following de Valera's stop in New Orleans, British official were repeatedly questioned in the House of Commons about whether the bond drive and the receptions de Valera was receiving didn't constitute "unfriendly acts" on the part of the United States. At one point de Valera was referred to as "this outlaw" and his visit to New Orleans as a "deliberate insult by a friendly power." Officials responded that they did not believe de Valera's successes represented the feelings of the U.S. government and further announced that Prime Minister David Lloyd George would ignore any resolutions by Congress concerning Irish independence.[36]

McGuire also kept his attention focused on shipping and trade issues during this period. He received a letter from the Irish delegation to America in which they reported,

We have just had a conversation with our friend, Frederick C. Howe, former Commissioner of Immigration, New York City . . . and he gives us some information and urges us to carry the same to you at once.

He tells us that the U.S. Shipping Board is "lousy with British Agents," and he fears that some morning your Irish commission may wake up and find that the vessels which are used to establish trade between America and Ireland, which you have mentioned in your conversation to us, have been taken over by British interests, and you will find your enterprise balked.

Mr. Howe was very urgent in this matter, and said that the danger to Irish interests in this situation could not possibly be over emphasized.

This information is pretty direct, and this matter was spoken of as having just reached Mr. Howe.

We trust this may help you in meeting the exigencies of the situation.[37]

This letter prompted McGuire to write Cohalan two days later from Philadelphia, telling him,

I expected to see you yesterday but found you were away.

Some 5 or 6 weeks ago Martin J. Gillen was nominated for member of the U.S. Shipping Board, and has not been confirmed. I have not seen him recently but I am told some powerful British influences do not want him in. Despite certain peculiarities which make him enemies he is determined to build a great merchant marine and include direct shipping to Ireland and thence to the continent.

I suggest that you say to Sen. Borah that those of us who observe his work have confidence in his stand on American interests. Senator Jones is Chairman of the Commerce Committee and a Progressive

Republican. Gillen is a Republican (Racine, Wis.) and named to fill
a Rep vacancy. There is some opposition to him in shipping circles.
At present he is advisor to the Chairman and his rejection would
not be well for the country now.[38]

As the two major political parties' conventions neared, both Cohalan and de Valera seized upon a common strategy to try and obtain
recognition for Ireland. Unfortunately their plans had a subtle distinction from each other and the two sides wound up working at cross-
purposes from each other, both ending in failure. Cohalan endeavored
to have a plank inserted into the Republican Party platform in which
the Republicans committed to the principle of self-determination for
Ireland. Cohalan's plank was approved by the Republican Party Platform Committee on June 9, at a meeting in Chicago, by a vote of 7–6.
The approval of the Platform Committee was something of a surprise,
since a watered-down version of the Mason bill, "expressing sympathy for the Irish people," had been defeated in late May. De Valera,
however, repudiated Cohalan's proposal and insisted that the plank
encompass nothing less than recognition of the Republic of Ireland.
As a result of the repudiation, the plank supporting self-determination
was withdrawn and the Republican Party took no position on the Irish
question going into the fall campaign. Undaunted by his experience
in Chicago, de Valera went to the Democratic Party Convention later
that month in San Francisco and tried to have the Democrats include
a plank in the party platform recognizing the Republic. This proposed
plank too was defeated.[39] While de Valera's foray directly into American politics inspired both criticism and recriminations, McGuire,
perhaps the most politically savvy of the lot, had never believed that
the mission to insert any plank favorable to Irish independence into
either party platform would be successful. In early June he had written Cohalan from Washington, DC, reminding him of a view he had
expressed several months before:

I wrote you several months ago that I had been informed that the
Chairman of the Rep. Nat. Committee and other leaders, including

Mills[40] & Parsons[41] of N.Y. had advised the House leaders to soft pedal or stop all Irish resolutions.

Since then the question has been one of battledove and shuttlecock between both parties. This I had tried to point out to the President but with no success. Mason is sincere but not the man in the House, to further any important resolution of that kind. The war reactionaries have not swung far enough to give him support in the Rep. party, they will come in time.

Porter and Gillette[42] were crude in their methods, hence the Democrats who are friendly, are jubilant over the unexpected way the Reps. have been outplayed on the Irish issue.

In the closing days of Congress in a Pres. year, there is nothing but petty partisanship and log rolling. The fate of Ireland is far from their thoughts.[43]

Following the debacle in Chicago but prior to the San Francisco convention, McGuire wrote Cohalan again, and this letter, although containing a kernel of optimism, inspires little hope of a resounding victory on the issue:

Several months back in one of my letters to you I said Big Business would select two-thirds of the delegates to the Rep. Convention and would nominate Lowden[44] or Harding. They would prefer Lowden as more capable but Harding "would stand unhitched."

From N.Y., Pa., New England, leading manufacturers, munition makers etc. were chosen as delegates for this purpose. I said to you the makeup of the convention would be the most reactionary in history. The platform is a fraud, a play of artful dodging in words. Banking on the weakness and mistakes of the President they assume the public is only interested in discrediting the Administration.

The newspapers have various headlines. "Irish Freedom Refused" "De Valera Walsh Cohalan Rebuked" etc. etc. not much detail. I was in Washington the last 3 days of the convention & yesterday rode around seeing a lot of Democrats to note what they think.

They are chortling with glee over the refusal of the Rep. Party to recognize Ireland. I was told that the failure in part is attributed to divisions of the leaders and lack of harmony. An Irish resolution of some sort is to be passed at San Francisco. The Rep. Party has ignored the Irish race believing the feeling against the Dem. Party is all sufficient and they are not specially needed. The treaty is far more important but not many people understand that plank as each faction in Senate is "satisfied." But the Irish friends who are watching Ireland daily do know that Ireland got it in the neck in Chicago. Elihu Root appears to have fathered the Treaty plank. Mills in his speech said "not a line had been changed from Mr. Root etc." Mr. Root is on the other side shaping up a treaty deal doubtless, in anticipation of a new Senate and Harding & Coolidge.

Washington opinion is to the effect that Mr. McAdoo[45] will be nominated, treaty plank approved with mild reservations & a big fight over "wine & beer." The Rep. Convention has brought hope to the Democrats.

I have met Mr. Harding several times, once at Marion[46]— genial, kindly, spread eagle, ultra-conservative light for these times. The best Rep. would have been Knox.[47]

McGuire was completely pessimistic about the Democratic Party platform's containing any plank favorable to Ireland two weeks prior to the convention opening, as he wrote Cohalan,

Virginia Democrats whom I have met feel that in view of the failure of the Republican party to make any reference to Ireland the Democratic convention ought to follow suit and one expressed it "Get the whole Irish business out of American politics." The Democratic politicians in southern Virginia are greatly relieved over the rejection of the Irish plan in Chicago. Local friends here and at Portsmouth, whom I met at a meeting last night are greatly chagrinned [*sic*] over the outcome and are concerned the movement of Irish Democrats to the Republican party has been arrested.

There is no longer any interest in the League of Nations, most people considering, perhaps unwisely, that the treaty is dead. Public interest, at least as I see it, is confined to the subject of high rents, scarcity of houses, food, clothing and taxes, beer & wine.

I hope you are well and get a good rest this summer.[48]

An interesting feature of this particular letter, aside from the fact that McGuire was in Virginia, is that it is on the letterhead of "McGuire Company General Contractors and Engineers." The stationary identifies McGuire as president of the company and his brother-in-law, Frank J. McGuire, Frances's brother, as vice president. Moreover it lists its principal address at 110 W. 40th Street with offices in New York; Syracuse; Norfolk, Virginia; and Lilington, North Carolina. Clearly he was expanding his business interests and continuing to provide opportunities for relatives.

Despite their differences over de Valera, McGuire continued to try and maintain cordial relations with the judge. He sent him a copy of Champ Clark's memoir with his own observations about it. Clark, the Senate minority leader and a Democrat from Missouri, had been a contender for the 1912 Democratic nomination for president, losing it to Wilson. Reviewing the work for Cohalan, McGuire observed,

> With my compliments am presenting you with a set of Champ Clark's new book. Of course it does not rank with Blaine's or Butters or compared with the vivid style of Waterson or John Sherman's book of memoirs. They lived in more stirring political times following the Civil War & reconstruction. / Then too Clark's party was mostly out of power since 1860 and his defeat in 1912 embitters him too deeply and he does not write much on events since 1912 other than to describe bitterly in the closing chapters of the last vol. the alleged treachery and cruelty of Bryan at Baltimore. But there are very many interesting reminiscences throughout the book—of more value in the 2nd Vol.
>
> His defeat in 1912 changed, probably, the fate of the world. He was one of the fifty in Congress who voted against the war, he would have striven for a settlement with Germany and would have led a less isolated life than President Wilson and met more people.

Edward G. Riggs, who is with R.R., was for 30 years political writer for The Sun. He wrote The Spur which I will send you,
superb English. Note the enclosed letter, reference to Blaine &
Hewitt amusing.[49]

The ongoing feud between de Valera, supported by McGarrity,
and Cohalan and Devoy, which was being conducted through their
respective weekly newspapers and in meetings of the Friends of Irish
Freedom, continued unabated. In the aftermath of the Republican Convention, Cohalan convened a meeting of the organization's
national council that adopted a report criticizing de Valera.[50] The
dispute was taking a toll on the spirit and enthusiasm of the Irish
American community elsewhere in the country, as evidenced by a letter McGuire received in early July from O'Neill Ryan, an attorney in
St. Louis. In it, Ryan wrote,

I am in conference here in my office with some of our friends . . .
with reference to the controversy that is going on in the East, of
which we know only through the Gaelic American, Irish World and
Irish Press, and which is having a very markedly bad effect on the
spirit here. None of us have heard anything whatever from the East,
except what we get via these newspapers, except that I had a communication from the Central Council of Irish County Associations,
Boston, Massachusetts, signed By John J. Foley, President, and others dated June 23, which I answered on July 1, and both letter and
answer I enclose with the request that you return them to me with
your answer to this letter.

It is needless to say to you what the effect generally must be on
this very bitter and unfortunate newspaper controversy upon the
rank and file throughout the country and upon people who generally sympathize with the movement. We are agreed that it may be
possible for you to do something to bring the parties together that
is, the leaders or the most important ones on either side, so that they
may personally thresh out their differences, as they did on March 19
last at the Conference held in the Park Avenue Hotel, at which Mr.
Michael J. Ryan presided. You and I know by long experience how

often men, if they are brought together and get in personal contact, can better hope to adjust their differences than if they are at long range and firing epithetical bullets through the press.

I have the greatest confidence in your judgment and what is just as important at this time in your discretion and tact. You are personally known to all these men and I am taking it for granted that you are in a position where, not having become party to either side of this disagreement, and having the confidence and respect of both, your efforts to bring about a conference will probably be more effective than any person of whom I can think. Your name has not appeared in connection with any of the meetings so far as I have read reports thereof, and hence my assumption that you are free to make the effort to bring the parties together.

Meanwhile, if you do see the way clear to do this, if it would be possible to have the newspaper controversy stopped until the conference can be held it would be highly advisable. It is not unlikely that you have thought over these matters, because I know how deeply you feel on the question of the success of this movement, in the progress of which so far you have borne so conspicuous, honorable and effective a part. I nevertheless feel that I should write you on the subject and we are all agreed in the sentiments I am expressing as my friends are sitting here while I dictate this letter.

I have not heard from Devoy in many moons and nothing from Cohalan since he advised me of the matters that occurred preliminary to the March 19th conference, sending me, as he did, copies of the letters that passed between him and President De Valera in February.

I have been ordered by my doctor to go to the West and camp out, etc. In other words "hit the trail" in the Rockies, and will probably take one of my sons and start in a week or two. The order is imperative and I have no choice but to obey. It is a good deal akin to the outing that you gave James, and while I have not his youth and vigor to call to my aid, I hope that at least measurably as good results to me will follow. I hope that he is getting along to your entire satisfaction at the Naval Academy.[51]

On July 21, Boland again recorded in his diary a meeting he had with McGuire in New Rochelle. In this entry he reported on the disagreement the two were having with him about instructions and proposals he was receiving from Ireland concerning a reorganization of Clan-na-Gael because of Cohalan's and Devoy's attacks on de Valera. Boland noted, "I fear serious opposition from Clan in our efforts to secure organization controlled from home, and decided in all matters of policy from home."[52]

While de Valera and Cohalan and Devoy continued to point fingers and blame each other for failing to get either major party to include Irish self-determination or recognition of the Republic of Ireland in its platform, they did meet with limited success in getting the New York State Democratic Party to include recognition of the Republic in its platform for the statewide elections that fall.[53] McGuire, however, was not at Saratoga for the state convention. Rather, he was in Montreal attending the Imperial Press Convention and monitoring British propaganda on the Irish issue. He reported to Cohalan,

On the first page of the Montreal Star yesterday appeared two leading articles enclosed, an art in British propaganda.

The Imperial Press Convention is here, newspaper editors from London to S. Africa. And not the least important are the American guests of the hands across the sea movement.

John R. Rathom of Providence Journal

C. H. K. Curtis owner of the Phil. Ledger Sat. Evening Post

M.E. Stone head Ass. Press

Ogden Mills N.Y. Tribune & others

This is part of the great Lord Harmsworth–Lord Burnham world wide press move. And at night the motion pictures do their part for the edification of millions. Right alongside of the convention story is the De Valera article designed to cast ridicule on the cause and read at the right moment by the hundreds of imperial newspaper men to the injury of Ireland. Last night I dropped into the hall after the dinner to listen to the speaking. Some of the quotations

"Sinn Fein and Bolshevism are dead in the U.S."

"The future is with the U.S. & Britain as allies."

John R. Rathom, who tried hard to have me locked up for the war, and did succeed in having me arrested temporarily & wanted you put away, rec'd a big reception. Enclosed find part of his speech.

The U.S. Shipping Board boats are landing here empty from Europe & are eating their heads off waiting for cargoes. The Old Dominion Ship Co. here failed yesterday (3000 men) they owe me some money for equipment sold them. And I suspect the boom is breaking in parts.[54]

McGuire's reference to Rathom's trying to have him locked up and succeeding in having him temporarily arrested is a hard one to fathom. Other than Bielaski's investigation into his wartime propaganda efforts and Roosevelt's advocating the internment of Irish American leaders, there is no record of McGuire's ever being taken into custody in connection with these issues.

McGuire was a keen student of propaganda and had come to appreciate the power that motion pictures could play in furthering Irish propaganda. Earlier in the year he had received an eleven-page abstract of a proposed movie script written by one Padraic Colum of Cos Cob, Connecticut, who was seeking financial and industry backing for the movie. The plot involved a romantic drama in which a young American travels to Ireland and falls in love with an Irish girl who is also being sought by an English officer. As the plot progresses she involves him in delivering arms on his yacht to the Irish Volunteers, which aids in the liberation of Ireland. In his letter to McGuire, Colum writes,

> I have not yet been able to find the extended scenario I made originally of the Movie. It should have been in a box of papers that has come to me from Chicago, but I have failed to find it there. I can make the extended scenario over again, but I am still hoping the original will turn up.
>
> I am sending you an outline of it, and I should like to let the President see it, as not finding the original, I have not sent him any.

You will understand that a great deal that is interesting and important does not appear in the short abstract—it is a mere outline of the story.

When you are in town again I want you to have a conference with a friend of mine, a Mr. Wilton Barrett, who is on the Board of Censorship of the Movies. Mr. Barrett has a great deal of experience in the Movie World, and it is his opinion that we could get Mr. Powers, who is Irish, and belongs to one of the great producing syndicates to take it up, and put if necessary $100,000 in it. Mr. Barrett has an approach to Mr. Powers. As I said before, I should like very much if you would join me in a conference with Mr. Barrett.

Of course, when it comes down to the actual production there will be alterations in the scenario and a great deal of new material will be brought in.[55]

The various meetings proposed by Colum apparently did not come to fruition since McGuire received a letter from one W. D. McGuire of the National Board of Review of Motion Pictures, apparently the "Board of Censorship" alluded to by Colum, two months later, in which the writer brought McGuire up to date:

As you know I have been in consultation with Mr. Michael Doherty of New Rochelle, and my friend, Patrick Powers, relative to the production of an Irish propaganda motion picture. I came back from Cleveland hoping that I would find a conference had been arranged but unfortunately a telegram which Mr. Doherty had sent me had miscarried.

I am now enclosing an outline of an Irish story written by Padrick Colum, the Irish dramatist. To my mind it needs to be built up considerably towards the end, but this can easily be accomplished giving the story the proper dramatic appeal which will drive home the argument.

I have been with the National board as its Secretary for over ten years and realize the value of pictures of this type in reaching the people and emotionalizing the various subjects. Unquestionably, a fine Irish picture can be made from Mr. Colum's story with some slight revision and as I said building up the dramatic element. I think you will recognize the sincerity of the atmosphere appearing in the story.

I had planned to return to Cleveland Wednesday or Thursday night. Mr. Doherty tells me that you expect to be back in New York on either Thursday or Friday. I will be glad to stay over if we can arrange a conference with the President either Thursday or Friday. I shall be at my home in Scarsdale, New York, which is just outside of New York City, on Wednesday evening after 7 p.m.; won't you get me the telephone from Washington so that, if possible, we can arrange matters. I would be willing to stay over until Saturday if necessary to get things started, but I would like very much to get out Saturday at the latest, but must know at the earliest possible moment so that I can wire my wife in Cleveland about my plans.[56]

It would appear that the proposed conference did not take place, since four days later McGuire, in a letter from Norfolk, Virginia, forwarded the outline of the movie to de Valera's secretary, Miss Katherine O'Connell, with a request that she give it to de Valera. He advised her that W. D. McGuire would like to have de Valera meet with Powers at a later date.[57] While nothing more appears to have occurred concerning the production of the movie, it is clear that McGuire was cognizant of how powerful propaganda movies could be, particularly since the British were already utilizing them.

McGuire continued to provide his political insight to Cohalan, writing him from Montreal, where he was still at the Imperial Press Convention, about an idea he had discussed with John D. Moore:

John D. Moore saw me recently and had a good argument urging that the Dem. Organization in New York and other cities nominate some known advocates of Irish Independence for Congress this fall who would honestly & actively support the cause in the House. Outside of Smith there is no one in the New York delegation who counts. I am writing C. F. Murphy today to that effect. Perhaps it is too late & the present incumbents are to be re-nominated but the slate could be changed in several districts. District leaders whom I have met think that Cox & wet[58] will give them at least 80,000 plurality in New York City & insure their judges & representatives. They are mistaken & resting in fancied security. There is no diminishment in the Rep. trend as far as I can observe and I see & hear from many people.

The feeling over the League of Nations and Ireland has not died out although the politicians think the divisions in our circles have nullified the fears of the "Irish vote." We ought to have at least a few good & true men in the House who can urge the other weak ones. Moore himself would make a useful member. The real work is done in committee and he is tireless & energetic.

Cockran, great orator, was a practical failure in Congress. He would talk on occasion but not work on a committee, hence his name was not identified with legislation or constructive work. Most all of our "90 men of Irish blood" are poor sticks & the least influential 90 in the House.[59]

The following day he wrote Cohalan again from the conference, ostensibly returning to the issue of British propaganda but which was a much more subtle plea for reconciliation with de Valera and company:

Am sending you under separate cover a lot of Canadian papers giving the English a/c of the alleged split in U.S.—you will see they only use the matter now to injure the movement with more than a hint that the fight is over money & politics.

A friend, Maitland, introduced me last evening to Sir Gilbert Parker & Lord Burnham leading lights of the propaganda. Neither would say much about Ireland beyond the view that you are already familiar with—their special aim here is to bind the imperial ties closer and increase trade with England.

I met some workmen at the Vickers ship yard who were strong for the Irish Republic, also some R.R. workers, constituents of Dan Gallery M.P. St. Anns division.

They are praying for unity & harmony in U.S. & having a hard time here in the face of diminishing numbers of our race.

Montreal & suburbs now has 800,000 pop. About all the many steamers I noticed loading on the wonderful harbor piers were British.

Montreal is the second largest port in the new world, manifesting greater enterprise & more improvements than N.Y. & much cheaper shipping.[60]

Eight days later, on August 12, from Albany, he tried again using a different tactic:

They will not consider Moore or "any other Irish agitator."[61] Nearly 10,000 A.P.A. votes helped to defeat Gore in Oklahoma because of his Irish stand in Senate while many Irish in the oil country & OK. City worked against him. The Missouri result in both parties is a disgrace to us. Not a man of parts of our race on either side is to be nominated for any important office in the land in 1920. This I predicted to you in a letter six months ago. While we are fighting among ourselves the old party machines note the divisions and have reverted to their old feelings of contemptuous indifference. Angling for the "Irish vote" is put over for a season.[62]

While McGuire concentrated most of his effort at brokering an agreement between the warring factions on Cohalan, he was not afraid to try with Devoy too. In a letter to Devoy dated August 17, 1920, he implored him,

The action taken last evening was most necessary to either avert or prevent a split which would cut off the old organization from the revolution and soon destroy it, hasten the end of the Gaelic American and shorten your own life under the strain of a deadly and useless struggle, falsely condemned as a traitor in Ireland while misunderstood and abused in this country. The writer in the long meeting with you on July 30th, noted many signs of the effect of more than worry, the heart-breaking agony from which you are suffering in a quarrel among patriots which is becoming a personal feud. The race on the pinnacle of unity in Ireland, divided in America at such a time as this, would see your hopes of sixty years turned into ashes of the old organization which you built up and maintained by a life-time of sacrifices, was permitted to be cut down by severing it from Ireland and pronouncing it Outlaw and an enemy to the Republic. No defense of "Americanism" would save it from the execration in the pages of Irish history and often the penalties of calumnies in history are heavy

The writer detached from the activities of meetings and discussions but familiar with the movement and the personalities on both sides, realizing the misery of factional strife after 30 years, while admiring and appreciating the vast and invaluable labors of Justice Cohalan in constructing the great movement and the high standing his intellect and energy has given in—for he has given the best in him to this cause and despite the deep affection I hold for you, always manifested not to cause you pain but in the end to help you, was compelled to ask you on my own responsibility to make sacrifices of your own views in the name of Irish solidarity. I consulted no one but yourself and our colleagues and the resolutions met half way the wishes of the Envoy and satisfied him. Some friend had to begin this and some true men like our colleagues had to pave the way for a re-union on a larger field where I am hopeful of witnessing the last act of what has been a sorrowful tragedy where the President and our great friend Justice Cohalan will part brothers who for some months had become estranged through misunderstandings.[63]

Two days later McGuire wrote to Cohalan recounting his meeting of July 30 with Devoy and touching upon some of the same themes in seeking to effect a reunification of the factions. In the letter, from Norfolk, Virginia, he writes,

I had expected to leave for Westport tonight and spend the day there but am obliged to return to Paterson and now I find some relatives are on the way from Norfolk and I shall have to look after them, my family being away and I will not be able to make Westport for four or five days as things now stand today. But you will see two men, in the meantime, who will have all papers & are best able to familiarize you with the discussions and the compromises agreed to. For several months I have been receiving many letters urging the importance of making further efforts to effect reconciliations and, if possible, eliminate much of the unhappy press controversies full of hates and bitterness of spirit. I was especially interested in what our friends at Syracuse, Norfolk, Portsmouth, Richmond, Utica, Scranton etc., etc. had to say to me and some letters from old friends in the movement like the one enclosed from O'Neill Ryan with whom I made addresses for Ireland in the West 30 years ago. I have also heard that his physical sufferings are increased by the worriment over the division. More than all though was I impressed by seven hours with John Devoy July 30 where in addition to old age I could see the heart of the great veteran was breaking and I resolved to do my utmost in a final effort to compose the differences as far as they could & make every sacrifice possible.

All Irish quarrels start over Issues or Principles or Methods but invariably wind up in Personalities where the vilest epithets & calumnies are uttered & the character of men aspersed or destroyed. The vile talk now going on over the country beggars description and the morale is very seriously affected. As the President is said to be leaving the country this fall the wisest plan will be to accept the proposals in good faith and your leadership in the F.O.I.F. will carry the ideas through in different form but effectively & no one but you can do this invaluable service.

Boland, working under great difficulties, made a lasting & most favorable impression on all present. His review of the conditions in his country and his give & take style, running all the gamut of Irish emotions and the evidence of the real fighting man that enkindles the spirit of our people, the human side—all in all profoundly affected those present. He has grown greatly in a year. Revolution is the only process by which such types are suddenly developed.

It looks now as though Ireland as an issue will not be an important factor in the national campaign here. If so, with Congress not in session and the new Congress not to meet until a year from December, unless called in extra session the danger is remote of internecine strife among our friends over the election. President De Valera has not consulted me as to his plan of asking the State Dept. to recognize the I.R.[64] But I should say, as long as he is here he is eminently the proper person to present the application with what help he can secure. The main thing that most all the friends of Ireland want is some semblance of Unity here while the bloody work is going on in Ireland & the next year Ireland seems likely to be the center of world interest, resisting coercion, especially if the wars in the east are settled.

You have made many sacrifices before & you must make them again. De Valera is the only one whom revolutionary, cleric, nationalist labor agrees on and regardless of temperament etc., etc., no effort should be spared to save the organizations here for useful work.[65]

The "proposal" and "resolution" that McGuire alluded to in his letters to Devoy and Cohalan are a matter of some historical dispute. Devoy's biographer describes a meeting in New York City at which there was to be a "tentative peace treaty" in which Devoy would publicly withdraw a charge that he had made in the *Gaelic American* that de Valera had misused funds at the Republican Convention in Chicago.[66] Cohalan's biographer alludes to a "truce" resulting from a meeting of the two sides and contends that de Valera and Boland never intended to keep it.[67] Michael Doorley, in his history of the Friends of Irish Freedom, contends that it was a wholesale restructuring of the organization that would have moved its center of power away from Cohalan in New York City to Detroit.[68] The most comprehensive discussion of the terms of the truce were disclosed by Harry Boland in a conference on the relations between the Irish Republican Brotherhood and Clan-na-Gael, held in New York City on March 20, 1921, at which Boland told the group that the agreement was as follows:

1. That on all subjects regarding the policy and interests of the Irish Republic the wishes of the President shall be respected and followed; that where the differences arise the final decision on such matters shall rest with the President to whom we pledge the support of the organization.

2. That the chairman appoint a committee to study out and submit plans to extend the active work on the part of this organization along the lines directed by the Envoy from Ireland.

3. That this organization hereby declares its opposition to all further newspaper controversies on the alleged differences existing between the President and the leaders of the Irish organizations in America; that in so far as we can influence all such newspapers to silence it shall be done.

4. That a committee of two of this organization be sent to Ireland.

5. That a committee of three be selected from this body to advise with the JC as to the accompanying resolutions and as to our opinions and desire to bring together in unity all elements concerned in close co-ordination and a working agreement.

6. That in our presence it was mutually agreed between Envoy Boland and John Devoy that, provided that Devoy through the columns of the Gaelic American withdraws the criticism of de Valera's use of monies at Chicago, and that the same action be taken in regard to the position of President de Valera's alleged lowering of the flag in the Westminster Gazette interview, Envoy Boland agrees to secure correction of the minutes of Dáil Éirann [*sic*] reflecting on the loyalty and devotion to the cause of the Irish Republic of John Devoy.[69] Boland further disclosed that he had approved the resolutions by signing his name but that Cohalan had "vetoed" the agreement.

The "correction of the minutes of Dáil Éirann" regarding the loyalty of Devoy concerned a report by the acting minister for foreign affairs, Boland, to the Dáil the previous June, which offended Devoy to the core of his being. Boland had accused both Cohalan and Devoy of trying to sabotage the bond drive because of their enmity for de Valera.[70]

Despite this apparent stalemate, McGuire continued to try and bring Cohalan to the table, as reflected in a letter to Cohalan after the August 15 meeting, in which he wrote, "Enjoyed the meeting & visit very much & profited thereby. Your courage & poise is admirable and we shall be able to work out of this frightful state of welter some lasting good for you as well as the cause I believe."[71]

As the feud continued, de Valera took a variety of steps to secure control of the Friends of Irish Freedom, including installing Bishop Michael Gallagher of Detroit in place of Diarmuid Lynch as its national secretary and reorganizing the governing structure of the organization. Lynch, in a letter to Cohalan, commented on the situation, writing,

> I am very much disappointed on learning that Mr. D.[72] while at Westport did not discuss with you the question of how far the agreement is to affect the policy of the F.O.I.F.
>
> As I see it, if the agreement becomes public—and it will without doubt—the position of the Race in America will be seriously jeopardized and perhaps ruined. And if the policy of the Friends is to be different from that of the other organization, the members of the latter will find themselves in an impossible situation
>
> The situation is more confused than it was before, and when the facts become known it seems to me that our Detroit friend and many other prominent men will withdraw altogether. Dick says that he's through—absolutely.
>
> I have not yet written to de V. about the proposed amendments will probably hear from Detroit on the subject tomorrow.
>
> No we must give de V. some answer on the proposition which he made. The question is what is the answer to be? With you at Westport, the Bishop at Detroit and Dick out of things I find myself in a more impossible situation than ever. McHugh says I ought to keep in close touch with Detroit, but that is a very difficult matter under the circumstances.
>
> While it is possible that the visitor appreciates the seriousness of the outlook better than he did, he may also consider himself in a stronger position to force the issue of a Convention.
>
> Our friends on the 15th committed themselves absolutely and got nothing in return. Verbal exchanges are worthless, and the written resolutions are all on one side. All of those present with the exception of two or possibly three had no proof that the Constitution of the home O. was changed in the manner stated. H. said he

brought a revised copy but gave it to McG for safe keeping and the latter did not bring it with him. Talk about buying a pig in a bag!!

Personally I desire our visiting friends to have every possible concession consistent with the safety of the cause from the American viewpoint, but that's the rub.

If you can possibly come down for a meeting of the Ex. I trust you will do so. I am very sorry that Detroit is not coming on Saturday as I think it is of the utmost importance that you discuss the situation with him.[73]

The "agreement" that Lynch alludes to in the letter was something that if implemented would alter the landscape of Irish–Irish American relations profoundly. While he had been in Ireland the previous June reporting to the Dáil, Boland had secured authorization from the Irish Republican Brotherhood to sever its relationship with Clan-na-Gael in America if de Valera's supremacy continued to be challenged.[74] According to Cohalan's biographer, both Cohalan and Devoy either knew or suspected that this action would be forthcoming but doubted that Boland had the actual authority to take such an action.[75] Nevertheless, it is apparent from Lynch's concern that if it became public, the Irish movement in the United States would suffer grievously.

On that same day, Devoy wrote to Cohalan in a letter laden with pessimism, complaining about the situation:

I don't like the look of things to-day. The I.W.[76] has the worst article yet, based entirely on that lie they got inserted in the records of Dail Eireann. Harry called up to get copies of this and last week's paper, apparently to have D.V. study them to see whether he will carry out the promise or not. It would not surprise me if he demanded that I should retract my comment of last week on the lie they sent over, which, of course, I will refuse to do. It also seems to me that Joe consulted them before writing that letter about the circular—of which I can't send you a copy until to-morrow. Evidently the things he doesn't like are those that vindicate the org. and incidentally you and me.

I have written McGuire telling him that if they fail to carry out their part of the bargain I will attend to the correction myself and get it to the people here and at home and get us out of the movement entirely.

I have also a notion that they got us to pass that resolution about sending two men over to get us in a trap. The men that they want are Joe, and the party who is not here and who according to John A., is worse than Joe. The stuff about me going, I think, was "taffy" to soothe me, but they had the others in view. Of course, we can foil that, but the trouble is to warn our men in time to keep them from falling into a trap.

I may be too pessimistic, on account of the irritation over the I.W. but my experience with these men makes me suspicious of everything they do.

The men I have heard from here think the article will put them in a bad position if they do not keep faith, and are satisfied that we have the best of it so far.

I am only hearing now piecemeal what occurred at the meeting on the 15th. The others failed to tell me, thinking I heard things I did not hear. It is absurd for me to continue in that position. My deafness makes me helpless, and I cannot continue much longer.[77]

During this period McGuire continued to try to allay Cohalan's concerns about de Valera. On August 26, he sent the judge a column that de Valera had published in the *Philadelphia Ledger* in which he suggested that Britain could establish its own Monroe Doctrine to safeguard an independent Ireland.[78] McGuire also tried to mediate between Devoy and Boland, meeting with them together to try to iron out their differences. Devoy reported on the meeting in a letter to Cohalan, writing,

Some things have occurred that I can tell you of better verbally than in writing, and I need your advice.

I had a talk with Harry last Sunday, with James. James told me next day that we got nowhere because I was as bad as Harry. Now I was easier with him than usual and he was not so bad, but he said several ridiculous things which I had to contradict. It is doubtless these things which James objected to. He wants peace at any price and everything which interferes with that is wrong. He is even ready to deplete our treasury to carry out very doubtful schemes by them. They have got Hugh into the same state of mind. Hugh and James were in to-day and James is coming again to-morrow, which will be his last call for awhile.

Among the foolish things that Harry said was that it was *Treason* for you to go to Chicago to upset the President's plans. But he admitted Frank is a failure because he has no organizing ability and *you have.* So he wants you as leader but evidently to do what you are told. Their notion of how things should be done would shame a schoolboy—and they are all the same. D.V. is obsessed with safeguarding *his prerogative* and they are all crazy on that point.

Lindsay and Dairmuid have told me of the amendments to the Constitution. They are all D.V.'s but are presented by the Massachusetts State Council. They would hamstring the National Council and deprive it of all financial resources. As Lindsay put it, they would create a number of Sovereign States.

They still insist on a National Council meeting in Chicago, or anywhere away from New York and they can conceal their purpose of overriding the present majority.

Harry wants to know what *you are going to do* and I asked them what *they* were going to do. This, I think was one of the things that James objected to. He calls it "fighting." Hugh thinks you are missing a great chance by not coming out and assuming the leadership. It is an opportunity to get rid of Jerry etc. Harry prevented Jerry from speaking last Friday night and Jerry is furious, so he and Fr. Powers are holding a meeting of them on to-morrow evening. They allowed a buffoon named Ryan who has been expelled by both organizations to stand out in front of the audience signaling when to cheer for D.V. . . .

I enclose an article I have written on Mick's interview.[79] I expect to be told it is an attack on D.V. Well, it is not an attack, but it is a suggestion about Mick. He must have an idea of the ultimate leadership in his Corkian head. I have sent proofs of it to the Independent and the Freeman and the Roscommon Herald. Pat Lee came in last night with a message from Harry and among many other interesting things told me that Fr. Flanagan told the American Delegates that D.V. was not the real leader, but Mick was and had all the qualities to fit him for it. That is how I came to make that allusion in the article.

Dealhanty is on vacation and won't be back till next week. I did not even know about the article on the second page of the I.W. and have not read it. It is a concoction by what we call the "Shirt factory Committee" because it was held in the Red Shirt Factory of George Spearman, a man who was drummed out of Colonel Kerwin's cavalry regiment for shooting one of his fingers off while skulking behind a tree. Kerwin told me himself. They had neither book nor any other data except some notes supplied Kevin Le Caron of the previous clan convention . . . The $10,000 to Kelly was an invention, based on nothing at all. He never got a dollar. I will tell you how Pat Ford fell foul of me because I insisted on the return of the $10,000 in bonds lent him during my absence in Ireland in 1879. The week following the return of the last installment he attacked us for "doing nothing" and I wrote him a letter telling him if he said another word I would expose the whole transaction.

One of John O'Leary's cases came before Magistrate Conyan last Friday and he brought them into the anteroom and told them to settle it out of court. He said he had read my article, praised it highly and told them to follow my example. I am told that feeling is very general among that class of men.[80]

While the fighting among the leaders of the Irish movement in America continued, fighting across the sea in Ireland continued in deadly earnest. The Lord Mayor of Cork, Terence MacSwiney, was arrested and went on a hunger strike that would end in his death while in British custody.[81] As the month of September progressed, de Valera and Boland proceeded with their plans to gain control of the Friends of Irish Freedom. The controversy came to a head at a meeting of the national council of the organization on September 17, which ended with de Valera and his supporters staging a walk-out. The following day, he announced that a rival organization would be formed.[82]

Although it appeared that de Valera and Cohalan-Devoy had reached a final parting of the ways, McGuire took another stab at trying to reconcile the parties with a visit to Devoy on September 20, to which he was accompanied by his daughter Gertrude. Devoy recounted the meeting in a letter to Cohalan:

> As we were getting ready to go to press yesterday James K. and Hugh came in with a request that I submit my report of the Council meeting to Harry, so that "agreements" might be arrived at as to its contents. I positively refused and told them very plainly I was done making agreements that were never kept: that they did their best to make a split and failed etc., etc. Harry had spent Sunday evening at James's house and made all sorts of promises, saying D.V. was anxious for "peace" would call a Convention etc. I told them that it was only because he had failed in a deliberate attempt to wreck the organization and cited the proof. The argument got very warm, and James got indignant at my "stubbornness" and said Harry and I were one as bad as the other and that I should accept his sugges-tion. I told him these "agreements" were shams and the only thing to do was to get D.V. to stop his warfare on us. His daughter (who is a very nice girl) was with him and I had to express regret that her first visit to the office should be to witness a scene like that, but she did not mind a bit. Ferriter got excited and told James he must not talk to me that way, but James was only excited, not in the least insulting. Hugh agreed with him in most things and insisted that the "agreement" was not being lived up to by us. I told him that, on the contrary, it was simply used by the other people as a means of making trouble for us and they must stop it.
>
> I submitted my report to them and they pleaded hard with me to leave out a description of Father Powers farcical attempt to stampede and break up the meeting, contending that it was making too much of the incident and would do harm. I told him it was to forestall the

carrying out of a threat by the I.W. to attack the Nat. Council this week and he answered that such an attack would hurt the I.W. not the Council. As there was something in his plea, I cut out that part and he was satisfied to leave in other portions which he and Hugh had first objected to. He said D.V. would not call a Convention and I told him I did not care whether he did or not, but that he alone was responsible for all the trouble, with his absurd notions of his Presidential Prerogative and his attempts to treat us as a pack of schoolboys or servants and that I would not stand it any longer. There was a lot more in the talk, but that is the substance of it. We went out to lunch together and he seemed to think he had accomplished a big thing.

Hugh said we ought to make sacrifices to preserve unity, on account of the situation in Ireland, I told him we were making all the sacrifices and the men from Ireland, who ought to be avoiding, instead of creating trouble, were making none and if they kept it up the responsibility must be put on them and the men at home appealed to,

Jerry called on Harry Saturday to demand recognition of his new organization and they had it hot and heavy. Harry at last ordered him out of his room and told him what he thought of him. Up at James house he talked for twenty minutes in eulogy of me, and James thought this ought to go a long way with me.

I enclose a copy of my report. I am sending it to the Irish papers this evening, as there is a mail tomorrow.[83]

McGuire, despite his best efforts, had not "accomplished a big thing" or even a little thing. There was no reconciliation between the feuding factions, and on October 18 Harry Boland carried out his threat to sever the connection between the Irish Republican Brotherhood and the American Clan-na-Gael. Ironically the letter severing the ties between the two organizations went to McGuire, who was the chairman of the Clan-na-Gael Executive Committee in the United States. In his letter to McGuire, Boland wrote,

I am reluctantly compelled to address the enclosed letter to you as Chairman of the Clan-na-Gael Executive.

Let me take this occasion to thank you in behalf of the men at home for the wholehearted and unselfish cooperation you have given to their representative in this country.

It is a sad duty that I am called upon to perform. You will realize that I have done my best consistent with the safety of our Republic to placate and unify the many divergent views held by the Executive of the Clan-na-Gael.

I would be false in my duties to the Members of the Home Organization if I tolerated a moment longer any affiliation with an Organization in America whose official organ has persistently, since last February, attempted to undermine and obstruct the elected President of Ireland and his work in this country.

You are aware that on August 19th last we entered into a solemn compact—compact unanimously approved by the Executive Committee of Cal-na-Gael—only to find the will of the Executive of this great organization had to give way before the veto of Judge Cohalan.

I take this drastic step in the best interest of Ireland.[84]

In the wake of this action, McGuire and Devoy may have had one final meeting, which Devoy recounted in notes he had taken:

Among the things McGuire told me was this.

An Irish Republican in Ohio went to Harding to urge him to make a declaration in favor of Ireland. He said that a lot of Irish were going to vote for him, but I was not *for him*. They would vote, but *against Wilson and the League of Nations.* Any declaration that he made would not add much to that vote, but it would lose him a lot of others. Besides interfering for Ireland would be against his Mexican policy of non-interference in Europe etc. Then he gave him the stuff that has been published about the Irish being a "Domestic British Question."[85]

Clearly this first recollection is of a piece of political intelligence that McGuire picked up involving advice the Republican standard-bearer was receiving from a member of his own party who was of Irish decent and not advice McGuire was imparting to Harding. Devoy then went on to recount,

> James also gave De Valera's reason for staying here. He has not been asked by Dail Eireiann [*sic*] to return. And he will stay until they tell him to go back. He did not say he is more comfortable here than he is in Ireland. He also has a story which I suppose he got from D.V. or Boland that an Irishman who is in business in England who is married to a relative of Lloyd George met him recently at a social function and put the Irish Question up to him in conversation. L.G., according to the story told him they would be able to wear out the Sinn Feiners in three years.
>
> McG. also spoke about the hopelessness of getting England to agree to an Irish Republic. Doubtless that is an echo of his talks with De Valera.
>
> I pointed out to him D.V.'s persistent efforts to split or break the Irish organizations here that stand irrevocably for a Republic were not explainable by his personal hatreds (which McG. freely admitted) and gave him my opinion that the only logical explanation was that he wanted to remove every obstacle to a compromise, which his Cuban interview showed he was in favor of. He remained silent at that and seemed to be pondering it. But all through he kept up the talk about the differences being entirely personal.

On November 10, McGuire shared his own recollection of the meeting with Boland in a letter from Washington, DC, recounting,

> I waited to see whether my talk with Mr. Devoy would be helpful prior to the last meeting and finding the results worse than ever have resigned as Chairman and member.
>
> Nor will I join any other Irish American Society as they all go bad in the end The worst traits of the Irish character seem to show themselves in their operations and I have taken no active interest in them in years. Of course any personal or individual aid I can give you or your colleagues will be furnished.

I have visited the State Dept. And have been assured there will be no interferences from there with the work. Will be in Wilmington and Philadelphia today & will see before my return to New York the persons named.[86]

De Valera's new organization was called the American Association for the Recognition of the Irish Republic. Its growth could largely be measured by the loss of membership in the Friends of Irish Freedom, which declined over a six-month period beginning in November 1920 from 100,749 members to approximately 20,000.[87] True to his word, McGuire rebuffed Boland's overtures for him to play a role in the new organization as evidenced by a telegram he sent to Boland in New York from Philadelphia, which stated, "Deeply regret that I must positively decline position but in addition to the objections outlined here last night my health is none too rugged and am having a hard time keeping up. Also my business affairs are in a critical state owing to the slump and my associates demand more of my attention. They seriously object to the time lost now. For the work required you need a few new strong young men unspoiled by age or associations. Am leaving this evening to consult Dr. Franklin Church at Salem, N.J. as I have not been well today."[88]

Boland continued to pursue McGuire, who continued to resist his overtures. In a November 16 letter from Syracuse, McGuire amplified his concerns about his own situation, spelled out how badly the feud between de Valera and Cohalan-Devoy had taken its toll on him, and offered an insightful, nuanced critique of de Valera:

> If I was ten years younger and possessed the necessary physical stamina I would not hesitate to undertake the work proposed and this might accomplish some results for Ireland. But I am not as well as I would wish and the business depression this year has seriously affected my interests which are suffering and there is some complaint on the part of my associates of a neglect of the concerns in which I am interested.
>
> Then too I have a horror of all Irish-American organizations as a result of 30 years experience with them and would not join another

one. The rivalries of individuals for leadership or control of our organizations are the curse and the bane of the movement. In the old days of the Clan-na-Gael, the Ancient Order of Hibernians, the Land League, the Irish National League, etc., three-fourths of the efforts put forth were fighting fellow members instead of fighting England. In every case there has been a boss or clique dominating and the struggle against the caucus and dictatorship has resulted in paralysis of the hopes and aims of pacific but earnest men.

In looking over the names of the 25 men who signed the call for the Chicago Meeting which has been abandoned I noticed the names of several ambitious disturbers who are invariably factional, quarrelsome and unworkable. Any new organization made up of "old timers" will be bound to be factional and barren of good results. The only hope is the enlistment of zealous young men untainted by old factional scars.

The President has done the greatest work of any Irishman of his time in dealing with the great issues and with people in the mass. I am sorry to observe that he is a lamentable failure in meeting delegations or committees or groups in conference. In devotion to principle he is unexcelled. In details and methods he appears to most of his visitors as lacking in decision, changeable, unsteady and many men go away feeling they cannot work with him or under him safely. This statement I make as the result of receiving replies in response to inquiries and after meeting various friends lately. Last evening I met a number of workers here. The young men were ready for a change but the old workers were determined to stick to the old organizations. It is my opinion that no effective organization can be formed out of the groups in the Friends of Irish Freedom or the Clan-na-Gael. The control of these two bodies will remain where it is, young and fresh men may clear the way in some localities. When I return in a few days I will see you and give you my views further, with kindest regards.[89]

McGuire's resignation from the Friends of Irish Freedom and the Clan-na-Gael brought to an end his correspondence with Cohalan and his dealings with Devoy, which were captured in their correspondence, closing a fascinating window into the Irish American movement on behalf of Irish freedom. Devoy would go on to make a number of disparaging observations about McGuire in his memoir *Recollections of an Irish Rebel*, published after McGuire's death. Within a month of McGuire's death, Devoy would offer his less than favorable opinions about McGuire in his newspaper, the *Gaelic-American*. In this piece he portrayed McGuire as a de Valera sycophant, while at the same time spinning a tale that McGuire had warned him of a de Valera plot to have Devoy killed.[90] It is easy to see why Devoy withheld his observations about McGuire until after his death.

The following month de Valera returned to Ireland.[91]

10

The End

The year 1921 would prove to be one in which divisions increased both in America and in Ireland.

With de Valera's return to Ireland, the relationship between McGuire and Harry Boland, who remained in America, grew closer. The two had developed a social relationship the previous year, attending mass together with Cohalan and going to the Metropolitan Opera House in New York City where McGuire had introduced Boland to the internationally famous tenor Caruso. As 1920 turned to 1921, Boland spent the New Year holiday with McGuire, Frances, and their children in New Rochelle. Despite McGuire's resignation from Clan-na-Gael and withdrawal from Irish American activity, he continued to be supportive of Boland. Indeed, at Boland's request he wrote Michael Collins to vouch for Boland's genuineness in trying to bring about a reconciliation with Cohalan and Devoy. The letter to Collins is particularly significant because, from Collins's standpoint, Boland's most important role in America was to clandestinely obtain weapons for use by the Irish Republican Army in its war against the British.[1] No less a personage than John Devoy would later recount that Boland, with the assistance of McGuire, engaged in the only successful gun-running mission from America during that struggle.[2] Clearly McGuire had established his loyalty and bona fides with the Irish leadership.

The winter of 1920–21 had seen some of the worst fighting and atrocities occur between the Irish Volunteers and the Black and Tan Auxiliaries in Ireland. On November 21, 1920, one of Michael

Collins's squads succeeded in assassinating the top echelon of the British Secret Service in Dublin. Eighteen of its members were shot and killed. In retaliation, that afternoon the Black and Tans shot indiscriminately into a crowd of spectators watching a football game in Croke Park, Dublin. Seventeen were killed and hundreds wounded. In the winter months that followed, each side engaged in an escalating campaign of ambushes and burning of the farms and properties of the enemy supporters.

While fighting raged in Ireland, the British government's propaganda machine sought to discredit Ireland's American supporters and leadership by issuing a "white paper" titled "Irish Intrigue" in which it claimed to document pro-German activities by the Americans before and during World War I. The paper was little more than a rehash of the charges made against Cohalan, Devoy, and Jeremiah O'Leary by the Wilson administration years before.[3] No mention of McGuire was made in the news account.

Anticipating the inauguration of Harding as president in March, the National Council of the Friends of Irish Freedom passed a resolution pledging the organization's support for the new administration and urging it to seek repayment of all loans made to the allied European governments during World War I.[4]

In February, a delegation authorized by Harry Boland, which included McGuire, called upon the apostolic delegate to the United States in Washington, DC, to dissuade the Vatican from issuing any statement condemning the Irish Volunteers or supportive of the British efforts in Ireland. In a letter to Boland dated February 28, Frank Walsh reported on the meeting, informing him,

Think the interview went very well.

He expressed very great sympathy for our effort, and said that if we could convince him of the urgency of the matter, he would send a cablegram to the Holy See. He explained, however, he had been led to do that before by what appeared to be the very grave urgency of the matter, and that he had received a mild rebuke for being so precipitate.

His personal view, expressed very strongly, is that the Vatican will not interfere in the Irish situation. He said that in any event, he would send the request of the Committee as a report to the Holy Father.

The committee concluded to make an oral presentation of the case, and then asked for the privilege of addressing a written memorial to him. Before the close of the interview, however, the Delegate himself made the suggestion that the request of the Committee be put in writing and transmitted to him.

Major Kinkead thought it well to have the signatures of Messrs. Hines and Maloney attached to the memorial before its formal presentation.

In accordance with the suggestion that you made yourself, and some additions taken from the letter of President De Valera to Archbishop Hayes, and some suggestions of my own, I drew up a memorial to have ready for presentation.

When the Committee arrived, they had also drafted one, so Major Kinkead took both documents with him, from which to draw the address that they propose to submit.

Major Kinkead thought that he might get authority from Mr. Hines by wire to sign his name, in which event the document ought to be back here today. As soon as it arrives I will lose no time in presenting it to the delegate.[5]

Walsh also enclosed a copy of the letter sent to the apostolic delegate by the committee. The "memorial" submitted to the apostolic delegate in Washington, DC, was a lengthy document that was designed to appeal to the Vatican on all levels. It pointed out that the Irish people were among the most faithful members of the Roman Catholic Church in Ireland, America, Australia, and throughout the world and that the Irish had the support of other ethnic Catholics in their struggle for independence. It argued that any pronouncement by the Vatican that it was hostile to both sides in the hostilities between the Irish and the British would damage the faith of the Irish and other Catholics and would further signal that the Protestant British influence was considered paramount to the interests of Irish Catholics. It went on to seek the endorsement of an independent inquiry by an American commission into the "atrocities" committed by the British forces in Ireland against the Irish populace, which it claimed had either been withheld or falsely reported to the world by the British government.

This appeal was signed by McGuire; Walsh; New York State Supreme Court justice John Goff; Major Eugene Kinkead and Thomas J. Maloney, both of New Jersey; and one J. J. Castellini of Cincinnati, Ohio.[6]

The "Commission" did indeed have accurate information about the British government's efforts to have the Vatican issue a proclamation calling for a cessation of hostilities in Ireland while condemning Sin Fein. Indeed, the British government left no rock unturned in its ongoing efforts to poison the Vatican's perception of Sinn Fein, including sending the Holy Father a copy of Roger Casement's diary, which was replete with descriptions of his homosexual encounters, suggesting that this was typical of the Irish leadership.

Despite the fact that Ireland was an overwhelmingly Catholic country and supported by many more Catholics worldwide, as described in the "memorial," "the Catholic Church had not been supportive of the republican forces trying to achieve independence from protestant England. Indeed on some levels it was downright hostile to them. On December 12, 1920 the Bishop of Cork had decreed that anyone who took part in ambushes, kidnaping, murder or attempted murder would be excommunicated from the Church."[7] Since the overwhelming number of Black and Tans and British troops were Protestant, and a like number of Irish Volunteers were Roman Catholic, it is not hard to see who this decree was designed to discourage from participating in the hostilities.

The efforts of the British government to co-opt the Vatican were apparently thwarted by the appeal to the apostolic delegate and additional appeals to the pope by other clergy sympathetic to the cause of Irish freedom. Ultimately when the pope did issue a statement calling for a cessation of hostilities, he put both combatants on an equal footing, to the consternation of the British government.[8] The pope's appeal, however, was not welcomed by the Friends of Irish Freedom, whose William Pearse Branch adopted a resolution criticizing the appeal and claiming that its wording bypassed the government of the Republic of Ireland and appealed directly to the people of Ireland. The criticism by the Friends of Irish Freedom notwithstanding, Harry Boland issued a statement welcoming the pontiff's statement and predicted that it would result in a peace process unfolding.[9]

While the war in Ireland had grown more deadly, the conflict between the Friends of Irish Freedom, still loyal to Cohalan and Devoy, and the supporters of de Valera continued unabated and sometimes bordered on the ludicrous. For example, both sides clashed over the appropriate way to mark St. Patrick's Day in New York City, with the former proposing a parade down Fifth Avenue that would be a "monster protest demonstration against English rule in Ireland" and the latter advocating that the money instead be spent for a relief fund for the people of Ireland who have been victims of the war.[10] The Harding administration found itself drawn into a similar controversy when it refused to allow any of the armed forces stationed in New England to march in Boston's St. Patrick's Day parade, lest it be construed as tacit support of the Republic of Ireland.[11] The split between these two factions would never be more apparent than when a peace conference, accompanied by a truce in the fighting, was proposed by British prime minister David Lloyd George in July.

Harry Boland was still in the United States on his thirty-fourth birthday on April 27, 1921. Frances presented him with a gift and a card that read, "a tie for one whom we all like and admire so much."[12]

Discussions between the combatants had been under way for months but did not culminate in a truce and agreed-upon conference until de Valera accepted Lloyd George's proposal on July 8, 1921.[13] Reaction in the United States, as expected, was mixed. Supporters of de Valera were convinced that he would insist on recognition of the Republic of Ireland, while supporters of Cohalan suspected that he would seek something less, such as dominion status.[14] Cohalan charged that de Valera "has been all the time working for a compromise with

Lloyd George to arrange a plebiscite, formally carrying out a plan agreed upon between them, which will remove from his shoulders the responsibility for lining up Ireland with England against America."[15]

Four days later de Valera and a number of his ministers traveled to London to conduct direct talks with Lloyd George. During the four sessions that they held, the prime minister tried to persuade de Valera to accept dominion status; however, the latter resolutely held out for Irish independence. The discussions prompted Lloyd George to observe that negotiating with de Valera was "like trying to pick up mercury with a fork."[16]

De Valera's unwillingness to accept anything less than independence prompted Cohalan and Devoy to publicly send him telegrams congratulating him on his stand. Privately, however, the two men in their correspondence with each other continued to question de Valera's motives and willingness to accept something less than full independence. As future events would reveal, Cohalan and Devoy's views of de Valera and the issue of Irish independence were capable of a revision that defied all logic and consistency. McGuire's view of this turn of events remains a mystery.

Ultimately after months of correspondence between the de Valera government and the British government, in which views were exchanged, another session was scheduled for London at the end of 1921. This time, however, de Valera would not attend. The Irish delegation would principally consist of Michael Collins, Arthur Griffith, and other members of Sinn Fein. In early December a treaty between the two sides was crafted that provided for dominion status for Ireland, an oath of allegiance to the Crown, external association between the two countries that guaranteed security, and exclusion of the northern six counties after establishment of a boundary commission.[17] On December 6, 1921, the members of the Irish delegation signed the treaty and returned home to present it to the Dáil.[18]

In Dublin de Valera was outraged that the treaty had been approved by the delegation. He claimed that they had agreed not to approve any agreement until he had approved it. Debate in the Dáil was intense. De Valera insisted that Ireland should accept nothing less than full independence, while Collins, Griffith, and those supporting the treaty viewed it as the first step toward eventual independence. After extensive debate, the Dáil approved the treaty by a vote of sixty-four to fifty-seven. De Valera resigned his presidency and seat in the Dáil, and the country would soon be plunged into civil war.[19]

The reaction in America to the split in Ireland on the part of Cohalan and Devoy can only be described as bizarre. They had pilloried de Valera for his interview in which he had proposed that Ireland be treated similarly to the status of Cuba; they had constantly questioned his commitment to an Irish Republic and repeatedly suggested that he would compromise for dominion status. No attack on his integrity or motives was too shrill. Now that de Valera had rejected the treaty, with its dominion status for Ireland, they aligned themselves with the pro-treaty forces and went on the attack again.[20] Devoy told a convention of the Friends of Irish Freedom held in New York City, "We knew a year ago that the man they sent here was engineering for a compromise with England and subsequent developments have shown this to be a fact. Éamon de Valera is an autocrat, or would-be autocrat, and the policy he adopted was deliberate and intentional and calculated to bring about a compromise with England."[21]

The Cohalan-Devoy criticism, as well as that of Diarmuid Lynch, was promptly answered by Harry Boland in a statement in which he declared,

> The statements of Justice Cohalan and Mr. Lynch, National Secretary, Friends of Irish Freedom anent the Anglo-Irish peace pact, would come from them with better grace had they stood by the Irish Republic in its hour of trial.
>
> Daniel F. Cohalan has consistently and persistently denied the existence of the Republic of Ireland from the day on which the Chairman of the Irish Race Convention, held in Philadelphia in February, 1919, and one month after Dail Eireann had formally declared the independence of Ireland, he bitterly opposed in committee a resolution urging the recognition of the Irish Republic—substituting in its stead a compromise resolution of self-determination, until

the Republican National Convention in Chicago last year, when President de Valera's resolution asking the Republican committee to adopt recognition of Ireland as a plank in their platform, he entered a compromise resolution, and thus by his action seriously hampered the Irish Republic.

Mr. Lynch can rest assured that those who remained faithful to Dail Eireann when resigned will not now shirk the responsibilities they have so splendidly maintained in the face of a terrible and brutal aggression, and if when Dail Eireann shall have passed and an Irish Free State shall have come into being, those who will carry on the struggle for an Irish Republic will not give support or countenance men who failed miserably to assist the Irish Republic during its life.[22]

In Ireland, debate continued between the pro-treaty and anti-treaty forces in the form of large rallies held by each side throughout the country. The first real military skirmishing did not occur until the anti-treaty forces sized the Four Courts complex in Dublin on April 13, 1922. Despite this provocation, the pro-treaty forces, commanded by Michael Collins, refrained from retaliating until June 28, when it shelled the Four Courts and drove out the occupants.[23]

While McGuire remained silent throughout the public recriminations between Cohalan-Devoy and Harry Boland, he did maintain a warm and personal correspondence with Boland, who had returned to Ireland, perhaps giving a clue as to where his loyalty and sympathy lay, although this too was tempered by his belief that the dispute should be settled by a plebiscite of some form of the Irish people.

On April 7, 1922, he wrote Boland at the Mansion House, Dublin, addressing him as "My dear Friend." He went on to keep him informed on a number of topics, telling him,

Since my last communication to you early last month, there are few developments in America outside the Big Four treaty and other treaties which have been adopted and the pending coal strike which has brought out 600,000 miners. I have been away from home more than ever, since you left and have visited twelve ship yards along the Atlantic coast. The shipping industry is in worse shape than ever and there is no market for engines.

A week ago Sunday when I was home Prof. Smiddy of Cork with Gilbert Ward and James Connolly, the Irish Council, called at the house and spent the afternoon with us; that night I sat on the platform at the Lexington Ave. opera house and I listened to Father O'Flanagan, Austin Stack and O'Kelly present in able fashion, their side of the controversy in Ireland. The meeting was very largely attended, several overflow meetings. I also heard them in Brooklyn at the Academy of Music.

Prof. Smiddy is a man of most pleasant manners, tactful, genial and so far as I can observe, does not discuss political matters at all. He arrived in Washington yesterday. I went to the station to meet him with Joe Begley as Joe had not seen him and I told the Professor in New York what an interesting character Joe was in many ways. We went over to the Willard Hotel together and took a walk with him on the Mall, and through Potomac Park; then I left him with Joe and will see him again when I return from Portsmouth. He has not given out any interviews and says that he is simply appointed to remain here as the representative of the Dail until after the elections in Ireland. I consider his selection a wise one under the circumstances.

The Alliance on the Treaties has tremendously increased the prestige of England in America. One cannot help but notice the changes in the motion picture audiences, who now vigorously applaud everything on the screen from Lloyd George down. If the British Premier should accomplish any practical results from the Genoa Economic Conference, his prestige would be further enhanced, but more or less of the industries of the world lie prostrate and it may be that none of the politicians can ever bring back peace and prosperity and that a new social order founded on a different system, of production, exchange and distribution must come before a restless world is quieted. All this leads to growing indifference in America to the fate of Ireland.

The American public and most of the people generally interested in Ireland, excepting the press reports and the settlement, view with mingled feelings of perplexity, disgust, amazement and mostly misunderstanding, what is going on in Ireland. And it will take sometime for thought to work in order to understand the conditions which have split the Irish nation. All who know De Valera and yourself know in their heart of hearts that you are pure minded patriots, but the feeling here among your friends is in effect that whatever the majority of people of Ireland should determine, is the best settlement to accept. We miss you greatly at home. Mrs. McGuire is disappointed in your not having returned as expected. I went to lunch with James O'Mara[24] on his invitation. He is very strongly opposed to your side, but of course had nothing personally unkind to say. I understand he has gone home and I have not met his colleagues.

With deepest personal regards and sincere wishes of hope to the President, I am with affectionate regards.[25]

Boland replied to this letter on April 20, greeting McGuire in the Gaelic phrase "A Chara" and telling him,

I am delighted to receive your letter of April 7th and must apologize for not communicating with you earlier. You will understand of course, that the present situation here makes it very difficult for us to keep up with our correspondence.

I am sorry to know that the shipping business is so bad in America. . . .

Very strong pressure was brought to bear on me to return to America with Austin Stack . . . but I really had not the heart to go back again particularly on such a Mission. I know that our representatives will have a very difficult and uphill task but I feel sure that the selection has been a wise one and if anyone can win support from America it will be Messrs. Stack and the other members of the Mission.

I have no doubt that Prof. Smiddy will fill the post in Washington satisfactorily. I have never met him but I understand that his connection with our movement began last November.

We all here agree that the Irish people are the final JUDGES of this controversy and we are insisting that the Irish people have free choice as between the "Free State" and the REPUBLIC. We demand that the threat of immediate and terrible war be removed by England and also insist on a vital matter such as this, that every man and woman over twenty-one years of age in this country is entitled to vote. I have no hesitation in saying that if an election takes place on this issue that the REPUBLIC proclaimed in '16 and maintained ever since will be again ratified by the Irish people.

Give my very kind regards to Mrs. Maguire [*sic*] and to all the family. I am looking forward to meet you all in Ireland. Mise, le meas mor.[26]

In a postscript, Boland informed McGuire that he would send him copies of the election literature being circulated by the anti-treaty forces.

The following month, McGuire wrote Boland again from Washington, DC, this time after the latter had attempted to devise a peace conference between the two opposing camps.[27] Congratulating him on the effort, McGuire wrote,

On the way up here from the south I read with satisfaction of the reconciliation accomplishments of the past ten days, which are the result of great effort and thought. I was also glad to see as one of the oldest and dearest of your American friends, that your own name was frequently mentioned in the press dispatches, as having been responsible for much of the beneficial results and that the pact or agreement, arrived at, was largely along the lines of your ideas and resolution. Hence my congratulatory cable to you today.

I may be able to get over to see you in August but the chances are against my coming as I have no one here to leave my work to and the business lines in which I have been interested in, show no improvement.

Joseph Connolly and Jos. Begley as well as his charming and pretty bride to be, were in to see me and Joe has certainly made a great find in this country. He tells me that he is leaving on June 14th for Dublin together with Gilbert Ward.

I missed seeing Steven O'Mara. Have been in New York very little and missed him. He did not come around to see us or call us up and I should like to have seen him before he got away. I met Austin Stack and he is certainly a fine type of man. Professor Smiddy is in New York and I will not be able to see him this trip.[28]

Boland replied the following month in a brief note filled with optimism about the impending peace talks and the better days that he and McGuire would enjoy:

I am writing to thank you for your cable and congratulatory letter of May 24th. I am very glad that a reconciliation has been brought about. However, it is a little early yet to prophecy as to whether the Coalition will be successful.

If at all possible you should take a trip to Ireland about August, as by that time things should be quieted down here. You would be in time for the Taillteann Games and I would be delighted to take care of you during your tour.

Give my kindest regards to Mrs. McGuire and the family.

As I write I received a post card sent by yourself, Mary and Gertrude. I trust you had an enjoyable holiday in Virginia.[29]

McGuire had applied for a passport the previous December. On his application he declared his intention to visit "Great Britain, Ireland, France, Sweden, Holland, Belgium, Italy." He further disclosed his plans to depart on December 24, 1921, from New York aboard the *Scythia*.[30] Although his planned departure was only a week from the date of his application, there is no information about whether the trip actually occurred. The tenor of his correspondence with Boland would suggest that it did not.

Harry Boland's hopes for peace and reconciliation were dashed. Following the shelling of the Four Courts and the capture of the anti-treaty forces occupying it, fighting escalated and civil war in Ireland broke out in earnest. August, the month in which McGuire and Boland hoped to reunite in Ireland and attend the Taillteann Games, would prove to be a particularly deadly one in which the cream of the Irish independence movement on both sides would die. On August 5, Harry Boland would die from wounds suffered in a raid on his hotel room in Dublin. One week later, on August 12, Arthur Griffith, the father of the Sinn Fein movement, who had succeeded de Valera as president of Ireland, died after suffering a stroke. On August 22, Michael Collins, the man whom the British feared the most, was killed in an ambush by anti-treaty forces.[31]

In America, McGuire would not live to see the end of the civil war or peace come to Ireland. He had taken a respite from his advocacy of Irish independence, having tired of the internecine disputes. The following year was spent traveling throughout the country conducting his various business enterprises. On June 9, 1923, he returned to Syracuse, where he gave an interview about the upcoming presidential election and the national issues of the day. The *Syracuse Journal* reported,

> Mr. McGuire is in the manufacturing business in the South and his duties bring him into practically all the Southeastern States. Although he has not been active in politics since he was Mayor of Syracuse, he has never failed to keep in touch with the political situation generally.
>
> [McGuire was quoted as saying,] "From my observations as traveler I am convinced that the prohibition law, in spite of the difficulties of enforcement, is a great blessing to the nation and that it will not be repealed, at least during the lifetime of the present generation. I judge from the talk of the Southerners that I meet that the states of Virginia, Georgia, Florida and the Carolinas and probably Alabama and Mississippi will send solid dry delegations to the Democratic national convention. The only doubtful state is Louisiana. Texas, the largest Southern state, will undoubtedly send a solid dry delegation. The people in the South have never cared much about beer. They drink strong liquor and have very little difficulty in getting from the moonshiners white corn liquor at low prices."

Turning to the 1924 presidential election, he observed, "The presidential sentiment in the south is divided between Secretary McAdoo and Senator Underwood. Among the small planters and storekeepers there is a tremendous undercurrent for Henry Ford. These people want cheap nitrates for the cotton fields and power from Muscle Shoals and other places all of which they believe Ford is trying to get them."

The article went on to report, "Mr. McGuire has entirely recovered from a serious attack of pneumonia last winter and his friends and acquaintances tell him he is looking better than ever. He has met many of his friends of 30 and 35 years ago and was delighted to recall the days when Syracuse was 'just getting started.' He leaves for New York City Saturday night."[32]

Slightly less than three weeks later, on June 29, he was found dead in bed at the Hotel Raleigh in Washington, DC, where he usually stayed while in the nation's capital. The coroner's verdict was that he died from a heart attack.[33]

Funeral services were held at St. John the Evangelist church on State Street in Syracuse, where the mass was celebrated by the pastor, Monsignor Albert J. Hayes, who had been McGuire's seatmate when they attended Christian Brothers School. In his eulogy, Father William Dougherty told the congregation,

> We are gathered here to express our sentiment in the premature and early death of the Boy Mayor of Syracuse, a man of state and nation. I hope the day is not far distant when a monument will be erected in our city in memory of Jimmie McGuire, the boy of Syracuse and a man of whom the community may well be proud. His deeds are written in the hearts of men and women, his charities were given in an exceedingly modest manner, but today in many places there stands a living memory to the goodness of Jimmie McGuire's heart. I am sure that when a monument is erected, and I hope it will be soon, every man and boy in passing would doff his hat out of respect to the memory of the man.
>
> Fit to be honored by his fellows and crowned on high, James K. McGuire carried out all of the injunctions of the Master. He carried

out the ideals of the true American to the marrow of his bones, to his country, this state and his city. Though young in years he was old beyond his years in experience by the many things crowded into that life.

As we are gathered here in this Christian civic assembly I make bold to say that such a marvelous and phenomenal boy has not arisen here during the past 30 years and during that time there has not been a man who deserves the honor and respect of this community more than James K. McGuire. He attained the highest heights of confidence among the people and if monuments are erected to inspire young people to patriotism and high ideals one should be built to the boy, the man, the mayor of whom we are all proud, one whose worthiness and integrity stamped him in our hearts.

The bell in City hall this morning tolled the tears of sorrow and sympathy of a city to a man we are all proud of. James K. McGuire was a citizen worthy of the name; the Christian who has gone to receive his eternal reward.[34]

At the conclusion of the service hundreds of people followed the honor guards of the police and fire departments through the city and up to Saint Agnes Cemetery on the city's south side. He was buried under a headstone with a bronze plaque provided by the city, which read, "Dutiful Son, Helpful bother, Devoted husband, Loving Father, Useful Citizen, Efficient Mayor, loyal Friend, Thinker, Orator and Lover of His fellow Man. Followed He the Master's rule Render Unto Caesar the Things that are Caesar's And unto God the Things that are God's."

Later that year, on October 23, 1923, the indictment pending against him in New York County was dismissed, ten years after it had been brought.[35]

McGuire wore the title of "Boy Mayor" with an air of bemusement as was reflected in a note he penned to the *Syracuse Herald*, which had erroneously reported his thirty-eighth birthday on his thirty-seventh, writing, "37 today not 38, getting old fast enough without you tacking on another year. Was 16 when nominated for

School Commissioner and 19 when nominated for Member of the Assembly, 27 when nominated for Mayor 'a boy wonder,' now 37 and a dead bird. Jim"[36]

Conclusion

Upon reflection, one might be tempted to think of James K. McGuire as an enigma. A poor boy that became rich. A child of an Irish immigrant, who walked the corridors of power, dealing with presidents both American and Irish. A grade school dropout who wrote books, tracts, and speeches on the issues of the day. A populist who became a lobbyist for the Asphalt Trust. A reformer, who was indicted twice. Nevertheless, there was a marvelous consistency about him.

In his three terms as mayor of Syracuse, he fought the political bosses and the entrenched power structure. He always stood on the side of the citizen, advocating for publicly owned franchises and utilities, reaching out to the ignored and marginalized African American community. He had special empathy for the "tramps," the unemployed, the penitentiary inmates, and the cursed souls that Clarence Darrow would later call "the damned and the despised." Educated by his mother, "home-schooled" if you will, he built schools and the Carnegie Library, and championed the arts. It didn't matter whether he was competing with the Ivy-educated Theodore Roosevelt, Theodore Hancock, or University Chancellor Day, he refused to allow his lack of formal education to handicap him in any way. A gifted speaker, candidate, and political leader who dominated Syracuse politics throughout the decades he lived there, he would later confess and lament the uses of the naked political power he wielded, even if the means topped a greater good.

McGuire was first, last, and always an Irishman. He would have resisted that description if it had been put to him, but the evidence is clearly there. Unlike Devoy and McGarrity, he was not a native of Ireland and, unlike Cohalan, he was ready, willing, and able to take whatever risks, popular or unpopular, legal or illegal, were needed to further the cause of Irish independence. He was willing to speak and write on the subject from his earliest adult years until his death. He didn't hesitate to advocate for Germany in the run-up to World War I if doing so would help Ireland and injure England. Where Cohalan was timid and feared a backlash and repression, McGuire was bold, public, and more than willing to incur the wrath of President Wilson and Congress as they probed his propaganda efforts. Like the "Defenders of the Realm" that Padraig Pearce scored in his eulogy of O'Donovan Rossa on the eve of the Rising, McGuire too would "work in secret and in the open" to break the yoke of British oppression, whether it involved raising money through the Friends of Irish Freedom, negotiating with the Wilson White House, managing de Valera's speaking tours or secretly managing the affairs of Clan-na-Gael, supplying a false identity to Roger Casement and running guns, or siding with Harry Boland during the Irish war against the Black and Tans. While publicly he would insist that he be "judged on his patriotism" after America entered the war against Germany, he never once shrank from any task that would achieve the goal of a free and independent Ireland, no matter what risk it involved to him. He would cross lines that Devoy, Cohalan, and McGarrity would not, even if it meant entering places where angels might fear to tread. In the end, forced to choose between his fellow Irish American leaders and de Valera and Boland, he chose the latter.

While McGuire did not preserve any of his correspondence, and left no diaries or other personal recollections of his journey, he left his mark everywhere on the city he headed for three terms and on the events that led to Irish freedom. His life was a truly fascinating odyssey in American history.

Notes

Glossary

Bibliography

Index

J M K

Notes

1. July 12, 1868

1. William S. McFeeley, *Grant* (New York: William Norton Co., 1981), 273.

2. *New York Times*, July 12, 1868.

3. "Death of Mrs. McGuire," *Syracuse Post-Standard*, Jan. 20, 1899.

4. Karl Bottigheimer, *Ireland and the Irish: A Short History* (New York: Columbia Univ. Press, 2001), 265.

5. Robert A. Slayton, *Empire Statesman: The Rise and Redemption of Al Smith* (New York: Free Press, 2001), 9.

6. "Obituary," *Catholic Sun*, Oct. 22, 1892. See also *Syracuse Daily Journal*, Oct. 22, 1892.

7. Ibid.

8. "The Crispins' Strike—Widening of the Breach," *New York Times*, Dec. 15, 1870, 4.

2. Life in the Salt City

1. *Boyd's City Directory* (Syracuse, NY: Andrew Boyd, 1870–71), 20.

2. Ibid.

3. Records of the U.S. Census, courtesy of the Onondaga Historical Society, Syracuse, NY.

4. *Boyd's City Directory*, 1870–71, 20, 54.

5. Ibid., 85–86.

6. "The Strike of the Crispins," *Syracuse Daily Journal*, Apr. 11, 1871, 1.

7. "City Notes," *Syracuse Daily Journal*, Apr. 21, 1871, 4.

8. Lock Street was later renamed North State Street.

9. *Boyd's City Directory*, 1870–71, 34, 70.

10. *Syracuse Herald Journal*, Apr. 20, 1947. In this article, the Simon Block is designated as being part of "North State Street," which is what Lock Street was later renamed.

11. James K. McGuire, *The King, the Kaiser and Irish Freedom* (New York: Devin-Adair, 1914), 9. This school could have been located in one of the two Lutheran churches at the

corners of Butternut Street and Union Street: the Evangelical Lutheran Church of St. John or the Zion Evangelical German Lutheran. See *Boyd's City Directory*, 1870–71, 70.

12. McGuire, *King, Kaiser, Irish Freedom*, 68–69.

13. "Christian Brothers in Syracuse Diocese," *Catholic Sun*, Nov. 30, 1961.

14. *Boyd's City Directory*, 1870–71, 27. The "Brothers School" would close in 1891 as a cost-cutting measure by the parish, which had become the cathedral in Syracuse, and the Brothers left Syracuse. They returned in 1900 and opened another school near the same site as the previous one and would provide continuous education throughout the next century; the school continues today in the adjacent town of Dewitt.

15. This anecdote was related to his daughter, Mary McGuire Fahey, the author's mother.

16. "Obituary," *Catholic Sun*, Oct. 29, 1892.

17. "Obituary, Mrs. Mary Jane McGuire," *Catholic Sun*, Feb. 9, 1899.

18. "Death of Mrs. McGuire," *Syracuse Post-Standard*, Jan. 20, 1899.

19. "Obituary," *Catholic Sun*, Feb. 9, 1899.

20. This anecdote was told by Charles McGuire to his daughter, Mary McGuire Fahey, the author's mother.

3. The Early Years: Tragedy, Triumph, and the Rise to Power

1. "A Boy's Early Death," *Syracuse Post-Standard*, May 23, 1881.

2. "Map of the City of Syracuse by H. Wadsworth Clarke," *Boyd's City Directory*, 1883.

3. "A Boy's Early Death."

4. "Accidents," *Syracuse Daily Journal*, May 23, 1881.

5. The author's grandfather. This account was shared with my mother, Mary McGuire Fahey.

6. William V. Shannon, *The American Irish, A Political and Social Portrait*, rev. ed. (New York: MacMillan, 1966).

7. Shannon, *American Irish*, 37.

8. M. J. Kingsley, J. J. Knauber, J. Neville, and J. Bruckheimer, *The Political Blue Book of Syracuse New York* (Syracuse, NY: Grover, 1902).

9. "Newsboys Who Have Risen to High Political Office, 2 Mayors," *New York World*, undated copy, 1898.

10. "Mayoral Rival Were Neighbors," *Syracuse Herald-Journal*, Apr. 20, 1947.

11. *Dictionary of American Biography*, vol. 7 (New York: Charles Scribner & Son, 1931), 19.

12. Ibid.

13. The same is true of each of his siblings upon their entry into the labor market.

14. "A Proud Record," *Syracuse Sunday Herald*, Feb. 5, 1893, 6.

15. *Boyd's City Directory*, 1883–84.

16. *Boyd's City Directory*, 1885–87.

17. The business became Bradford, Kennedy, Sons, & McGuire, and was located at 210 South Clinton Street. *Boyd's City Directory*, 1893.

18. California Department of Health Information and Research, Vital Statistics Section.

19. *Boyd's City Directory*, 1882–83, 1883–84, 1884–85, 1885–86, 1886–87, 1887–88, 1888–89, 1889–90.

20. "A Proud Record," 6.

21. Shannon, *American Irish*, 133.

22. "A Proud Record."

23. "A Proud Record." See also *Dictionary of American Biography*, 7:19.

24. *Dictionary of American Biography*, vol. 7.

25. "A Proud Record."

26. *Boyd's City Directory*, 1886–87.

27. "Records of Conviction in Police Court, City of Syracuse Court of General Sessions." Provided by the Onondaga county clerk.

28. "A Slippery Maniac," *Syracuse Journal*, Mar. 29, 1888, 4.

29. "A Proud Record."

30. H. Paul Jeffers, *An Honest President: The Life and Presidencies of Grover Cleveland* (New York: William Morrow, 2000), 219.

31. "A Proud Record."

32. Jeffers, *An Honest President*, 219.

33. "A Proud Record."

34. "Records of the Police Court, City of Syracuse," June 24, 1887.

35. "Frauds in the Asylum," *Syracuse Standard*, Apr. 4, 1888.

36. This account of his conversation with his family was furnished by his granddaughter, Mary McGuire Fahey, the author's mother.

37. "Frauds in the Asylum."

38. "Record of Conviction, Police Court, City of Syracuse Court of General Sessions," Aug. 20, 1888.

39. *Boyd's City Directory*, 1888–89.

40. Ibid.

41. "A Proud Record."

42. Ibid.

43. Jeffers, *An Honest President*, 33–34, 42–55.

44. "A Proud Record."

45. *Boyd's City Directory*, 1888–89.

46. "Petition for Writ of Habeas Corpus," filed in the Office of the County Clerk, Syracuse, NY.

47. *Boyd's City Directory*, 1888–89.

48. "Frauds in the Asylum."

49. "Penitentiary Punishments," *Syracuse Courier*, Dec. 28, 1890.

50. "He Had the Wrong Key," *Syracuse Standard*, July 1, 1882.

51. "Cruel Treatment of Prisoners," *New York World*, Dec. 31, 1880. "Bucked" is not otherwise described.

52. Records of the Onondaga County Penitentiary, Onondaga County Department of Corrections, Jamesville, New York.

53. Records of the Police Court, City of Syracuse.

54. *Boyd's City Directory*, 1890–91.

55. "Talking to Irishmen," *Chicago Sun-Times*, Aug. 16, 1891.

56. Undated and untitled article courtesy of the archives of the Onondaga Historical Society.

57. "A Proud Record."

58. Jack Bellamy, *The Rascal King: The Life and Times of James Michael Curley (1874–1958)* (Reading, MA: Addison-Wesley, 1992), 318–23.

59. "List of Stockholders," *Catholic Sun*, July 1, 1892, 6.

60. *Catholic Sun*, June 24, 1892, 1.

61. *Syracuse Daily Journal*, Saturday, Oct. 22, 1892.

62. "Obituary," *Catholic Sun*, Oct. 28, 1892, 6; *Syracuse Daily Journal*, Saturday, Oct. 22, 1892.

63. "Deaths of the Day, James K. McGuire," *Syracuse Herald*, June 30, 1923.

64. "Obituary," *Catholic Sun*, Oct. 28, 1892.

65. "A Proud Record."

66. Jeffers, *An Honest President*, 234.

67. "A Proud Record."

68. Jeffers, *An Honest President*, 242–43.

69. "Hill's Man Kirk Carries Through His Slate in Onondaga," *New York Times*, Feb. 21, 1892, 2.

70. "Work of the Hill Crowd," *New York Times*, Feb. 23, 1892, 1.

71. "A Proud Record."

72. Ibid.

73. "William B. Kirk Dies After Illness of Months," *Syracuse Herald*, Aug. 26, 1911.

74. "Long Ill, W. B. Kirk Dies," *Syracuse Journal*, Aug. 26, 1911.

75. "A Proud Record."

76. "Work of the Hill Crowd."

77. Shannon, *American Irish*, 77.

78. "Sheehan Took Flight," *Catholic Sun*, June 24, 1892, 8.

79. "Work of the Hill Crowd," *New York Times*, Feb. 21, 1892, 1.

80. Jeffers, *An Honest President*, 251.

81. "In Business Circles," *Syracuse Evening Herald*, Feb. 11, 1893, 4.

82. In addition to the assembly seat in 1889, he was nominated as a candidate for supervisor of the Fourth Ward in the municipal election in 1890 but declined two days later. See "General Caucus Day," *Syracuse Evening Herald*, Feb. 15, 1890, 1; and "Tomorrow's the Day," *Syracuse Evening Herald*, Feb. 17, 1890, 1.

83. *Catholic Sun*, Oct. 28, 1892, 4.

84. "In Business Circles," *Syracuse Evening Herald*, Feb. 11, 1893, 4.

85. "Mowry Men Absent," *Syracuse Standard*, Sept. 22, 1895, 16.

86. "The Busy Democrat," *Syracuse Standard*, Sept. 20, 1895, 6.

87. "Mowry Men Absent."

88. "James Is in the Way," *Syracuse Standard*, Sept. 30, 1895, 6.

89. "Kirk a Little Ahead," *Syracuse Standard*, Oct. 1, 1895, 1.

90. "Fun in the Ninth," *Syracuse Standard*, Oct. 5, 1895, 6.

91. "McGuire Ahead," *Syracuse Standard*, Oct. 8, 1895, 6.

92. "McGuire Ahead."

93. "Young Democrats Won," *Syracuse Post*, Oct. 9, 1895, 2.

94. "Captured by Young Men," *New York Times*, Oct. 9, 1895, 9.

95. "Politics in the City," *Syracuse Standard*, Oct. 2, 1895, 6.

96. "Business in Politics," *Syracuse Evening Herald*, Oct. 3, 1895, 6.

97. "Melange of Politics," *Syracuse Post*, Oct. 9, 1895, 5.

98. "String Was Pulled," *Syracuse Post*, Oct. 10, 1895, 6.

99. "It Was Rather Chilly," *Syracuse Evening Herald*, Oct. 10, 1895, 11.

100. "The Democratic Candidate," *Syracuse Courier*, Oct. 9, 1895, 4.

101. "The Republican Candidate," *Syracuse Courier*, Oct. 10, 1895, 4.

102. "For Mayor Charles F. Saul," *Syracuse Standard*, Oct. 10, 1895, 4–6.

103. The microfiche for the year 1895 for the *Journal* were not held by the Onondaga County Public Library, from which all of the other reporting was available.

104. *Syracuse Standard*, Oct. 11, 1895, 4.

105. "Fishing with Minnows," *Syracuse Courier*, Oct. 11, 1895, 4.

106. "Put Up a Full Ticket," *Syracuse Courier*, Oct. 11, 1895, 8.

107. "Baldwin Named," *Syracuse Post*, Oct. 17, 1895, 3.

108. "A Belden Candidate," *Syracuse Standard*, Oct. 17, 1895, 4.

109. "Praise for McGuire," *Syracuse Courier*, Oct. 17, 1895, 2.

110. "Holding Back on Black Heritage," *Syracuse Post-Standard*, Feb. 27, 1991.

111. "Over a Million a Year," *Syracuse Courier*, Oct. 21, 1895, 1.

112. "The Time Isn't Ripe," *Syracuse Standard*, Oct. 13, 1895, 6.

113. "Democrats Ratify," *Syracuse Standard*, Oct. 20, 1895, 6.

114. "Up in a Tree," *Syracuse Post*, Oct. 22, 1895, 3.

115. "More Hot Shot," *Syracuse Post*, Oct. 23, 1895, 3.

116. "Bishop Ludden's Letter," *Syracuse Post*, Oct. 23, 1895, 4.

117. "Baldwin the Winner," *Syracuse Evening Herald*, Nov. 1, 1895, 6.

118. Franklin Chase, *Syracuse and Its Environs: A History*, vol. 2 (New York: Lewis Publishing Co., 1924), 696.

119. "Campaign Lie Nailed," *Syracuse Courier*, Nov. 1, 1895, 2.

120. *Syracuse Evening Herald*, Nov. 2, 1895, 6.

121. "Bets on the Result," *Syracuse Courier*, Nov. 2, 1895, 5.

122. "Some Charges," *Syracuse Courier*, Nov. 4, 1895, 4.

123. "Ready for the Fray," *Syracuse Courier*, Nov. 4, 1895, 1.

124. *Dictionary of American Biography*, 7:19.

125. "Soule Won't Take It," *Syracuse Evening Herald*, Nov. 12, 1895, 6.

126. "Heavy Vote Cast," *Syracuse Evening Herald*, Nov. 5, 1895, 6.

127. "McGuire Is Elected," *Syracuse Post*, Nov. 6, 1895, 2.

128. "Ovation for McGuire," *Syracuse Courier*, Nov. 6, 1895, 2.

129. "Death of Mrs. McGuire," *Syracuse Post-Standard*, Jan. 20, 1899.

130. "The New Mayor," *Syracuse Courier*, Nov. 6, 1895, 4.

131. "Mayor-Elect McGuire," *Syracuse Evening Herald*, Nov. 6, 1895, 4.

132. "Mr. McGuire's Opportunity," *Syracuse Post*, Nov. 7, 1895, 4.

133. "The Results in the City," *Syracuse Standard*, Nov. 6, 1895, 4.

134. An anti-Catholic nativist society.

135. "Mayoral Rivals Were Neighbors," *Syracuse Herald-Journal*, Apr. 20, 1947.

136. "After the Battle," *Syracuse Post*, Nov. 7, 1895, 3.

137. "James K. McGuire: The Comment Produced by His Election," *Syracuse Courier*, Nov. 9, 1895, 4.

138. "McGuire Will Fool Them," *Syracuse Evening Herald*, Nov. 11, 1895, 6.

139. "McGuire Is Elected," *Syracuse Post*, Nov. 6, 1895, 2.

140. "McGuire the Leader," *Syracuse Standard*, Nov. 7, 1895, 6.

141. "Soule Won't Take It."

142. "To Get Ide Out," *Syracuse Evening Herald*, Nov. 17, 1895, 11.

143. Daniel Wager, *Our County and Its People*, part 3: *Family Sketches* ([Boston]: Boston History Co., 1896), 17.

144. "McGuire in New York," *Catholic Sun*, Nov. 29, 1895, 1, 4.

145. "This Is McGuire," *Sunday Herald*, Dec. 22, 1895, 5.

4. The Mayoral Years: Boy Mayor

1. This commission would investigate the laying of electric light, telephone, and other cables under the streets. It is not to be confused with a transit company operating subterranean railway lines.

2. Letter to the Common Council, Jan. 6, 1896, Communications file, Syracuse City Hall Archives.

3. "The Garbage Question," *Syracuse Evening Herald*, Jan. 17, 1896, 10.

4. "Standing Committees," *Syracuse Evening Herald*, Jan. 21, 1896, 7.

5. "Hendricks Wants a Man," *Syracuse Evening Herald*, Jan. 27, 1896, 6.

6. "For Public Bath," *Syracuse Evening Herald*, Feb. 9, 1896, 11.

7. "The Mayor on Saloons," *Syracuse Evening Herald*, Feb. 11, 1896, 6.

8. *Catholic Sun*, Feb. 28, 1896, 4.

9. "Why Bishop Is Kept," *Syracuse Evening Herald*, Apr. 14, 1896.

10. "Suburban's Franchise," *Syracuse Evening Herald*, Apr. 21, 1896, 10.

11. "Mayor and Suburban," *Syracuse Evening Herald*, May 4, 1896, 6.

12. "Mayor's Ideas Are All In," *Syracuse Evening Herald*, May 7, 1896, 12.

13. "Mayor's Cabinet," *Syracuse Evening Herald*, May 10, 1896, 13.

14. Chapter 559 of the Laws of the State of New York, enacted June 21, 1881.

15. "The New Police Board," *Syracuse Evening Herald*, May 1, 1896, 6.

16. "Suburban and Lakeside," *Syracuse Evening Herald*, May 12, 1896, 9.

17. "Lakeside's Directors," *Syracuse Evening Herald*, May 15, 1896, 6.

18. "Mayor McGuire's Wedding," *Syracuse Evening Herald*, June 24, 1896, 6.

19. "Bonds Keep Him Home," *New York Times*, July 2, 1896.

20. "Blame Hendricks," *Syracuse Evening Herald*, June 28, 1896, 13.

21. "They Say They Will Pay," *Syracuse Evening Herald*, Aug. 4, 1896, 6.

22. "Mayor's Silver Census," *Syracuse Evening Herald*, Aug. 7, 1896, 6.

23. "On a Still Hunt," *Syracuse Evening Herald*, Aug. 9, 1896, 13.

24. "Does It No Little Harm," *Syracuse Evening Herald*, Aug. 10, 1896, 6.

25. "Bryan to Come Here," *Syracuse Evening Herald*, Aug. 14, 1896, 6.

26. "Off for the Islands," *Syracuse Evening Herald*, Aug. 20, 1896, 6.

27. "Onondagans at Buffalo," *Syracuse Evening Herald*, Sept. 18, 1896, 6.

28. "McGuire Offended Tammany," *Syracuse Evening Herald*, Sept. 18, 1896, 6.

29. Letters to the Common Council, Sept. 22, 1896, Communications file, Syracuse City Hall Archives.

30. "Mayor Vetoes Budget," *Syracuse Evening Herald*, Sept. 22, 1896, 6.

31. "To Sustain the Mayor," *Syracuse Evening Herald*, Sept. 26, 1896, 6.

32. "Lively Argument," *Syracuse Evening Herald*, Sept. 29, 1896, 7.

33. "Belden's Sweeping Victory," *Syracuse Evening Herald*, Nov. 6, 1896, 6.

34. "Too Much Power," *Syracuse Evening Herald*, Jan. 3, 1897, 13.

35. "His Appointees," *Syracuse Evening Herald*, Jan. 17, 1897, 13.

36. "Cold Comfort for Him," *Syracuse Evening Herald*, Jan. 19, 1897, 7.

37. "Mayor Can't Help Them," *Syracuse Evening Herald*, Jan. 21, 1897, 6.

38. "Taxpayer Notes," *Syracuse Evening Herald*, Mar. 10, 1897, 6.

39. "Newell's Vain Wait," *Syracuse Post*, Apr. 29, 1897, 3.

40. "They Enter the Field," *Syracuse Post*, May 18, 1897, 3.

41. "At Odds Over a Park," *Syracuse Post*, May 18, 1897, 3.

42. "Up on the Same Horse," *Syracuse Post*, May 19, 1897, 3.

43. "McGuire Starts It Up," *Syracuse Evening Herald*, June 5, 1897, 7.

44. "Cunning Scheme," *Syracuse Evening Herald*, June 13, 1897, 13.

45. "Democrats Preparing," *Syracuse Evening Herald*, June 22, 1897, 6.

46. "Nothing for the City," *Syracuse Evening Herald*, July 4, 1897, 13.

47. Ibid.

48. McGuire to the Common Council, July 10, 1897, Communications file, Syracuse City Hall Archives.

49. "Reform Candidate," *Syracuse Evening Herald*, July 18, 1897, 13.

50. "Hadn't Enough Votes," *Syracuse Evening Herald*, July 20, 1897, 7.

51. "Signs of Activity," *Syracuse Evening Herald*, Aug. 8, 1897, 13.

52. "Mayor's Mishap," *Syracuse Evening Herald*, Aug. 8, 1897, 13.

53. "Confirmed by Council," *Syracuse Evening Herald*, Aug. 8, 1897, 7.

54. McGuire letter to the Common Council, Aug. 18, 1897, Communications file, Syracuse City Hall Archives.

55. "Fifteen Voted for It," *Syracuse Evening Herald*, Aug. 31, 1897, 7.

56. "Mayor McGuire a Daddy," *Syracuse Evening Herald*, Aug. 27, 1897, 6.

57. Edward S. McGuire, the mayor's youngest brother.

58. "Talk of Harmony," *Syracuse Evening Herald*, Sept. 5, 1897, 13.

59. "For Good Government," *Syracuse Evening Herald*, Oct. 8, 1897, 7.

60. "Political Gossip," *Syracuse Evening Herald*, Oct. 10, 1897, 13.

61. "In the Republican Twelfth," *Syracuse Evening Herald*, Oct. 21, 1897, 7.

62. "Crowds Cheer McGuire," *Syracuse Evening Herald*, Oct. 23, 1897, 7.

63. "Spoke Five Times," *Syracuse Evening Herald*, Oct. 14, 1897, 13.

64. Letter provided to the author by Joan Carey.

65. *Boyd's City Directory*, 1898–99.

66. "Ovation for Dey," *Syracuse Evening Herald*, Oct. 28, 1897, 7.

67. "Only Another Day," *Syracuse Evening Herald*, Oct. 31, 1897, 13.

68. "Unlucky Number," *Syracuse Evening Herald*, Oct. 31, 1897, 13.

69. "Democrats Win," *Syracuse Evening Herald*, Nov. 3, 1897, 7.

70. Ibid.

71. "Aldermen Do Figuring," *Syracuse Evening Herald*, Nov. 5, 1897, 6.

72. "The Next Common Council," *Syracuse Evening Herald*, Nov. 3, 1897, 6.

73. "Mayor Off for New York," *Syracuse Evening Herald*, Nov. 5, 1897, 6.

74. "He Will Drop Out," *Syracuse Evening Herald*, Nov. 14, 1897, 13.

75. "Strife Is Ahead," *Syracuse Evening Herald*, Nov. 21, 1897, 13.

76. "Filling the Lake," *Syracuse Evening Herald*, Dec. 12, 1897, 13.

77. "Ready to Take Offices," *Syracuse Evening Herald*, Dec. 24, 1897, 7.

78. "Democrats Are in Town," *Syracuse Evening Herald*, Jan. 3, 1898, 6.

79. "Matty the Common Council's President," *Syracuse Evening Herald*, Jan. 4, 1898, 6.

80. "Mack Is Elected," *Syracuse Evening Herald*, Jan. 6, 1898, 10.

81. "An Investigation," *Syracuse Evening Herald*, Jan. 7, 1898, 6.

82. "Offer Declined," *Syracuse Evening Herald*, Jan. 9, 1898, 13.

83. "Matty the Common Council's President," 6.

84. McGuire letter to the Common Council, Jan. 3, 1898, Communications file, Syracuse City Hall Archives.

85. "What It Hinges On," *Syracuse Evening Herald*, Jan. 16, 1898, 13.

86. "To Give Public Succor," *Syracuse Evening Herald*, Jan. 22, 1898, 6.

87. "Nine Democrats Are Indicted," *Syracuse Evening Herald*, Jan. 28, 1898, 6.

88. "The Indictments," *Syracuse Evening Herald*, Jan. 29, 1898, 4.

89. "Jurors Politics," *Syracuse Evening Herald*, Jan. 30, 1898, 13.

90. "Council Does Nothing," *Syracuse Evening Herald*, Feb. 1, 1898, 7.

91. "High School Bill," *Syracuse Evening Herald*, Feb. 13, 1898, 13.

92. "Legislators to Decide," *Syracuse Evening Herald*, Feb. 22, 1898, 6.

93. "They'll not Interfere," *Syracuse Evening Herald*, Feb. 25, 1898, 6.

94. "Mayor Must Accept It," *Syracuse Evening Herald*, Mar. 9, 1898, 7.

95. "Wow, Wow, Wow," *Catholic Sun*, Jan. 14, 1898, 1.

96. "Political Gossip," *Syracuse Evening Herald*, Mar. 20, 1898, 13.

97. "One Democrat on the Jury," *Syracuse Evening Herald*, Mar. 22, 1898, 6.

98. "Mack Helped Stuff Hat," *Syracuse Evening Herald*, Mar. 23, 1898, 6.

99. "Jurors Disagreed," *Syracuse Evening Herald*, Mar. 26, 1898, 7.

100. "Not a Lower One," *Syracuse Evening Herald*, Apr. 17, 1898, 13.

101. "To Have an Organ," *Syracuse Evening Herald*, May 1, 1898, 17.

102. "Kirk's Mission," *Syracuse Evening Herald*, May 8, 1898, 13.

103. "Political Gossip," *Syracuse Evening Herald*, May 15, 1898, 17.

104. "Mayor to Ministers," *Syracuse Evening Herald*, May 10, 1898, 6.

105. "Austin Got Too Bold," *Syracuse Evening Herald*, May 17, 1898, 17.

106. "Political Gossip," *Syracuse Evening Herald*, July 3, 1898, 13.

107. "Political Gossip," *Syracuse Evening Herald*, July 10, 1898, 13.

108. "Eyes on Belden," *Syracuse Evening Herald*, July 24, 1898, 13.

109. "Political Gossip," *Syracuse Evening Herald*, July 31, 1898, 13.

110. "Silver Men Are Active," *Syracuse Evening Herald*, Aug. 10, 1898, 6.

111. "City's Victory," *Syracuse Evening Herald*, Aug. 14, 1898, 13.

112. "Favor Roosevelt," *Syracuse Evening Herald*, Aug. 21, 1898, 13.

113. "Will He Go West," *Syracuse Evening Herald*, Aug. 28, 1898, 13.

114. "Is Well Received," *Syracuse Evening Herald*, Sept. 4, 1898, 13.

115. Official Records, U.S. Census Bureau, Washington, DC, 1900.

116. "McGuire for Governor," *Syracuse Evening Herald*, Sept. 21, 1898, 6.

117. "They Came To-day," *Syracuse Evening Herald*, Sept. 25, 1898, 13.

118. "Roosevelt and Woodruff," *Syracuse Evening Herald*, Sept. 26, 1898, 1.

119. "Silver Men Ready to Bolt," *Syracuse Evening Herald*, Sept. 28, 1898, 2.

120. "Croker the Man of the Hour," *Syracuse Evening Herald*, Sept. 28, 1898, 3.

121. "Hill the Man of the Night," *Syracuse Evening Herald*, Sept. 29, 1898, 3.

122. "There's Fun Ahead," *Syracuse Evening Herald*, Oct. 2, 1898, 13.

123. "Democrats Also," *Syracuse Evening Herald*, Oct. 7, 1898, 6.

124. "Belden's Refusal," *Syracuse Evening Herald*, Oct. 10, 1898, 6.

125. "McGuire on the Situation," *Syracuse Evening Herald*, Oct. 11, 1898, 6.

126. "Van Wyck Is Here," *Syracuse Evening Herald*, Oct. 26, 1898, 6.

127. "Van Wyck at Alhambra," *Syracuse Evening Herald*, Oct. 27, 1898, 7.

128. Roosevelt Takes Alhambra by Storm, *Syracuse Evening Herald*, Oct. 28, 1898, 9.

129. William H. Manz, "Tammany Had a Right to Expect Proper Consideration: The Judicial Nominations Controversy of 1898," *New York State Bar Association Journal* 81, no. 3 (Mar./Apr. 2009): 11–23.

130. "Closing the Lines," *Syracuse Evening Herald*, Nov. 6, 1898, 13.

131. "It Is Roosevelt by 20,000 Votes," *Syracuse Evening Herald*, Nov. 9, 1898, 1.

132. "Croker on McGuire," *Syracuse Herald*, Mar. 15, 1909, 2.

133. "Joy and Sorrow," *Syracuse Evening Herald*, Nov. 13, 1898, 13.

134. "Fifty Machines," *Syracuse Evening Herald*, Nov. 20, 1898, 13.

135. "What McGuire Would Do," *Syracuse Evening Herald*, Dec. 2, 1898, 6.

136. "Demand for Work or Bread," *Syracuse Evening Herald*, Dec. 16, 1898, 6.

137. "Assessors Work," *Syracuse Evening Herald*, Dec. 18, 1898, 13.

138. "Death of Mrs. McGuire," *Syracuse Post-Standard*, Jan. 20, 1899.

139. "Clear Field for Mack," *Syracuse Evening Herald*, Jan. 4, 1899, 6.

140. "Not To Be So Easy," *Syracuse Evening Herald*, Jan. 8, 1899, 13.

141. "Second Class City Charter," *New York Times*, Jan. 13, 1899.

142. Mayor's Annual Address to the Common Council, Feb. 1, 1899, *Common Council Manual, City of Syracuse* (Syracuse, NY: E. M. Grover Printers and Binders, 1899), 51–104.

143. "Looking for a Candidate," *Syracuse Evening Herald*, Feb. 13, 1899, 6.

144. "Deficiency Is Growing," *Syracuse Evening Herald*, Mar. 11, 1899, 7.

145. "Enormous Deficit in City Funds," *Syracuse Evening Herald*, Mar. 12, 1899, 7.

146. "Tracks Entirely Out," *Syracuse Evening Herald*, Apr. 12, 1899, 6.

147. "Tracks Torn Up," *Syracuse Evening Herald*, Apr. 22, 1899, 6.

148. "City Is Liable," *Syracuse Evening Herald*, Apr. 23, 1899, 13.

149. "Hendricks's Trip," *Syracuse Evening Herald*, Apr. 24, 1899, 6.

150. "Hendricks in Albany," *Syracuse Evening Herald*, Apr. 25, 1899, 6.

151. "It Will Enjoin," *Syracuse Evening Herald*, Apr. 25, 1899, 6.

152. "No Fight on Haven," *Syracuse Evening Herald*, Apr. 23, 1899, 13.

153. "Hard Nut to Crack," *Syracuse Evening Herald*, Apr. 3, 1899, 13.

154. "Who'll Be Named," *Syracuse Evening Herald*, May 7, 1899, 13.

155. "This View Bright," *Syracuse Evening Herald*, June 4, 1899, 13.

156. "Now It's Sager," *Syracuse Evening Herald*, June 18, 1899, 13.

157. "City Should Own," *Syracuse Evening Herald*, July 11, 1899, 6.

158. "At Last He Speaks," *Syracuse Evening Herald*, Oct. 8, 1899, 13.

159. "Mayor McGuire's Opening Gun," *Syracuse Evening Herald*, Oct. 13, 1899, 9.

160. "Spoke in the Nineteenth," *Syracuse Evening Herald*, Oct. 14, 1899, 7.

161. "Syracuse Republicans Have Opened Their Municipal Campaign," *Syracuse Evening Herald*, Oct. 18, 1899, 10.

162. "McGuire Answers," *Syracuse Evening Herald*, Oct. 19, 1899, 9.

163. "Havens Big Talk," *Syracuse Evening Herald*, Oct. 21, 1899, 12.

164. "In Thirteenth," *Syracuse Evening Herald*, Oct. 26, 1899, 7.

165. "Hancock Figures," *Syracuse Evening Herald*, Oct. 24, 1899, 9.

166. "Hotel Is Cheaper," *Syracuse Evening Herald*, Oct. 25, 1899, 7.

167. "Value for Money," *Syracuse Evening Herald*, Oct. 25, 1899, 9.

168. "Under a Tent," *Syracuse Evening Herald*, Oct. 28, 1899, 7.

169. "Should Retire," *Syracuse Evening Herald*, Oct. 28, 1899, 9.

170. "Crowds in Rain," *Syracuse Evening Herald*, Nov. 1, 1899, 9.

171. "Wet, but Lively," *Syracuse Evening Herald*, 1899, Nov. 1, 10.

172. "In Three Wards," *Syracuse Evening Herald*, Nov. 2, 1899, 9.

173. "Bets on the Election," *Syracuse Evening Herald*, Nov. 6, 1899, 6.

174. "For Pure Ballot," *Syracuse Evening Herald*, Nov. 3, 1899, 9.

175. "Special Police," *Syracuse Evening Herald*, Nov. 3, 1899, 13.

176. "Vote Is Heavy," *Syracuse Evening Herald*, Nov. 7, 1899, 6.

177. "Mayor McGuire's Great Victory," *Syracuse Evening Herald*, Nov. 8, 1899, 7.

178. "Vote in the City on State, Senatorial and County Tickets," *Syracuse Post*, Nov. 6, 1895, 3.

179. "Now in Official Life," *Syracuse Evening Herald*, Jan. 2, 1900, 6.

180. "It Looks Like Saunders," *Syracuse Evening Herald*, Nov. 8, 1900, 6.

181. "To California," *Syracuse Evening Herald*, Jan. 21, 1900, 13.

182. New York State Bureau of Vital Statistics, New York Department of Health, Menands, New York.

183. "Mayor on Overdrafts," *Syracuse Evening Herald*, Jan. 22, 1900, 6.

184. "If Mayor Were Older," *Syracuse Evening Herald*, Feb. 10, 1900, 6.

185. "New Plan of Campaign," *Syracuse Evening Herald*, Feb. 11, 1900, 13.

186. "Is It a Political Device?" *Syracuse Evening Herald*, Feb. 15, 1900, 6.

187. "Pressure Is Great," *Syracuse Evening Herald*, Feb. 18, 1900, 13.

188. "Legislators to Probe Here," *Syracuse Evening Herald*, Feb. 22, 1900, 6.

189. "Friends See Him Off," *Syracuse Evening Herald*, Apr. 26, 1900, 6.

190. "Will Sail To-morrow," *Catholic Sun*, Apr. 27, 1900, 1.

191. "Returns To-morrow," *Catholic Sun*, May 18, 1900, 1.

192. "An Irish Army," *Catholic Sun*, Dec. 20, 1895, 1.

193. "Will Act Monday," *Syracuse Evening Herald*, May 5, 1900, 6.

194. Edmund Morris, *Theodore Rex* (New York: Random House, 2001), 425.

195. "This Afternoon," *Syracuse Evening Herald*, May 7, 1900, 6.

196. "Talks of His Trip," *Syracuse Evening Herald*, May 28, 1900, 6.

197. "Buffalo Politicians," *Syracuse Evening Herald*, May 31, 1900, 6.

198. "Who Told Jury Secrets," *Syracuse Evening Herald*, June 20, 1900, 6.

199. "Matty's Dream," *Syracuse Evening Herald*, June 21, 1900, 6.

200. "To Run Once More," *Syracuse Evening Herald*, June 24, 1900, 13.

201. *Billingsgate*, n. Meaning vulgar or abusive language; coarse vituperation; an allusion to Billingsgate market, London, where formerly the fish women were notorious for scurrility. *Funk & Wagnalls New Standard Dictionary of the English Language* (New York: Funk & Wagnalls, 1926), 268.

202. "Mayor Wants O'Neill Abated," *Syracuse Evening Herald*, June 29, 1900, 8.

203. "Indicted," *Syracuse Evening Herald*, July 5, 1900, 6. See also "Syracuse Mayor Indicted," *New York Times*, July 3, 1900.

204. "An Early Trial," *Syracuse Evening Herald*, July 8, 1900, 13.

205. "Three Days Each Week," *Syracuse Evening Herald*, July 1, 1900, 6.

206. "McGuire Taken Ill While Speaking," *Syracuse Evening Herald*, Oct. 7, 1900, 17.

207. "McGuire's Views," *Syracuse Evening Herald*, Nov. 8, 1900, 6.

208. "State Chairman," *Syracuse Evening Herald*, Nov. 16, 1900, 6.

209. "Public Golf Links," *Syracuse Evening Herald*, Nov. 26, 1900, 13.

210. "Not to Run Again," *Syracuse Evening Herald*, Dec. 1, 1900, 6.

211. "Mayor's Decision," *Syracuse Evening Herald*, Dec. 2, 1900, 13.

212. "Fifteen Defendants," *Syracuse Evening Herald*, Dec. 4, 1900, 6.

213. "With the Jury," *Syracuse Evening Herald*, Dec. 4, 1900, 8.

214. "Jury Failed to Agree," *Syracuse Evening Herald*, Dec. 5, 1900, 7.

215. "Given to the Jury," *Syracuse Evening Herald*, Dec. 7, 1900, 7.

216. "Mayor Talks of Trial," *Syracuse Evening Herald*, Dec. 8, 1900, 6.

217. "Effort for Plant," *Syracuse Evening Herald*, Dec. 13, 1900, 6.

218. "It Is Larger than Expected," *Syracuse Evening Herald*, Jan. 1, 1901, 16.

219. "Carnegie Will Give City a Library," *Syracuse Evening Herald*, Jan. 17, 1901, 6.

220. McGuire to George Fisk Comfort, Mar. 17, 1899, courtesy of the George Fisk Comfort Papers, Syracuse University Archives, box 5, 7112: 1898–99 folder; and the Onondaga Historical Association.

221. "Were They Mixed," *Syracuse Evening Herald*, Jan. 21, 1901, 6.

222. "Carnegie's Gift," *Syracuse Evening Herald*, Jan. 26, 1901, 6.

223. "Talk Mandamus," *Syracuse Evening Herald*, Jan. 27, 1901, 13.

224. "McGuire Wants Meagher," *Syracuse Evening Herald*, Feb. 1, 1901, 6.

225. "Political Gossip," *Syracuse Evening Herald*, Mar. 10, 1901, 13.

226. "Political Gossip," *Syracuse Evening Herald*, Mar. 24, 1901, 13.

227. "They Urge Kline," *Syracuse Evening Herald*, Mar. 31, 1901, 13.

228. "Mayor McGuire Invests," *Syracuse Evening Herald*, Apr. 30, 1901, 7.

229. "Mayor Is Home," *Syracuse Evening Herald*, May 2, 1901, 6.

230. "Old Men's Home," *Syracuse Evening Herald*, May 26, 1901, 13.

231. "Mayor Talks on Home," *Syracuse Evening Herald*, May 28, 1901, 6.

232. "Deficiency Goes In," *Syracuse Evening Herald*, June 24, 1901, 6.

233. "Tax Rate, $21.30," *Syracuse Evening Herald*, Sept. 23, 1901, 6.

234. "McGuire on Tax Rate," *Syracuse Evening Herald*, Sept. 24, 1901, 7.

235. "Will McGuire Accept," *Syracuse Evening Herald*, Oct. 10, 1901, 6.

236. "Hendricks Surrendered; Kline Chosen," *Syracuse Evening Herald*, Oct. 10, 1901, 7.

237. "McGuire Protested; Convention Insisted," *Syracuse Evening Herald*, Oct. 11, 1901, 8.

238. "Mrs. McGuire Yields," *Syracuse Evening Herald*, Oct. 12, 1901, 6.

239. "Record Broken," *Syracuse Evening Herald*, Oct. 20, 1901, 13.

240. "Talk of the Pay Roll," *Syracuse Evening Herald*, Oct. 23, 1901, 8.

241. "McGuire Is Willing," *Syracuse Evening Herald*, Oct. 24, 1901, 7.

242. "His Second Challenge," *Syracuse Evening Herald*, Oct. 25, 1901, 9.

243. "McGuire Is Rich, Says Magee," *Syracuse Evening Herald*, Oct. 25, 1901, 10.

244. "Mayor in the West End," *Syracuse Evening Herald*, Oct. 26, 1901, 9.

245. "Marnell Bets 2 to 1," *Syracuse Evening Herald*, Oct. 26, 1901, 6.

246. "1,700 Indictments," *Syracuse Evening Herald*, Oct. 19, 1901, 7.

247. "Kline Is Severe Too," *Syracuse Evening Herald*, Oct. 30, 1901, 10.

248. "Election Betting," *Syracuse Evening Herald*, Oct. 31, 1901, 6.

249. "McGuire Is Favorite," *Syracuse Evening Herald*, Nov. 3, 1901, 1.

250. "The Vote in Early," *Syracuse Evening Herald*, Nov. 5, 1901, 6.

251. McGuire to George Fisk Comfort, Nov. 29, 1901, courtesy of the George Fisk Comfort Papers, Syracuse University Archives, box 5, 7113: 1901 folder; and the Onondaga Historical Association.

252. "Mayoral Rivals Were Neighbors."

5. The "Wilderness" Years

1. New York State Bureau of Vital Statistics.

2. James K. McGuire, ed., *Democratic Party of the State of New York* (New York: United States History Co., J. R. Tapley Co., 1905).

3. "He Visited Hill," *Syracuse Evening Herald*, Mar. 30, 1902, 13.

4. "Democratic Chairman McGuire, Resigns," *New York Times*, July 9, 1902.

5. "Waited Half an Hour," *Syracuse Evening Herald*, Aug. 2, 1902, 7.

6. "Bird S. Coler for Governor," *Syracuse Evening Herald*, Oct. 1, 1902, 1.

7. See H. W. Brands, *T.R.: The Last Romantic* (New York: Basic Books, 1997), 450–60.

8. "McGuire on His Plank," *Syracuse Evening Herald*, Oct. 4, 1902, 7.

9. "McGuire's First Speech," *Syracuse Evening Herald*, Oct. 22, 1902, 7.

10. "Governor Odell in Auburn," *Syracuse Evening Herald*, Oct. 23, 1902, 1.

11. "Ready to Retire," *Syracuse Evening Herald*, Nov. 23, 1902, 13.

12. "He Is Out of Politics," *Syracuse Evening Herald*, May 20, 1903, 6.

13. "He Quits as Leader," *Syracuse Evening Herald*, Jan. 3, 1904, 13.

14. "All Records Broken in Onondaga County," *Syracuse Evening Herald*, Nov. 12, 1904, 6.

15. "Cummins Will Quit," *Syracuse Evening Herald*, Nov. 9, 1904, 6.

16. "Party in a Bad Way," *Syracuse Evening Herald*, Nov. 13, 1904, 13.

17. "McGuire Will Keep Out," *Syracuse Evening Herald*, Jan. 30, 1905, 6.

18. McGuire, *Democratic Party of the State Of New York*.

19. "Asphalt Row in Albany," *Syracuse Evening Herald*, Apr. 5, 1905, 6.

20. "Politicians Bad," *Syracuse Evening Herald*, May 1, 1905, 6.

21. "Haven Makes Case," *Syracuse Evening Herald*, Jan. 7, 1906, 6.

22. Ben Procter, *William Randolph Hearst: The Early Years, 1863–1910* (New York: Oxford Univ. Press, 1998), 173, 182, 184, 197, 203, 205.

23. "Hearst Writes Grays," *Syracuse Evening Herald*, Mar. 25, 1906, 6.

24. "Chancellor Renews His Attack on the President; McGuire's Visit to the White House," *Syracuse Evening Herald*, May 10, 1906, 12.

25. "Hearst Can Win; And Only Hearst," *Syracuse Evening Herald*, May 20, 1906, 6.

26. "It Is Hearst Now against Higgins," *Syracuse Evening Herald*, May 21, 1906, 1.

27. "Hearst Men to Meet," *Syracuse Evening Herald*, May 27, 1906, 6.

28. "McGuire Scores the Chancellor," *Syracuse Evening Herald*, June 12, 1906, 6.

29. "No Longer a Partisan," *Syracuse Evening Herald*, June 25, 1906, 6.

30. "Hearst a Prophet," *Syracuse Evening Herald*, July 15, 1906, 8.

31. Procter, *William Randolph Hearst: The Early Years*, 163.

32. "Mayor's Right to Seat May Not Be Tested," *New York Times*, July 16, 1906.

33. "To Nominate Hearst before Democrats Act," *New York Times*, Aug. 1, 1906.

34. "Hearst Must Run for Governor Alone," *New York Times*, Aug. 1, 1906.

35. "To Draft McGuire," *Syracuse Evening Herald*, Aug. 5, 1906, 6.

36. "It Is Hearst for Sure," *Syracuse Evening Herald*, Aug. 12, 1906, 7.

37. "Few Are Enrolled," *Syracuse Evening Herald*, Aug. 27, 1906, 6.

38. "New Morning Paper," *Syracuse Evening Herald*, Aug. 31, 1906, 6.

39. Procter, *William Randolph Hearst: The Early Years*, 153.

40. "At Home to Fight," *Syracuse Evening Herald*, Sept. 1, 1906, 6.

41. "Haven Is in Albany," *Syracuse Evening Herald*, Sept. 5, 1906, 6.

42. "Trim Murphy Too," *Syracuse Evening Herald*, Sept. 9, 1906, 6.

43. "An Old Time Battle," *Syracuse Evening Herald*, Sept. 18, 1906, 6–7.

44. "Parsons and Murphy," *Syracuse Evening Herald*, Sept. 19, 1906, 1.

45. "Hearst Named by Democrats," *New York Times*, Sept. 27, 1906.

46. "Hughes Nominated," *Syracuse Evening Herald*, Sept. 26, 1906, 1.

47. "McGuire to Make Run for Congress," *New York Times*, Oct. 9, 1906.

48. "Now for the Ballots," *Syracuse Evening Herald*, Nov. 15, 1906, 6.

49. "Wild Cheers Follow Hughes about the City," *New York Times*, Nov. 6, 1906.

50. "Hughes Wins," *New York Times*, Nov. 7, 1906.

51. "About 8,600 for Hughes," *Syracuse Evening Herald*, Nov. 7, 1906, 6.

52. "Big Plurality for Driscoll," *Syracuse Post-Standard*, Nov. 7, 1906, 14.

53. "McGuire to Make Run for Congress," *Syracuse Post-Standard*, Oct. 9, 1906, 6.

54. "The Floaters Did It," *Syracuse Evening Herald*, Nov. 8, 1906, 7.

55. "Hungry for Office," *Syracuse Evening Herald*, Nov. 19, 1906, 6.

56. "Campaign Statements Fail to State All," *New York Times*, Nov. 30, 1906.

57. "Matty Is in Earnest," *Syracuse Evening Herald*, June 7, 1907, 6.

58. "To Renominate All," *Syracuse Evening Herald*, Sept. 22, 1907, 6.

59. "McGuire on Mayoralty," *Syracuse Evening Herald*, Sept. 23, 1907, 6.

60. "Matty for Mayor," *Syracuse Evening Herald*, Oct. 10, 1907, 6.

61. "I Wasn't a Cheap Guy Anyway, Matty on the Alleged $7,000 Hold Up," *Syracuse Evening Herald*, Oct. 30, 1907, 6.

62. "Ballot Box Stuffed for Matty Election as President of the Council," *Syracuse Evening Herald*, Oct. 29, 1907, 6.

63. "Marked Cards," *Syracuse Evening Herald*, Nov. 2, 1907, 6.

64. "Matty Has Pull on Rapid Transit," *Syracuse Evening Herald*, Oct. 23, 1907, 7.

65. "Matty Got Electric Lights for Nothing Evidence before State Gas Commission," *Syracuse Evening Herald*, Oct. 22, 1907, 6.

66. "Matty's Dream of the Grand Jury His Examination by Justice Smith," *Syracuse Evening Herald*, Oct. 25, 1907, 7.

67. "Matty's Tax Marked 'Erroneous' Saved $606.10 in 1898," *Syracuse Evening Herald*, Oct. 24, 1907, 6.

68. "The Raid on Matty's," *Syracuse Evening Herald*, Oct. 28, 1907, 6.

69. "Marked Cards."

70. "McGuire on Matty," *Syracuse Evening Herald*, Oct. 20, 1907, 6.

71. "McGuire Not to Vote," *Syracuse Evening Herald*, Oct. 21, 1907, 6.

72. "McGuire Not to Speak," *Syracuse Evening Herald*, Oct. 28, 1907, 7.

73. "Matty Falls Down," *Syracuse Evening Herald*, Nov. 3, 1907, 6.

74. "Fobes Wins by 2,326," *Syracuse Evening Herald*, Nov. 6, 1907, 6.

75. "Is After McGuire," *Syracuse Evening Herald*, Feb. 24, 1908, 6.

76. "Burglar Alarms Rang, Says McGuire," *Syracuse Evening Herald*, Feb. 26, 1908, 6.

77. "He Asks Definition," *Syracuse Evening Herald*, Feb. 27, 1908, 6.

78. "Goes to Meet Bryan," *Syracuse Evening Herald*, June 15, 1908, 6.

79. "McGuire Won't Be Swerved," *Syracuse Evening Herald*, June 28, 1908, 6.

80. "McGuire's Idea of a Platform," *Syracuse Evening Herald*, June 29, 1908, 6.

81. "To Get State in Line," *Syracuse Evening Herald*, July 16, 1908, 1.

82. "Say They'll Help," *Syracuse Evening Herald*, July 1, 1908, 6.

83. "The Effect of Hearst Party," *Syracuse Evening Herald*, July 24, 1908, 6.

84. Procter, *William Randolph Hearst: The Early Years*, 240.

85. "On Move for Bryan," *Syracuse Evening Herald*, Aug. 17, 1908, 6.

86. "Are Watching Debs," *Syracuse Evening Herald*, Oct. 5, 1908, 7.

87. "Own Money, He Says," *Syracuse Evening Herald*, Oct. 24, 1908, 6.

88. "Now After Thomas," *Syracuse Evening Herald*, Oct. 26, 1908, 6.

89. Procter, *William Randolph Hearst: The Early Years*, 246–51.

90. Ibid., 253.

91. "Big Crowd in Fifth," *Syracuse Evening Herald*, Oct. 17, 1909, c-1-2.

92. "McGuire's Speech," *Syracuse Evening Herald*, Oct. 18, 1909, 4.

93. "McGuire Retires from Leadership," *Syracuse Evening Herald*, July 6, 1910, 6.

94. Ben Procter, *William Randolph Hearst: The Later Years, 1911–1951* (New York: Oxford Univ. Press, 2007), 19–25.

95. "Sulzer Will Start with Clean Slate," *New York Times*, Oct. 4, 1912.

96. "Sulzer Too," *New York Times*, Nov. 6, 1912.

97. "Sulzer in Open War with Tammany Boss," *New York Times*, Mar. 1, 1913.

98. "Contracts Held Up; Road Work Waste," *New York Times*, Apr. 8, 1913.

99. "Eight Articles of Impeachment against Governor Sulzer," *New York Times*, Aug. 14, 1913.

100. "Four Acquittal Ballots," *New York Times*, Oct. 18, 1913.

101. "Murphy to Be a Witness at Graft Hearing," *Syracuse Herald*, Oct. 31, 1913, 1.

102. "Republicans May Call on Whitman," *Syracuse Herald*, Oct. 23, 1913, 3.

103. "McGuire Denies Hennessy Story," *Syracuse Herald*, Nov. 2, 1913, 25.

104. "Wanted Hennessy to Attack Kelley to Hurt Syracuse Democrats," *Syracuse Herald*, Nov. 7, 1913, 1.

105. "Whitman Asks Glynn for Help in Graft Probe," *Syracuse Herald*, Nov. 1, 1913, 6.

106. "McGuire's Confession Leads to State-Wide Investigation of Graft in Connection with Road Contracts and Campaign Gifts," *Syracuse Herald*, Nov. 12, 1913, 1.

107. "Fowler Is Accused of Extortion," *Syracuse Herald*, Nov. 14, 1913, 3.

108. "Whitman Wants McGuire to Make a Clean Breast," *Syracuse Herald*, Nov. 19, 1913, 3.

109. "McGuire Must Tell All He Knows about Graft, Is Whitman Message," *Syracuse Herald*, Nov. 20, 1913, 1.

110. "Four Contractors Say They Gave Up Money to Fowler in Syracuse," *Syracuse Herald*, Nov. 21, 1913, 2.

111. "Whitman Prepares New List of Questions to Ask George McGuire," *Syracuse Herald*, Nov. 22, 1913, 3.

112. "James K. McGuire Under Indictment in New York on a Charge of Illegally Soliciting Contributions for a Political Campaign," *Syracuse Herald*, Nov. 24, 1923, 1.

113. "District Attorney Whitman Puts Guard Over New Rochelle Home of Former Mayor J. K. McGuire," *Syracuse Herald*, Nov. 25, 1913, 1.

114. "J. K. McGuire Calls Charge an Incident," *New York Times*, Nov. 28, 1913.

115. "Contractors Are Asked to Tell of Campaign Gifts," *Syracuse Herald*, Dec. 1, 1913, 2.

116. "M'Guire Denounces Charges as 'Lie,'" *New York Times*, Dec. 3, 1913.

117. "James K. M'Guire Replies 'Liar' To Fillmore Condit," *Syracuse Herald*, Dec. 4, 1913, 2.

118. "McGuire Blames Brother's Mania," *New York Times*, Dec. 8, 1913.

119. "J. K. McGuire Says George Is Mentally Unbalanced," *Syracuse Herald*, Dec. 8, 1913, 1.

120. "M'Guire Says He Told Brother to Support Dolan," *Syracuse Herald*, Dec. 9, 1913, 3.

121. "McGuire Clears Sullivan from Any Wrongdoing," *Syracuse Herald*, Dec. 14, 1913, 1.

122. "Probers Are Unable to Find McGuire," *Syracuse Herald*, Dec. 20, 1913, 1.

123. "J. W. Osborne Gives the Lie to Whitman," *Syracuse Herald*, Dec. 22, 1913, 1; "Glynn Speaks His Last Word in Whitman Case," *Syracuse Herald*, Dec. 24, 1913, 1.

124. "The McGuires Own $70,000 stock in Asphalt Company," *Syracuse Herald*, Dec. 27, 1913, 1.

125. "McGuire Says He Was offered Job by C. M. Warner," *Syracuse Post-Standard*, Dec. 29, 1913.

126. "Whitman Clears Hassett," *New York Times*, Jan. 13, 1914.

127. "Murphy Ready to Follow Sulzer on Witness Stand," *Syracuse Herald*, Jan. 21, 1914, 1.

128. "Sulzer's Story Causes Fight among Democratic Leaders of the State," *Syracuse Herald*, Jan. 22, 1914, 2.

129. "McGuire Telegram Gone," *New York Times*, Jan. 25, 1914.

130. "Seeks Old Picture of 'Jim' Gaffney," *New York Times*, Feb. 1, 1914.

131. "Bench and Bar Join in Lauding Whitman," *New York Times*, Dec. 30, 1914.

6. The King, the Kaiser, and the President

1. Patrick McCartan, *With De Valera in America* (New York: Brentano, 1931), 13. See also Terry Golway, *Irish Rebel: John Devoy and America's Fight for Freedom* (New York: St. Martin's Press, 1998), 24.

2. *Syracuse Post-Standard*, Sept. 18, 1914.

3. Joseph Finnan, *John Redmond and Irish Unity, 1912–1918* (Syracuse, NY: Syracuse Univ. Press, 2004), 21.

4. Charles Callan Tansill, *America and the Fight for Irish Freedom, 1866–1922* (New York: Devin-Adair, 1957), 138–45, 148–50, 156.

5. Published by Devin-Adair Co., New York (1915).

6. Published by Wolfe Tone Co., New York (1916).

7. Finnan, *John Redmond,* 129.

8. See "James K. McGuire's Graphic Letter from the War Zone," *Catholic Sun,* Aug. 21, 1914, 2; and "Mr. McGuire in London," *Catholic Sun,* Aug. 28, 1914, 5.

9. McGuire, *King, Kaiser and Irish Freedom,* 62, 156, 239, 285,303.

10. "James K. McGuire's Book," *Syracuse Post-Standard,* Apr. 20, 1915.

11. James K. McGuire, *What Could Germany Do for Ireland?* (New York: Wolfe Tone Co., 1916), 32, 46–47, 54, 70, 73.

12. See, e.g., John Devoy, *Recollections of an Irish Rebel* (New York: Charles D. Young, 1929), 3–4.

13. McGuire, *What Could Germany Do for Ireland?,* 74–76, 113, 163, 203–4, 247, 248, 98, 264, 82.

14. Tansill, *America and the Fight for Irish Freedom,* 151–52, 157, 166–67.

15. "Former Mayor McGuire Doesn't Like Redmond's Attitude on the War," *Marcellus Observer,* Oct. 14, 1914.

16. Tansill, *America and the Fight for Irish Freedom,* 33.

17. Golway, *Irish Rebel,* 69, 16, 42, 43, 44, 45–50, 55, 66–67.

18. "O'Donovan Rossa, Patriot Dies at 83," *New York Times,* June 30, 1915.

19. Golway, *Irish Rebel,* 67–71.

20. Kenneth D. Ackerman, *Boss Tweed: The Rise and Fall of the Corrupt Pol Who Conceived the Soul of Modern New York* (New York: Carroll & Graf, 2005), 254–55, 72, 79, 94.

21. "O'Donovan Rossa, Patriot, Dies at 83."

22. Golway, *Irish Rebel,* 73–85, 186–87.

23. Tansill, *America and the Fight for Irish Freedom,* 172–73, 176.

24. Devoy, *Recollections,* 403.

25. Tansill, *America and the Fight for Irish Freedom,* 176–77. See also Golway, *Irish Rebel,* 202–3.

26. Sean Cronin, *The McGarrity Papers* (County Kerry, Ireland: Anvil Books, 1972), 70.

27. Tansill, *America and the Fight for Irish Freedom,* 175.

28. Golway, *Irish Rebel,* 203.

29. Cronin, *McGarrity Papers,* 53; Golway, *Irish Rebel,* 203–4.

30. Cronin, *McGarrity Papers,* 53; Golway, *Irish Rebel,* 203–4.

31. Golway, *Irish Rebel,* 203.

32. Tansill, *America and the Fight for Irish Freedom,* 179–86.

33. Devoy, *Recollections,* 429–30, 442–48.

34. Christopher Andrew, *Defend the Realm: The Authorized History of MI5* (London: Penguin Books, 2009), 86.

35. "O'Donovan Ross, Patriot, Dies at 83."

36. "Irish Rebels in English Prisons," *Catholic Sun*, July 10, 1914, 3.

37. Golway, *Irish Rebel*, 207–8. See also Tim Pat Coogan, *Eamon de Valera: The Man Who Was Ireland* (New York: Harper Collins, 1993), 60.

38. Golway, *Irish Rebel*, 210–21.

39. Tansill, *America and the Fight for Irish Freedom*, 121.

40. Procter, *William Randolph Hearst: The Later Years*, 10–12.

41. Golway, *Irish Rebel*, 187, 205, 209, 210, 218, 220.

42. Michael Doorley, *Irish-American Diaspora Nationalism: The Friends of Irish Freedom, 1916–1935* (Portland, OR: Four Courts Press, 2005), 184.

43. Golway, *Irish Rebel*, 220–23.

7. Fellow Traveler

1. Tansill, *America and the Fight for Irish Freedom*, 185; Golway, *Irish Rebel*, 218.

2. Tansill, *America and the Fight for Irish Freedom*, 185. See also Devoy, *Recollections*, 472.

3. Golway, *Irish Rebel*, 227; Devoy, *Recollections*, 472.

4. Tansill, *America and the Fight for Irish Freedom*, 199.

5. Golway, *Irish Rebel*, 228; Coogan, *Eamon de Valera*, 65–66.

6. Golway, *Irish Rebel*, 234; Coogan, *Eamon de Valera*, 73–74.

7. Coogan, *Eamon de Valera*, 55–57.

8. Coogan, *Eamon de Valera*, 74. See also Tansill, *America and the Fight for Irish Freedom*, 200–202.

9. Golway, *Irish Rebel*, 234; Tansill, *America and the Fight for Irish Freedom*, 202–4.

10. Golway, *Irish Rebel*, 235.

11. Ibid., 235.

12. Doorley, *Irish-American Diaspora*, 46.

13. Golway, *Irish Rebel*, 235–37.

14. Doorley, *Irish-American Diaspora*, 46–47.

15. Golway, *Irish Rebel*, 236–37.

16. Tansill, *America and the Fight for Irish Freedom*, 202.

17. Coogan, *Eamon de Valera*, 78. See also Golway, *Irish Rebel*, 237; and Tansill, *America and the Fight for Irish Freedom*, 202.

18. Coogan, *Eamon de Valera*, 78–79.

19. Charles Seymour, *The Intimate Papers of Colonel House*, vol. 2 (Boston: Houghton Mifflin, 1926), 78–79.

20. Tansill, *America and the Fight for Irish Freedom*, 204.

21. Golway, *Irish Rebel*, 236–39.

22. Tansill, *America and the Fight for Irish Freedom*, 206, 208–11, 213.

23. Doorley, *Irish-American Diaspora*, 55.

24. Tansill, *America and the Fight for Irish Freedom*, 212–13; Golway, *Irish Rebel*, 238–40.

25. Doorley, *Irish-American Diaspora*, 56.

26. Tansill, *America and the Fight for Irish Freedom*, 220.

27. Doorley, *Irish-American Diaspora*, 53.

28. Golway, *Irish Rebel*, 240.

29. Tansill, *America and the Fight for Irish Freedom*, 227–29.

30. Doorley, *Irish-American Diaspora*, 67.

31. Tansill, *America and the Fight for Irish Freedom*, 230–33.

32. Golway, *Irish Rebel*, 243.

33. Tansill, *America and the Fight for Irish Freedom*, 213.

34. Tansill, *America and the Fight for Irish Freedom*, 243–44; Golway, *Irish Rebel*, 237.

35. Golway, *Irish Rebel*, 238–39.

36. Ibid., 239.

37. Ibid.

38. Tansill, *America and the Fight for Irish Freedom*, 239.

39. Doorley, *Irish-American Diaspora*, 74.

40. "Many Books Barred from Army Reading," *New York Times*, Sept. 1, 1918.

41. Doorley, *Irish-American Diaspora*, 67.

42. Cohalan to McGuire, July 21, 1917, courtesy of the American Irish Historical Society, New York.

43. Jeremiah O'Leary, *My Political Trials and Experiences* (New York: Jefferson Publishing Co., 1919), 490–99.

44. Doorley, *Irish-American Diaspora*, 67–71, 74–76.

45. Tansill, *America and the Fight for Irish Freedom*, 255.

46. Ibid., 255–57. See also Doorley, *Irish-American Diaspora*, 76.

47. Doorley, *Irish-American Diaspora*, 76–77.

48. Tansill, *America and the Fight for Irish Freedom*, 261–70. See also Golway, *Irish Rebel*, 248.

49. Bielaski to Ford, June 12, 1916, U.S. Department of Justice, Bureau of Investigation file #1898, National Archives and Records Administration, Washington, DC.

50. Ford to Bielaski, June 19, 1916, U.S. Department of Justice, Bureau of Investigation file #1898.

51. Bielaski to Harrison, June 24, 1916, U.S. Department of Justice, Bureau of Investigation file #1898.

52. H. G. Pratt to Harry A. Taylor, Dec. 26, 1917, U.S. Department of Justice, Bureau of Investigation file #1898.

53. F. T. Walters to Taylor, Dec. 31, 1917, U.S. Department of Justice, Bureau of Investigation file #1898.

54. Walters to Taylor, confidential memorandum, Jan. 19, 1918, U.S. Department of Justice, Bureau of Investigation file #1898.

55. R. H. Van Daman to Bielaski, Feb. 4, 1918, U.S. Department of Justice, Bureau of Investigation file #1898.

56. Bielaski to Lamar, Feb. 8, 1918, U.S. Department of Justice, Bureau of Investigation file #1898.

57. Bielaski to Van Daman, Feb. 18, 1918, U.S. Department of Justice, Bureau of Investigation file #1898.

58. Bielaski to Tormey, Feb. 18, 1918, U.S. Department of Justice, Bureau of Investigation file #1898.

59. "James C. Tormey Succumbs at Hospital," *Syracuse Post-Standard*, Oct. 9, 1974.

60. Barkey to Bielaski, Dec. 17, 1917, U.S. Department of Justice, Bureau of Investigation file #1898.

61. Bielaski to the Attorney General, Dec. 24, 1917, U.S. Department of Justice, Bureau of Investigation file #1898.

62. Tormey to Bielaski, Feb. 26, 1918, U.S. Department of Justice, Bureau of Investigation file #1898.

63. Lamar to Bielaski, Feb. 26, 1918, U.S. Department of Justice, Bureau of Investigation file #1898.

64. Bielaski to DeWoody, May 29, 1918, U.S. Department of Justice, Bureau of Investigation file #1898.

65. "60,175 Men Taken in Slacker Raids," *New York Times*, Sept. 8, 1918.

66. Abbreviation for the International Workers of the World, a labor organization.

67. Report of J. P. Robinson, June 10, 1918, U.S. Department of Justice, Bureau of Investigation file #1898.

68. Report of Norman L. Gifford, July 23, 1918, U.S. Department of Justice, Bureau of Investigation file #1898.

69. Tim Weir, *Enemies: A History of the FBI* (New York: Random House, 2012), 13–16.

70. Report of S. C. Endicott, Aug. 13, 1918, U.S. Department of Justice, Bureau of Investigation file #1898.

71. Johnstone to Bielaski, Sept. 28, 1918, U.S. Department of Justice, Bureau of Investigation file #1898.

72. Presumably this is a reference to Jeremiah O'Leary.

73. DeWoody to Bielaski, Oct. 14, 1918, U.S. Department of Justice, Bureau of Investigation file #1898.

74. E. J. Wells report, Oct. 30, 1918, U.S. Department of Justice, Bureau of Investigation file #1898.

75. Reports of the U.S. Department of Justice, Bureau of Investigation file #1898.

76. Tormey report, Feb. 26, 1918, U.S. Department of Justice, Bureau of Investigation file #1898.

77. McCarver to Bielaski, Dec. 1, 1918, U.S. Department of Justice, Bureau of Investigation file #1898.

78. *Hearing Minutes of the U.S. Senate Judiciary Subcommittee to Investigate Brewing and Liquor Interests and German Propaganda*, Dec. 7, 1918, 65th U.S. Congress, Washington, DC, 1392.

79. A commercial attaché at the German embassy.

80. *Hearing Minutes*, 1392–99.

81. A German official in charge of propaganda.

82. German ambassador.

83. German military attaché.

84. H. G. Peterson, *Propaganda for War* (Norman: Univ. of Oklahoma Press, 1939), 138.

85. "Former Mayor of Syracuse, Says Bielaski, Received Money for Pamphlets and Organizing Societies Favoring Huns," *Syracuse Post-Standard*, Dec. 7, 1918.

86. "Former Mayor McGuire Asks to Be Judged by Patriotism Shown Since We Entered the War," *Syracuse Post-Standard*, Dec. 16, 1918, 7–8.

87. Tansill, *America and the Fight for Irish Freedom*, 279–81; Golway, *Irish Rebel*, 249–50.

88. Golway, *Irish Rebel*, 250.

89. Tansill, *America and the Fight for Irish Freedom*, 292–93.

90. U.S. Congressman Henry Flood.

91. U.S. Congressman Thomas Gallagher from Chicago, Illinois.

92. A reference to one McLaughlin, an Irish American leader from Philadelphia.

93. John Devoy to Daniel Cohalan, Dec. 16, 1918, courtesy of the American Irish Historical Society.

94. Legislation introduced by Congressman William E. Mason of Illinois to authorize an appropriation for salaried minister or consul to the "Republic of Ireland."

95. Diarmuid Fawsitt, Irish trade consul to America.

96. Patrick McCartan, Irish envoy to America.

97. McGuire to Cohalan, undated, courtesy of the American Irish Historical Society.

98. Diarmuid Lynch, president of the Friends of Irish Freedom.

99. McGuire to Cohalan, Dec. 22, 1918, courtesy of the American Irish Historical Society.

100. Golway, *Irish Rebel*, 251.

101. Coogan, *Eamon de Valera*, 125–26.

102. Golway, *Irish Rebel*, 252.

8. Campaign Manager

1. "Convention Asks Peace Conference to Free Ireland," *New York Times*, Feb. 24, 1919.

2. "Wilson Will Hear Plea for Ireland," *New York Times*, Mar. 2, 1919.

3. "Wilson Won't Meet Cohalan with Irish," *New York Times*, Mar. 5, 1919.

4. Tansill, *America and the Fight for Irish Freedom*, 212–13, 302.

5. "Will Go to Paris to Plead for Erin," *New York Times*, 1919, Mar. 29.

6. McGuire to Cohalan, Mar. 31, 1919, courtesy of the American Irish Historical Society.

7. T. Frank Dolan to McGuire, May 9, 1919, courtesy of the American Irish Historical Society.

8. McGuire to Cohalan, May 10, 1919, courtesy of the American Irish Historical Society.

9. McGuire to Cohalan, Jan. 18, 1902, courtesy of the American Irish Historical Society.

10. McGuire to Cohalan, Jan. 14, 1914, courtesy of the American Irish Historical Society.

11. McGuire to Cohalan, Oct. 21, 1918, courtesy of the American Irish Historical Society.

12. McGuire to Cohalan, Nov. 6, 1918, courtesy of the American Irish Historical Society.

13. Coogan, *Eamon de Valera*, 137–39.

14. Tansill, *America and the Fight for Irish Freedom*, 340.

15. Coogan, *Eamon de Valera*, 147.

16. Tansill, *America and the Fight for Irish Freedom*, 344–45.

17. Coogan, *Eamon de Valera*, 147.

18. McGuire to Cohalan, July 7, 1919, courtesy of the American Irish Historical Society.

19. Thomas to McGuire, July 15, 1919, courtesy of the American Irish Historical Society.

20. Mayor John Grace of Charleston, South Carolina.

21. McGuire to Cohalan, July 19, 1919, courtesy of the American Irish Historical Society.

22. Coogan, *Eamon de Valera*, 148, 150–52.

23. McGuire to Cohalan, July 19, 1919, courtesy of the American Irish Historical Society.

24. McGuire to Diarmuid Lynch, July 31, 1919, courtesy of the UCD-OFM Partnership.

25. Diarmuid Lynch to McGuire, Aug. 1, 1919, courtesy of the UCD-OFM Partnership.

26. "Ireland Will Accept Only Absolute Freedom at Hands of Britain Says De Valera," *Syracuse Evening Herald*, Aug. 28, 1919, 4.

27. McGuire to Cohalan, July 31, 1919, courtesy of the American Irish Historical Society.

28. "Walsh and Dunne See Irish Victory," *New York Times*, July 9, 1919.

29. "F. P. Walsh Assails Treaty," *New York Times*, Aug. 4, 1919.

30. McGuire to Cohalan, Aug. 22, 1919, courtesy of the American Irish Historical Society.

31. Coogan, *Eamon de Valera*, 148.

32. De Valera was awarded an honorary degree from St. Paul University.

33. McGuire to Cohalan, Aug. 31, 1919, courtesy of the American Irish Historical Society.

34. Tansill, *America and the Fight for Irish Freedom*, 345, 347–48.

35. Golway, *Irish Rebel*, 265.

36. Tansill, *America and the Fight for Irish Freedom*, 351.

37. Boland to McGuire, Sept. 11, 1919, courtesy of the American Irish Historical Society.

38. Golway, *Irish Rebel*, 267.

39. McGuire to Cohalan, Sept. 17, 1919, courtesy of the American Irish Historical Society.

40. McGuire to Cohalan, Sept. 18, 1919, courtesy of the American Irish Historical Society.

41. John D. Moore, national secretary of Friends of Irish Freedom, 1916–18.

42. McGuire to Cohalan, Sept. 20, 1919, courtesy of the American Irish Historical Society.

43. Justice of the New York State Supreme Court.

44. U.S. congressman from New York.

45. McGuire to Cohalan, Sept. 22, 1919, courtesy of the American Irish Historical Society.

46. Manton to McGuire, Sept. 27, 1919, courtesy of the Irish American Historical Society.

47. "Manton Assails De Valera," *New York Times*, Sept. 24, 1919.

48. Coogan, *Eamon de Valera*, 6.

49. "Wilson Names Hough to Succeed Lacombe," *New York Times*, Aug. 16, 1916.

50. James Chace, *1912: Wilson, Roosevelt, Taft, Debs—The Election That Changed the Country* (New York: Simon and Schuster, 2004), 169–70.

51. J. B. Shannon to McGuire by Western Union telegram, Sept. 30, 1919, courtesy of the UCD-OFM Partnership.

52. Thomas Lysaght to McGuire, Sept. 29, 1919, courtesy of UCD-OFM Partnership.

53. McGuire to Cohalan, Oct. 3, 1919, courtesy of the American Irish Historical Society.

54. McGuire to Cohalan, Oct. 6, 1919, courtesy of the American Irish Historical Society.

55. McGuire to Cohalan, Oct. 17, 1919, courtesy of the American Irish Historical Society.

56. Daniel T. O'Connell, head of the Friends of Irish Freedom Speakers Bureau in Washington, DC.

57. McGuire to Cohalan, Oct. 24, 1919, courtesy of the American Irish Historical Society

58. Tansill, *America and the Fight for Irish Freedom*, 325–26.

59. Borah to McGurrin, Oct. 27, 1919, courtesy of the American Irish Historical Society.

60. A possible reference to McGarrity.

61. McGuire to Cohalan, Nov. 14, 1919, courtesy of the American Irish Historical Society.

62. Tansill, *America and the Fight for Irish Freedom*, 337.

63. McGuire to Cohalan, Nov. 19, 1919, courtesy of the American Irish Historical Society.

64. Wilson's attorney general.

65. Senator Frank Kellogg, Republican from Minnesota.

66. Senator Walter Edge, Republican from New Jersey.

67. Senator Irvine Lenroot, Republican from Wisconsin.

68. McGuire to Cohalan, Nov. 21, 1919, courtesy of the American Irish Historical Society.

69. McGuire to Cohalan, Dec. 19, 1919, first letter, courtesy of the American Irish Historical Society.

70. Senator Oscar Underwood, Democrat from Alabama.

71. Senator Lee Overman, Democrat from North Carolina.

72. McGuire to Cohalan, Dec. 19, 1919, second letter, courtesy of the American Irish Historical Society.

9. The Mediator

1. Tansill, *America and the Fight for Irish Freedom*, 359–60.

2. McCartan, *With De Valera*, 153.

3. Tansill, *America and the Fight for Irish Freedom*, 348.

4. Golway, *Irish Rebel*, 271.

5. Tansill, *America and the Fight for Irish Freedom*, 362–63. See also Golway, *Irish Rebel*, 271–72.

6. Tansill, *America and the Fight for Irish Freedom*, 363–64.

7. McGuire to Cohalan, Feb. 8, 1920, courtesy of the American Irish Historical Society.

8. William Jennings Bryan, Wilson's secretary of state.

9. McGuire to Cohalan, Feb. 10, 1920, courtesy of the American Irish Historical Society.

10. McCartan, *With De Valera*, 152.

11. David Fitzpatrick, *Harry Boland's Irish Revolution* (Cork, Ireland: Cork Univ. Press, 2003), 154.

12. Frank Lansing, Wilson's second secretary of state.

13. McGuire to Cohalan, Feb. 18, 1920, courtesy of the American Irish Historical Society.

14. Fitzpatrick, *Harry Boland's Irish Revolution*, 154.

15. McGuire to Cohalan, Feb. 23, 1920, courtesy of the American Irish Historical Society.

16. Coogan, *Eamon de Valera*, 139.

17. Joseph McGarrity.

18. *Gaelic American*, Devoy's newspaper.

19. Tansill, *America and the Fight for Irish Freedom*, 364–65.

20. McGuire to Cohalan, Feb. 28, 1920, courtesy of the American Irish Historical Society.

21. Georgetown University.

22. The resolution that would authorize the creation of a paid envoy to Ireland and that would implicitly result in recognition of the Republic of Ireland.

23. McGuire to Cohalan, Mar. 8, 1920, courtesy of the American Irish Historical Society.

24. Boland to Anderson, Mar. 10, 1920, courtesy of the American Irish Historical Society.

25. Sean Cronin, *The McGarrity Papers* (Tralee, Ireland: Anvil Books, 1992), appendix 8, 11.

26. McGuire to Cohalan, Mar. 11, 1920, courtesy of the American Irish Historical Society.

27. McCartan, *With De Valera*, 156.

28. Tansill, *America and the Fight for Irish Freedom*, 365–68.

29. Golway, *Irish Rebel*, 273.

30. Coogan, *Eamon de Valera*, 173–75.

31. Jim Maher, *Harry Boland: A Biography* (Dublin, Ireland: Mercier Press, 1998), 109.

32. Coogan, *Eamon de Valera*, 167.

33. McGuire to Cohalan, Apr. 5, 1920, courtesy of the American Irish Historical Society.

34. McGuire to Cohalan, Apr. 8, 1920, courtesy of the American Irish Historical Society.

35. McGuire to Cohalan, Apr. 16, 1920, courtesy of the American Irish Historical Society.

36. "Demand Protests on Irish Aid Here," *New York Times*, May 7, 1920.

37. American Delegation, Republic of Ireland, to McGuire, May 14, 1920, courtesy of the American Irish Historical Society.

38. McGuire to Cohalan, May 16, 1920, courtesy of the American Irish Historical Society.

39. Tansill, *America and the Fight for Irish Freedom*, 356–58, 361–64, 380–82.

40. Ogden Mills, congressman from New York.

41. Herbert Parsons, former Republican national committeeman from New York.

42. Frederick Gillet, Republican Speaker of the House of Representatives.

43. McGuire to Cohalan, June 5, 1920, courtesy of the American Irish Historical Society.

44. Frank O. Lowden, governor of Illinois.

45. William Gibbs McAdoo, Wilson's son-in-law.

46. Marion, Ohio, where Harding resided.

47. Philander Knox, U.S. senator from Pennsylvania; McGuire to Cohalan, June 5, 1920, courtesy of the American Irish Historical Society.

48. McGuire to Cohalan, June 14, 1920, courtesy of the American Irish Historical Society.

49. McGuire to Cohalan, June 21, 1920, courtesy of the American Irish Historical Society.

50. Doorley, *Irish-American Diaspora*, 131.

51. Ryan to McGuire, July 8, 1920, courtesy of the American Irish Historical Society.

52. Fitzpatrick, *Harry Boland's Irish Revolution*, 184.

53. "2.75 Beer Plank Wins at Saratoga: Backing for Irish," *New York Times*, Aug. 5, 1920.

54. McGuire to Cohalan, Aug. 2, 1920, courtesy of the American Irish Historical Society.

55. Colum to McGuire, May 27, 1920, courtesy of the UCD-OFM Partnership.

56. W. D. McGuire to McGuire, July 27, 1920, courtesy of the UCD-OFM Partnership.

57. McGuire to O'Connell, Aug. 1, 1920, courtesy of the UCD-OFM Partnership.

58. James Cox, the Democratic presidential nominee; "wet," the Party platform plank favoring the sale of beer and wine.

59. McGuire to Cohalan, Aug. 4, 1920, courtesy of the American Irish Historical Society.

60. McGuire to Cohalan, Aug. 5, 1920, courtesy of the American Irish Historical Society.

61. An apparent reference to John D. Moore's incipient candidacy for Congress.

62. McGuire to Cohalan, Aug. 12, 1920, courtesy of the American Irish Historical Society.

63. McGuire to Devoy, Aug. 17, 1920, courtesy of the American Irish Historical Society.

64. Irish Republic.

65. McGuire to Cohalan, Aug. 19, 1920, courtesy of the American Irish Historical Society.

66. Golway, *Irish Rebel*, 280.

67. Tansill, *America and the Fight for Irish Freedom*, 389.

68. Doorley, *Irish-American Diaspora*, 132.

69. Cronin, *McGarrity Papers*, appendix 8, 12–13.

70. Tansill, *America and the Fight for Irish Freedom*, 388–89.

71. McGuire to Cohalan, Aug. 24, 1920, courtesy of the American Irish Historical Society.

72. This may be a reference to Edward Doheny, an American oil magnate and confidante of de Valera's.

73. Lynch to Cohalan, Aug. 25, 1920, courtesy of the American Irish Historical Society.

74. Maher, *Harry Boland*, 119.

75. Tansill, *America and the Fight for Irish Freedom*, 384–85.

76. *Irish World*, published by McGarrity.

77. Devoy to Cohalan, Aug. 25, 1920, courtesy of the American Irish Historical Society.

78. McGuire to Cohalan, Aug. 26, 1920, courtesy of the American Irish Historical Society.

79. Michael Collins.

80. Devoy to Cohalan, Aug. 31, 1920, courtesy of the American Irish Historical Society.

81. Golway, *Irish Rebel*, 280.

82. Doorley, *Irish-American Diaspora*, 133.

83. Devoy to Cohalan, Sept. 21, 1920, courtesy of the American Irish Historical Society.

84. Boland to McGuire, Oct. 18, 1920, courtesy of the UCD-OFM Partnership.

85. Devoy notes, Oct. 31, 1920, courtesy of the American Irish Historical Society.

86. McGuire to Boland, Nov. 10, 1920, courtesy of the UCD-OFM Partnership.

87. Doorley, *Irish-American Diaspora*, 134.

88. McGuire to Boland, Nov. 11, 1920, courtesy of the UCD-OFM Partnership.

89. McGuire to Boland, Nov. 16, 1920, courtesy of the UCD-OFM Partnership.

90. "Fenian Chief's Estimate of James K. McGuire," *Catholic Sun*, July 19, 1923, 7.

91. Coogan, *Eamon de Valera*, 194–95.

10. The End

1. Fitzpatrick, *Harry Boland's Irish Revolution*, 161, 220, 214, 148.

2. "Fenian Chief's Estimate of James K. McGuire."

3. "Says Irish Plotted Here After 1917," *New York Times*, Jan. 11, 1921.

4. "Telling Harding What to Do," *New York Times*, Feb. 26, 1921.

5. Walsh to Boland, Feb. 28, 1920, courtesy of the UCD-OFM Partnership.

6. Walsh to Boland enclosure in the letter of Feb. 28, 1920, courtesy of the UCD-OFM Partnership.

7. Tim Pat Coogan, *The Man Who Made Ireland: The Life and Times of Michael Collins* (Niwot, CO: Roberts Rinehart, 1992), 201–3.

8. Coogan, *Eamon de Valera*, 218–19.

9. "Pope Is Criticized by Friends of Irish," *New York Times*, May 23, 1921.

10. "St. Patrick's Parade Splits Irish Ranks," *New York Times*, Mar. 3, 1921.

11. "Harding Rejects Boston Irish Plea," *New York Times*, Mar. 18, 1921.

12. Fitzpatrick, *Harry Boland's Irish Revolution*, 220.

13. Tansill, *America and the Fight for Irish Freedom*, 418–19.

14. "Irish Here Pleased over Monday Truce," *New York Times*, July 9, 1921.

15. "Cohalan Attacks De Valera's Stand," *New York Times*, July 10, 1921.

16. Tansill, *America and the Fight for Irish Freedom*, 419–20.

17. Ibid., 422–23, 426, 431–33.

18. Coogan, *Man Who Made Ireland*, 272–73.

19. Ibid., 272–73, 294–309. See also Tansill, *America and the Fight for Irish Freedom*, 431–35.

20. Tansill, *America and the Fight for Irish Freedom*, 436–42.

21. "Irish Pledge Fund to Fight Here," *New York Times*, Dec. 12, 1921.

22. "Assails Cohalan's Stand," *New York Times*, Dec. 9, 1921.

23. Coogan, *Eamon de Valera*, 312, 324.

24. O'Mara managed the bond drive for de Valera.

25. McGuire to Boland, Apr. 7, 1922, courtesy of the UCD-OFM Partnership.

26. Boland to McGuire, Apr. 20, 1922, courtesy of the UCD-OFM Partnership.

27. Maher, *Harry Boland*, 198–205.

28. McGuire to Boland, May 24, 1922, courtesy of the UCD-OFM Partnership.

29. Boland to McGuire, June 8, 1922, courtesy of the UCD-OFM Partnership.

30. Passport application, Dec. 17, 1921, U.S. National Archives and Records Administration, Washington, DC.

31. Coogan, *Eamon de Valera*, 329.

32. "South Really Dry Asserts J. K. McGuire," *Syracuse Journal*, June 9, 1923.

33. "Find Former Mayor of Syracuse Dead Here," *Washington Post*, June 30, 1923.

34. "Tribute to Its Former Leader," *Syracuse Herald*, July 2, 1923.

35. Court records of these proceedings were provided by the Office of the District Attorney for New York County and the chief clerk of the New York State Supreme Court, Criminal Term, 100 Centre Street, New York, NY.

36. *Syracuse Herald*, July 15, 1915.

J M K

Glossary

Amos, Jacob. Mayor of Syracuse, 1893–95

Baldwin, Charles. Independent candidate for mayor of Syracuse and member of the Board of Police Commissioners

Barber Asphalt Company. James K. McGuire employer

Belden, James J. Congressman from central New York and former mayor of Syracuse

Bielaski, A. Bruce. U.S. Justice Department, Bureau of Investigation Chief

Bishop, Thomas. Superintendent of Parks, City of Syracuse

Black, Frank. 32nd governor of New York, Republican

Black and Tans. British militia sent to Ireland to suppress the Irish rebellion

Boland, Harry. Secretary to the president of Ireland and member of the Irish Republican Brotherhood

Bryan, William Jennings. Democratic candidate for president and secretary of state in Woodrow Wilson administration

Carnegie, Andrew. Philanthropist who contributed funds for Central Library in Syracuse

Casement, Roger. British diplomat executed by Britain for treason

Catholic Sun. Roman Catholic newspaper published by James K. McGuire in Syracuse

Clan-Na-Gael. A secret organization of Irish American political and business leaders to support the Irish Republican Brotherhood

Cleveland, Grover. 22nd and 24th president of the United States and 28th governor of New York

Cockran, Bourke. Congressman from New York and Irish American activist

Cohalan, Daniel. New York State Supreme Court justice and executive committee member of Friends of Irish Freedom

293

Coler, Bird S. New York State comptroller and Democratic candidate for governor

Collins, Michael. Commander of Irish Republican Army and secretary of finance for Irish Republic

Comfort, George Fisk. Founding director of the Syracuse Museum of Art

Condit, Filmore. Officer of Union Oil Company

Croker, Richard. Tammany Hall political club leader

Cummins, John J. Onondaga County Democratic Party chairman

Daly, Joseph. New York State Supreme Court justice

Day, James. Chancellor of Syracuse University

Debs, Eugene. Socialist candidate for president in 1908 and 1912

De Valera, Éamon. First president of the Republic of Ireland

Devoy, John. Publisher of the *Gaelic American* and Irish independence activist

Dey, Donald. Republican candidate for mayor of Syracuse in 1897

Dolan, T. Frank. Member of the City of Syracuse Board of Health and McGuire supporter

Doyle, Michael. Philadelphia attorney for Roger Casement

Driscoll, George. Attorney and Democratic candidate for mayor of Syracuse

Driscoll, Michael. Republican congressman from central New York

Dunfee, John. New York state committeeman and McGuire supporter

Ford, Patrick. Publisher of the *Irish World*

Friends of Irish Freedom. American organization that raised money for the Irish Republican Brotherhood

Gaffney, Jim. Tammany hall member and associate of Charles Murphy

Gaynor, William. Mayor of New York City elected in 1909

George, David Lloyd. British prime minister

Glynn, Martin. 40th governor of New York upon the impeachment of William Sulzer

Gray Brothers. Syracuse boot and shoe manufacturer that employed James McGuire

Griffith, Arthur. Founder of Sinn Fein and president of the Irish Free State

Hancock, Theodore. New York State attorney general and Republican candidate for mayor of Syracuse in 1899

Harding, Warren. 29th president of the United States

Haven Melvin Z. Corporation counsel, city clerk for City of Syracuse, and McGuire supporter

Hearst, William Randolph. Newspaper magnate; member of congress from New York; and candidate for mayor of New York City, candidate for governor of New York, and candidate for president of the United States

Hendricks, Francis. Former mayor of Syracuse, New York state senator, New York state insurance commissioner, and Onondaga County Republican Party leader

Hennessy, John. Special investigator for Governor William Sulzer

Hill, David. U.S. senator from New York, 29th governor of New York, and Democratic Party leader

Hiscock, Frank. U.S. senator from New York and Onondaga County Republican leader

Hisgen, Thomas. Independence League candidate for president in 1908

Hughes, Charles Evans. Judge of the New York Court of Appeals, 36th governor of New York, Republican candidate for president of the United States, and justice of the U.S. Supreme Court

Hughes, Katherine. Administrator and researcher, Bureau of Friends of Irish Freedom, Washington, DC.

Hyde, Salem. Onondaga County commissioner of jurors

Independence League. Political party organized by William Randolph Hearst

Kelley, William. Onondaga County Democratic Party chairman

Kirk, William B. Mayor of Syracuse, 1888–89, and Democratic Party political boss of Onondaga County

Kline, Jay B. District attorney of Onondaga County and mayor of Syracuse, 1901–3

Ludden, Patrick. Bishop of the Diocese of Syracuse

Lynch, Diarmuid. Member of the Irish Republican Brotherhood and national secretary of the Friends of Irish Freedom

Mack, E. J. Republican alderman for the City of Syracuse

Mack, John. Asphalt baron and employer of James K. McGuire

Mann, Dewitt. Accountant for the McGuire administration

Manz, G. Adolph. Comptroller of the City of Syracuse

Matty, Frank. Democratic president of the Syracuse Board of Aldermen and candidate for mayor

McAdoo, William. New York City chief magistrate

McCartan, Patrick. Envoy from the Republic of Ireland

McGarrity, Joseph. Publisher of the *Irish Press* in Philadelphia

McGuire, Charles Matthew. Brother of James K. McGuire

McGuire, Edward Sarsfield. Brother of James K. McGuire

McGuire, Elizabeth. Sister of James K. McGuire

McGuire, Frances. Wife of James K. McGuire

McGuire, George Henry Moore. Brother of James K. McGuire

McGuire, Gertrude. Daughter of James K. McGuire

McGuire, James Phillip. Son of James K. McGuire

McGuire, James. Father of James K. McGuire

McGuire, John Francis, "Frankie". Brother of James K. McGuire who died during childhood

McGuire, Mary Frances. Daughter of James K. McGuire

McGuire, Mary Jane. Mother of James K. McGuire, wife of James McGuire

McGuire, Phillip. Father-in-law of James K. McGuire

McGuire, Rosalind. Daughter of James K. McGuire

McKinley, William. 25th president of the United States

McLaughlin, Hugh. New York state senator and Kings County Democratic leader

McLellan, George S., Jr. Mayor of New York City

Meagher, James A. Overseer of the poor and director of public works for the City of Syracuse

Moore, John D. President of the Friends of Irish Freedom

Murphy, Charles. Tammany Hall leader

Murphy, Edward. U.S. senator from New York

Murphy, Jr., Charles F. Nephew of Tammany hall leader and insurance broker

Newell, James. Corporation counsel for the City of Syracuse

Odell, Benjamin. 34th governor of New York

O'Donovan Rossa, Jeremiah. Irish activist

O'Leary, Jeremiah. Attorney and Irish American activist and author

O'Mara, James. Irish banker who managed the Friends of Irish Freedom funds

Osborne, James. Special investigator for Governor Martin Glynn

Parker, Alton. Judge of the New York Court of Appeals and Democratic Party candidate for president

Pearse, Pádraig. Irish leader of the 1916 Rising

Peck, Duncan. Democratic candidate for mayor and commissioner of public safety for the City of Syracuse

Platt, Thomas. New York state senator and Republican Party leader

Rafferty, William. New York State Democratic committeeman and McGuire ally

Redmond, John. Irish Parliamentary Party leader

Root, Elihu. Attorney, secretary of war, and 1912 Nobel Peace Prize winner

Rosenbloom, Daniel. Republican member of the Syracuse Board of Education

Roosevelt, Franklin. 32nd president of the United States and bond attorney for Friends of Irish Freedom

Roosevelt, Theodore. 33rd governor of New York and 26th president of the United States

Rubino, Henry. Attorney for Warner-Quinlan Company

Ryan, John T. Buffalo, New York, attorney and Irish American activist

Saul, Charles. Republican candidate for mayor of Syracuse in 1895

Sehl, Jacob. Syracuse overseer of the poor

Smith, Carroll E. Editor and publisher of the *Syracuse Journal*

Smith, Wilbur. New York State Supreme Court justice from Queens and Nassau County

Sulzer, William. 39th governor of New York and congressman from New York City

St. Crispin Society. Shoemakers Union

Taft, William Howard. 27th president of the United States

Tammany Hall. New York City political club

Tormey, James. Agent of the Bureau of Investigation, U.S. Department of Justice

Tumulty, Joseph. Secretary to President Woodrow Wilson

Tweed, William. New York state senator and Tammany Hall leader

Van Wyck, Augustus. New York State Supreme Court justice and Democratic candidate for governor of New York in 1898

Van Wyck, Robert. Mayor of New York City

White, Horace. New York state senator from central New York and 37th governor of New York

Whitman, Charles. 41st governor of New York

Wilson, Woodrow. 28th president of the United States and governor of New Jersey

Warner-Quinlan Company. Asphalt manufacturer

JMK

Bibliography

Books and Periodicals

Ackerman, Kenneth D. *Boss Tweed: The Rise and Fall of the Corrupt Pol Who Conceived the Soul of Modern New York.* Cambridge, MA: Da Capo Press, 2005.

Beatty, Jack. *The Rascal King: The Life and Times of James Michael Curley (1874–1958).* Reading, MA: Addison-Wesley, 1992.

Bottigheimer, Karl. *Ireland and the Irish: A Short History.* New York: Columbia Univ. Press, 1982.

Brands, H. W. *T. R., The Last Romantic.* New York: Basic Books, 1997.

Chace, James. *1912: Wilson, Roosevelt, Taft, Debs—The Election That Changed the Country.* New York: Simon and Schuster, 2004.

Coogan, Tim Pat. *Eamon de Valera: The Man Who Was Ireland.* New York: Harper Collins, 1993.

———. *The Man Who Made Ireland: The Life and Death of Michael Collins.* Niwot, CO: Roberts Rinehart, 1992.

Cronin, Sean. *The McGarrity Papers.* Tralee, Ireland: Anvil Books, 1992.

Devoy, John. *Recollections of an Irish Rebel.* New York: Charles D. Young, 1929.

Dictionary of American Biography. Vol. 7. New York: Charles Scribner & Son, 1931.

Doorley, Michael. *Irish-American Diaspora Nationalism: The Friends of Irish Freedom, 1916–1935.* Portland, OR: Four Courts Press, 2005.

Finnan, Joseph. *John Redmond and Irish Unity, 1912–1918.* Syracuse, NY: Syracuse Univ. Press, 2004.

Fitzpatrick, David. *Harry Boland's Irish Revolution.* Cork, Ireland: Cork Univ. Press, 2003.

Golway, Terry. *Irish Rebel: John Devoy and America's Fight for Ireland's Freedom.* New York: St. Martin's Press, 1998.

Jeffers, H. Paul. *An Honest President: The Life and Times of Grover Cleveland.* New York: Harper Collins, 2000.

Kingsley, M., J. Knauber, J. J. Neville, and J. Bruckheimer. *The Political Blue Book of Syracuse, New York.* Syracuse, NY: Grover, 1902.

Maher, Jim. *Harry Boland: A Biography.* Dublin, Ireland: Mercier Press, 1998.

Manz, William H. "Tammany Had a Right to Expect Proper Consideration: The Judicial Nominations Controversy of 1898." *New York State Bar Association Journal* 81, no. 3 (Mar./Apr. 2009): 11–23.

McCartan, Patrick. *With De Valera in America.* New York: Brentano, 1931.

McFeeley, William S. *Grant.* New York: William Norton Co., 1981.

McGuire, James K., ed. *Democratic Party of the State of New York.* New York: U.S. History Company, J. F. Tapley Co., 1905.

———. *The King, the Kaiser and Irish Freedom.* New York: Devlin-Adair, 1915.

———. *What Could Germany Do for Ireland?* New York: Wolfe Tone Co., 1916.

Morris, Edmund. *Theodore Rex.* New York: Random House, 2001.

O'Leary, Jeremiah. *My Political Trials and Experiences.* New York: Jefferson Publishing Co., 1919.

Peterson, H. G. *Propaganda for War.* Norman: Univ. of Oklahoma Press, 1939.

Procter, Ben. *William Randolph Hearst: The Early Years, 1863–1910.* New York: Oxford Univ. Press, 1998.

———. *William Randolph Hearst: The Later Years, 1911–1951.* New York: Oxford Univ. Press, 2007.

Seymour, Charles. *The Intimate Papers of Colonel House.* Vol. 2. Boston: Houghton Mifflin, 1926.

Shannon, William V. *The American Irish.* Rev. ed. New York: McMillan, 1966.

Slyden, Robert A. *Empire Statesman: The Rise and Redemption of Al Smith.* New York: Simon and Schuster, 2001.

Tansill, Charles Callan. *America and the Fight for Irish Freedom, 1866–1922.* New York: Devin-Adair, 1957.

Wager, Daniel. *Our Country and Its People.* Part 3: *Family Sketches.* [Boston]: Boston History Company, 1896.

Archives

Onondaga County Public Library, Local History Section
Onondaga Historical Association
City Hall Archives, City of Syracuse
Irish American Historical Society, New York

University College, Dublin, Ireland, Éamon de Valera Collection and Harry Boland
    papers
National Archives and Records Administration, Washington, DC

Newspapers

Catholic Sun (Syracuse, NY)
Irish World
New York Times
New York World
Syracuse Courier
Syracuse Evening Herald
Syracuse Journal
Syracuse Post
Syracuse Post-Standard
Syracuse Standard

J M K

Index

303